TEACHING AS THE ART OF STAGING

TEACHING AS THE ART OF STAGING

A Scenario-Based College Pedagogy in Action

Anthony Weston

Foreword by Peter Felten

STERLING, VIRGINIA

Published by Stylus Publishing, LLC.
22883 Quicksilver Drive
Sterling, Virginia 20166-2019

Library of Congress Cataloging-in-Publication Data
Names: Weston, Anthony, 1954- author.
Title: Teaching as the art of staging : a scenario-based college
pedagogy in action / Anthony Weston ; foreword by Peter
Felten.
Description: First edition. |
Sterling, Virginia : Stylus Publishing, LLC., 2018. | Includes
bibliographical references and index.
Identifiers: LCCN 2018009432 (print) |
LCCN 2018026752 (ebook) |
ISBN 9781620365229 (Library networkable e-edition) |
ISBN 9781620365236 (Consumer e-edition) |
ISBN 9781620365212 (paperback) |
ISBN 9781620365205 (cloth)
Subjects: LCSH: College teaching--Methodology. | Teacher
effectiveness. | Active learning. | Lecture method in education.
Classification: LCC LB2331 (ebook) |
LCC LB2331 .W43 2018 (print) |
DDC 378.1/25--dc23
LC record available at https://lccn.loc.gov/2018009432

13-digit ISBN: 978-1-62036-520-5 (cloth)
13-digit ISBN: 978-1-62036-521-2 (paperback)
13-digit ISBN: 978-1-62036-522-9 (library networkable
e-edition)
13-digit ISBN: 978-1-62036-523-6 (consumer e-edition)

Printed in the United States of America

All first editions printed on acid-free paper
that meets the American National Standards Institute
Z39-48 Standard.

Bulk Purchases
Quantity discounts are available for use in workshops and
for staff development.
Call 1-800-232-0223

First Edition, 2019

CONTENTS

FOREWORD

In this book, Anthony Weston critically and practically unpacks what happens when we plunge our students into unfolding and urgently engaging educational scenarios. This is a book about possibilities, illustrating what can happen in a single class meeting or an entire course devoted to deeply situated and radically active learning.

As I read this manuscript, I vividly recalled an experience from my own teaching. One cold January day some years ago, a former student e-mailed: "I thought you might find this interesting." She explained that as part of her internship in a law firm, she had attended a legal hearing about a complex case. The experience reminded her of a course she had taken with me in which students played a three-week role-based game set in the royal court of the Ming Emperor in 1587:

> Just like in the China game, the attorneys sort of bowed to the judge, always saying in an exaggerated way, "Your Honor." And each attorney, there were 11 different ones, stood up and spoke with their own agendas and motives. Some (like the annoying Confucian purists) blamed unethical and incompetent individuals so they argued for personal punishments to settle the case. Others (the more pragmatistic *[sic]* ones, like me!) said the problems were rooted in legal and business structures, not individual behavior, so the court should respond in structural ways. (Personal communication, January 20, 2008)

The e-mail went on, but I stopped reading at that point, stunned. I remembered this student, but my recollection did not lead me to believe that long after the course she would make insightful connections between the U.S. legal system in the twenty-first century and the succession crisis of the Wanli emperor. In fact, though, she not only had learned but also still cared—and she couldn't resist getting in one more dig at those pesky Confucian purists.

This student's experience is not unusual. I've taught for more than a decade with Reacting to the Past games, and I find that experiences like hers are the norm when classes immerse students in a rich, challenging scenario. Indeed, in an end-of-semester survey I give my students, the majority every term tell me, to quote one: "This course is different because I care so much about the arguments we are making." That's in a general education course focused on the trial of Anne Hutchinson in Puritan New England and the debate over which son should succeed the Wanli emperor. Students didn't start the class caring about the purity of Hutchinson's religious beliefs or the merits of the emperor's first versus third son. The game's the thing! The pedagogy of the scenario steeps them in the historical situation, sparking their curiosity and empathy—and, sometimes, their competitiveness—as they inhabit the role of a character with a personal stake in the outcome of debates about how to apply what they've learned about a topic, such as Puritan theology or Confucian philosophy, in a dynamic situation.

Such methods are transformative. To teach with immersive scenarios, large or small, is not merely to tweak a traditional pedagogy or to do the routine and familiar things just a little better. In this book, Weston advances a distinctive and new conception of teaching and learning in higher education. This book invites us to take big, bold steps into a fundamentally different kind of classroom, where teaching is staging and learning is a form of becoming.

You do have to trust the pedagogy. Dedicating a day or a week or a month on your syllabus to a Reacting to the Past game, a Problem-Based Learning project, or a Model United Nations experience takes a leap of pedagogical faith. This book not only outlines the research that allows you to confidently make that leap but also shows you how to stage such scenarios to fit your own learning goals and teaching contexts. It may inspire you to stretch your goals and ambitions as well.

Teaching with scenarios also requires trusting your students. You need to believe your students can and will engage deeply. This book's scholarly foundation and personal stories demonstrate what is possible when you trust your students —and yourself!—enough to create opportunities for them to really immerse themselves in provocative and dynamic learning experiences.

As you may suspect by now, this is no ordinary book on teaching and learning. "Something dramatically different—something edgy, something a little unsettling and yet deeply intriguing and inviting at the same time and for the same reason—is afoot here" (p. 2, this volume). The stage is set to transform your teaching and your students' learning.

Peter Felten
Center for Engaged Learning
Elon University

ON BECOMING AN IMPRESARIO
A Personal Preface

Almost immediately upon becoming a college professor, I forswore lecturing entirely. This was not exactly the reaction expected by the teaching center staff who put together the conference that prompted my decision. Their aim was only to improve large-class lectures, a little, at the state university where I had just begun my career. Just project some images, they said. Put students into buzz groups for a break. Do anything, really, besides talk for an hour straight. But I was young, impatient, and not prone to half-measures. Their own data seemed to show that lecturing is shockingly ineffective even by its own standards, which could and should be questioned to boot. So why lecture at all?

The implications were immediate and acute. More or less on the spot, and in every class, I had to find alternatives to simply telling my students what I thought they should know. But just what were these alternatives to be? Indeed, what did I really think I was doing? What *was* my role as a college professor?

In the pedagogical literature of the time, there was basically one answer: a model of the professor as a kind of facilitator, or what later came to be called the Guide on the Side (King, 1993). The move still seems completely logical. If you forswear teacher-centered teaching, then obviously you must make your teaching *student*-centered instead. No longer what King cheekily labeled a Sage on the Stage, you need to check your ego and, like a good coach, put yourself on the side. It's not about you.

I embraced the facilitative model and tried to bring it full scale and persistently to my teaching. For some time I really did manage to conceive myself as a kind of guide. It helped that the Force was with me, so to say. I watched *student-centered* become the byword of an entire cohort of professors and even many whole schools, including my own, while the pedagogical literature elaborated and diversified myriad models of the teacher as facilitator or coach.

Yet the facilitative model was never a perfect fit for me or even, in the end, a very good one. What gradually happened over those years in my own teaching practice turns out to have been a move toward something quite different.

My colleagues noticed it even before I did. For almost every meeting of every class, they started to see me rearranging the desks, tables, and chairs, often bringing in props or doing other kinds of staging as well. Increasingly, I might set varied formats like impromptu debates and talk shows, or drop-ins by unexpected and provocative visitors, looking surprisingly like me in various degrees of costume. Later came role-plays that could last from minutes to months. Colleagues, friends, former students, and even confederates within a given class found themselves conscripted into these projects, as well. Willy-nilly, I was becoming an *arranger*, an organizer, and a stage-setter behind the scenes, as well as usually *in* the scenes.

Through this practice, evolving in its own way, I finally arrived at the point of articulating a corresponding, alternative general conceptualization of teaching. I now call this model *Teaching as the Art of Staging*. The aim, put in the most general terms, is to set up and work through self-unfolding learning challenges for and with my students. Broadly—but only loosely, roughly, just as a first approximation—the paradigms of stage-setting are improvisational theatrical approaches that create open-ended but highly structured situations that collectively we can call, again in the broadest terms, *scenarios*. No scripts, however. All participants find themselves challenged to take part at the very top of their thinking game.

Beyond Sage on the Stage and Guide on the Side, what developed for me is another distinctive and inviting model of the teacher, which I now propose to call an *Impresario with a Scenario* (Weston, 2015).

Even before I had the label, I began to discover other teachers on parallel paths. New colleagues brought the Reacting to the Past model to Elon University, with its elaborate and compelling historical scenarios. Instantly I was drawn to them, adapting them in my own ways and later co-teaching with a leading Reacting teacher, my esteemed astronomical colleague Tony Crider. You will meet Tony regularly in the pages to come. I joined Elon's Model United Nations activities with my first-year seminars, prompting me to develop my own role-playing simulations in turn. My next first-year seminars turned entirely into a series of model *worlds*. I adopted the Case Method in my ethics classes and adapted some Problem-Based Learning methods—building student work around specific and multilayered problems and challenges addressed collaboratively—to my Critical Thinking and Environmental Studies classes.

All of these alternative and broadly scenario-based pedagogies opened new horizons for me and prompted new adaptations and experiments. I saw no need to embrace just one. In today's pedagogical literature and practice, unfortunately, they tend to silo themselves, focusing on differences rather than congruencies, and sometimes even set themselves up as competitors. In my view, they are all close cousins, if not actual siblings, and complementary.

I argue that we would be better served by a conception that highlights their similarities within a broader shared framework.

To be clear from the start, however, I certainly do not mean that all teachers should now make themselves Impresarios with Scenarios or that all teaching should be some kind of staging. Since this point seems to be regularly missed, I want to say it again with emphasis: The last thing I want is to replace one one-size-fits-all orthodoxy with another. Many practicing teachers are committed syncretists—a little bit of everything—and rightly so (Cranton, 1998; Sandy, 1998). Still, this book aims to show that it is possible to teach in a *primarily* scenario-centered way across a *wide range* of topics and disciplines, and that the energies such a method can engage are unique and often electrifying. That is quite enough!

Indeed I don't always teach by staging myself, even when I consider myself at the top of my game. In the broadest way, almost all of my teaching is experiential. I have taught study abroad courses, for example, and regularly take my classes out of the classroom for all manner of alternative activities. But not all experiential teaching is acting like an impresario. Teaching abroad is more like fellow-traveling with your charges within a far grander scenario that is mostly not of your making. I have all manner of stories about that, too, but they will have to wait for another time. In this book, the para-digmatic methods are tightly structured, dialectically unfolding classroom activities that are accessible to nearly any teacher without going anywhere, certainly not anywhere far—except in imagination and, yes, with a certain degree of daring.

I am continuously grateful to my students over the years, co-adventurers in teaching and learning. Heartfelt thanks also to many pedagogical col-leagues, fellow travelers, and provocateurs, again over many years. Elon University has been my main professional and pedagogical home and has been supportive in many ways, especially my philosophical colleagues Nim Batchelor, Stephen Bloch-Schulman, Ann Cahill, Martin Fowler, Amy Glaser, Ryan Johnson, Yoram Lubling, and John Sullivan. Ann was kind enough to read entirely through an earlier version and make many helpful suggestions. Thanks also to biologist Amanda Chunco; historian Michael Carignan; literaturist Prudence Layne; and, as just mentioned, astronomer Tony Crider. Frances Bottenberg co-taught my 2012 Philosophy of Educa-tion course (Chapter 8). At Elon's Center for Engaged Learning, Peter Felten and Deandra Little have been consistently supportive. Facilitating a Zen course for many years with Sandy Gentei Stewart, Osho, has reshaped some of my other teaching, as well. At SUNY–Stony Brook, somewhere back in the mists of the last millennium, my colleague Peter Williams first set me off on these paths; Jim McKenna brought me into federated learning community work; and Ted Goldfarb, then assistant vice provost for undergraduate education, brought Lily Endowment programs to campus, and some of us young faculty to Lily, at just the most fertile time for me. This book is one kind of return on Lily's investment, as well as an offering of thanks.

I have consistently been inspired by books by other teachers and writers about teaching, going all the way back to Rousseau and John Dewey but including contemporaries as varied as bell hooks, Mark Carnes, Parker Palmer, Inge Bell, and others. In particular, I have been inspired by their stories, framed as they usually are by larger pedagogical philosophies, but vivid and suggestive in their own rights, as well. Even when I might wish to go beyond or in a different direction from their philosophies, the stories stayed with me and often enough provoked specific designs for my own classes. It is my fond hope that this book in turn may inspire and provoke others, paying my own way forward by the same means. Thirty years ago, a book like this might have saved me a lot of time. It is dedicated to the young teacher for whom it might save some time today. Take what you can use from it, and take it still further.

Many thanks also to treasured co-teachers abroad: Linda Holland and her Institute for Central American Studies in San José, Costa Rica; Bob Jickling of Yukon College and latterly of Lakehead University School of Education in Thunder Bay, Ontario, whose primary place of education was always the wild; Rick Kool, director of the master's program in environmental education and communication at Royal Roads University in Victoria, British Columbia, first to characterize my pedagogical style as "high wire"; and Patsy Hallen of the Institute for Science and Technology Policy at Murdoch University, Perth, Australia, who hauled me and our gallant band of eco-philosophy students off for weeks into the endlessly enigmatic Australian bush. I am deeply grateful as well to my partner Amy Halberstadt and our children Anna Ruth and Molly for their eagerness, curiosity, and inspirations and provocations of many sorts.

At Stylus Publishing, David Brightman's editorial support for this project has been stalwart, perceptive, and good humored from the start—all very much appreciated—and production editor McKenzie Baker and her team have been extraordinarily responsive and masterful in moving the work from complex manuscript to the final realization. At Elon University, kudos go to my indefatigable research assistant maggie castor, who took on the spirit of this work and systematically sifted reams of articles, made connections, and offered suggestions that repeatedly expanded its reach. Hali Tauxe-Stewart contributed the cover photo, which shows a number of her fellow students (and me) at a key moment in one of our "Contact" simulations (Chapter 7). I am grateful also to Rendi and Joe Mann-Stadt for making their mountain home the perfect snowy retreat for the penultimate editing of this manuscript.

A number of anonymous reviewers for earlier versions gave detailed feedback that persuaded me to dramatically restructure and refocus this book, greatly improving it and curbing some excesses in the process—although, for better or worse, certainly not all of them.

Anthony Weston
Durham, North Carolina
Spring Equinox 2018

I

A DIFFERENT KIND
OF TEACHING

Picture a college teacher who regularly sets up classroom scenarios—challenging problems, unscripted dramas, role-plays, simulations, and the like—such that the scenario frames and drives most of the action and learning that follows. Sometimes these scenarios can be seen coming. Other times they happen unexpectedly and on the spot. Students quickly learn to just go with the flow, and by design, that flow can often be powerful indeed.

It may be that the scene changes—or rather that suddenly there *is* a scene, whereas a moment ago there was just the usual class. A microphone suddenly appears out of the teacher's pocket, maybe, and students find themselves being interviewed on some kind of edgy and probing talk show about a theme of the day: what Socrates or Freud would make of our times, or new ideas for addressing global climate change, or the ethics of alternative forms of marriage, or of breeding back the mammoths. Maybe certain unexpected but challenging visitors turn up, such as an old-style Anglican clergyman ranting against the theory of evolution in a history of ideas class, mocked at first but in the end posing unexpectedly difficult challenges, so much so that Darwin himself has to show up later to respond—and be questioned in turn.

Traditional teachers might approach such debates by describing their dialectics in a lecture. Gun control, geoengineering, evolution: The norm would be to review the various sides, comment, try for a degree of objectivity, maybe argue for a position at the end of the review. There are places and times for this approach, and it can certainly, and laudably, model a kind of care and objectivity that are essential but rare in public discourse today. Yet the kinds of teachers I have in mind do something dramatically different. They bring students into the debate by actually staging it. They do not describe and review the various sides but rather set up the students them-selves to formulate and enact the debate, and in the course of doing so take the students' measures as well.

Such staging can take many different forms. Sometimes it may be entirely and obviously impromptu. Students find room to move in their own positions, chances to think on their feet, and a welcome freedom about their contributions, since everyone knows that they are doing this on the fly. Other times there is warning. In that case, students can prepare and hone their arguments, with assigned or developed positions. Other times still, per-haps they have done the background preparation but do not realize how it is to be applied until they walk into the day's classroom, where a debate is already set up, and just to sit down is to take a side. They can be quite sure they will be called on to speak up for it.

Reacting to the Past pedagogy, Model United Nations (UN), and a number of other contemporary role-play pedagogies take preparation another step. Model UN, for example, assigns students in teams to rep-resent a UN member country in a variety of settings and in the face of unpredictable crises. They know very well that there *will* be crises, but they do not know what the crises will be or what capacities or posi-tions they will call on or challenge. They may prepare for weeks or even months. Then the conference arrives—the simulation itself—24/7, coffee jitters, all-night conferences and negotiations, maybe on one's campus with a wide variety of other student groups that have also been preparing, partly in secret, in similar ways, or maybe at regional or even national gatherings. Then closing sessions, success, defeat, or both, debrief, and finally some sleep.

Some of this could certainly be described in readings and lectures. The students could simply be told what their teachers think they should know about how the UN works. Today that is how it almost always goes. The Model UN alternative, by contrast, is for the class, in concert with others, to actually *become* the UN.

Savor that thought for a second. The class, together with others, *becomes* the UN. Something dramatically different—something edgy, something a little unsettling and yet deeply intriguing and inviting at the same time and for the same reason—is afoot here.

Teaching as Staging

There is method behind these events and happenings. Most obviously, they are *staged*. They are planned, organized, and set up in advance. Work and inventiveness on the teacher's part is certainly required, but it is radically dif-ferent than preparing a lecture or even setting up the usual kind of classroom discussion. Talk-show hosts need to have their microphones ready to go and their patter and questions on the tips of their tongues. For debates, chairs and tables can be set up to tell the whole story the moment students walk into the room. Some urgent problem might be posed simply by setting up worktables with certain materials. For Model UN, whole buildings and weekends may be thoroughly staged. Entire Model UN conferences have even decamped to local government council chambers on weekends (Obendorf & Randerson, 2013).

This kind of staging is designed to be particularly provocative and insistent. It already embodies a certain dynamic and energy. There is not much room left for the usually lamented student passivity when to just take a seat in the room is already to take a side, to literally put yourself in the middle of an intense encounter or debate. And there are no other seats! Or perhaps you are not even in your classroom anymore. Or maybe what seemed like some dry and dated piece of writing is now being challenged with gusto, and even some good points, by a visitor who looks strangely like your professor but seems to be disturbingly unaware of the usual conventions and accommodations of the classroom, such as the sacred imperative not to get in students' faces or disturb someone who is discreetly FaceTiming her boyfriend. In such situations, as the genial but insistent host, I am more likely to start interviewing the boyfriend. Not to be punitive: I genuinely invite him to join in. But the FaceTiming is not likely to happen again—more likely, the boyfriend shows up in person for the next class.

You can already see, then, that such a teacher has a distinctive and deliberate pedagogy. In this book, I call it *Teaching as Staging*. The metaphor is theatrical, but it is also only a metaphor. Such teachers can be said to "set the stage," but this does not mean that fixed scripts are being followed or that anyone necessarily appears in costume. The basic goal is to put students into a self-unfolding and urgently engaging setting, scenario, or simulation, and then trust it, and them, to carry it forward, helping or even spark-plugging or provoking at times if needed. In the end, the teacher may even become more like the classic Guide on the Side (King, 1993), but only in the *end,* and typically not for long. Again, actually, *no* one is "on the side." Everybody is in—the teacher, too.

Chapter 4 elaborates the conceptual infrastructure I am sketching here. For a provisional definition, we may put it like this (Box 1.1):

BOX 1.1
Defining *Teaching as Staging*

Teaching as Staging is regularly setting up classroom scenarios such that the dynamics of the scenario frame and drive most of the action and learning that follow.

Provisionally, let us say that a *scenario* is some kind of dynamically structured situation. A *situation* is some kind of happening or state of affairs. Scenarios are *dynamic* when they contain some tension, opposition, or pattern of unfolding—an inner logic, in short, that structures but does not simply dictate the direction of the situation's movement or eventual resolution, if there is one. Teaching as Staging is an attempt to bring such situations to life in the classroom: to place oneself and one's students within them and let the dynamics of those situations do their work.

Out of the Silos

For Teaching as Staging, staging such scenarios is the primary work of the teacher. Many teachers today do stage occasional debates, of course, or set engaging problems, but these are often brought in with apologetics and elaborate explanations, and probably only seldom and as a break from what's supposed to be the real work. Such teachers would not define themselves by such methods or describe themselves as teachers who regularly do such things. Part of what I intend to show here is that it is possible to go much farther in this direction. *Staging* is meant as a comprehensive, widely encompassing characterization. It can take different forms in practice: There are many kinds of scenarios that a teacher might stage and many ways to stage each kind.

I emphasize this widely encompassing character in part because at present many scenario-based pedagogies tend to enthusiastically silo themselves. Both Reacting to the Past and Problem-Based Learning (PBL), to again cite two prominent and different examples that we will explore more fully in Chapter 5, are often advanced as singular and sui generis. Each maintains devoted communities of practitioners along with exclusive websites, clearinghouses, and dedicated conferences, and the literature about each tends to frame the question of pedagogical method as essentially what mix there might be between the one favored method and the usual default methods, primarily lecture or lecture and discussion.

In the PBL literature, for example, there are elaborate efforts to distinguish PBL from seemingly closely related methods such as Enquiry-Based Learning (Deignan, 2009) and the Case Method (Merseth, 1996). In addition, the courses described are either entirely problem-based (Barrows, 1996) or hybrid courses that mix group-based PBL and lecture (Armstrong, 1997; Clark, 2001) or conventional courses that use one or two such simulations as episodes or supplements (Duch, 2001; Harland, 2002; Stevens, 2015). Some article titles, such as "Some Difficulties in Implementation in an Otherwise Conventional Programme" (Woods, 1997), give the whole show away. Otherwise conventional programs? What about possible implementations in otherwise *un*conventional programs—intermixing them, in particular, with other similarly ambitious scenario-type methods?

A wide-ranging alternative conception like Teaching as Staging can redirect the pedagogical imagination toward complementary kinds of staging and other kinds of scenarios as well. A teacher might only use a few of any one particular kind but would not be tempted to think that somehow any one specific scenario-based pedagogy is the whole story. The variations among different kinds of staging might matter a great deal less than their parallels and potential synergies (Savin-Baden, 2014). A much wider community of practitioners, with broadly parallel and cross-fertilizing methods, might also develop its own community resources and more inclusive pedagogical toolbox. Anyone interested in going all the way—teaching this way all or almost all the time—would then have at hand a much more varied and inclusive set of methods, a pedagogical toolbox that may enable them to teach with problems *and* cases *and* role-plays, as well as simulations and a range of other methods still, and on a wide range of scales, from parts of a single class meeting to an entire semester or more.

Moreover, the literature across many of today's scenario-based pedagogies also continues to picture the teacher as essentially a guide or facilitator, when it specifically addresses the role of the teacher at all (Burgess & Taylor, 2000). Although this picture may seem like no more than a logical necessity, I will try to show that it is unnecessarily but profoundly limiting. There are far more dramatic possibilities for the teacher too. In the end, a more inclusive and wide-ranging pedagogical toolbox may change the character of teachers' whole approach to their work and even, in the end, who we think we are.

Why Teach by Staging?

This book elaborates and explains Teaching as Staging from its conceptual infrastructure through paradigmatic examples, ending "under the open skies" (Chapter 9). The first question, however, is simply *Why?* Why teach this way—in general or (for that matter) ever? What is the attraction? This entire book is my answer, but here at the beginning we can schematically sketch six interrelated reasons.

Staging Scenarios Mandates Active Learning

Students learn actively when they are "doing things and thinking about the things they are doing" (Bonwell & Eison, 1991, p. 5; see also Felder & Brent, 2009). And students doing things—engaging dynamic situations, often urgently, in carefully structured and progressive ways—is the very point of staging scenarios (Pettenger, West, & Young, 2014). Of necessity, students are moving and up on their feet, working with each other to solve urgent design challenges that are then cashed out with the whole class, or they are engaging in role-playing, simulations, or debates, resolving international crises or failing to do so, or applying Freud's theories on the spot to the Republican presidential field or the debate over gay rights. They are emphatically *not* merely passive recipients of information.

Today, the old empiricist idea of the mind as tabula rasa—a blank slate on which experience simply writes—is decisively gone, however influential it remains in the shadows and background of our actual pedagogies. Both modern epistemology and cognitive psychology understand the mind instead as essentially active (Bransford, Brown, & Cocking, 2000). Thus it is no surprise that multiple studies decisively show that students learn even the most traditionally defined content—discrete and often seemingly unconnected facts—just as well, or almost as well, using active rather than passive methods, whereas active methods serve far better for a vastly wider range of attitudes and skills we are now recognizing as even more essential, such as critical thinking, independence of thought, effective problem-solving, collaboration, zest for learning, interest in studying the subject further, enthusiasm, optimism about their own lives and the world, cognitive flexibility, and openness to new ways of thinking (Auman, 2011; Boud & Feletti, 1997; Carnes, 2014; Schwartz, Mennin, & Webb, 2001; Viachopoulos & Makri, 2017). They become ready to contribute to knowledge and not just consume it (Harland, 2002; Stevens, 2015).

Active learning's list of demonstrated advantages is actually stunning. Yet none of these points is a surprise. They have been staples in the diet of every university's Teaching and Learning Centers for decades (Hertel & Millis, 2002). Too often in application, however, the shifts are small: a little tweaking of traditional and still relatively inactive pedagogies, breakout groups during lectures maybe, or the occasional case study. *Much* bigger steps are possible.

Student Engagement Is Immediate and Immersive

Zeeman and Lotriet (2013) describe a University of Pretoria lecture class in classical Greek drama in which Zeeman had been struggling for weeks to explain the sociocultural setting of Greek drama, such as the sexual politics underlying plays such as *Lysistrata*. The students were listless. It was all just ancient history, literally. Then, suddenly and unexpectedly, they found themselves having a furious argument between the sexes. It was a day that the class happened to meet outside under a thorn tree:

An incident with a worm dangling from a small branch of the thorn tree and a passing bird that made a few dives at it caused opposite reactions from the male and female students—resulting in an argument between the two sexes. The lecturer suddenly realized that she was witnessing drama in the making, with the whole class participating, and the question arose "Why not use drama to teach ancient drama?" (Zeeman & Lotriet, 2013, pp. 180–181)

Suddenly, by accident, they were in the middle of a real *Lysistrata*-like debate, right then and there. It was a transformative moment. Zeeman now sets up groups of students to perform for each other not the old dramas word for word, but rather their own contemporary adaptations of those classics, accounting for their adaptations as they do so. And, she reports, her class has come alive.

To put the point more generally: in the default pedagogies, students typically have to summon a commitment to be engaged, if active engagement is welcome at all. Scenarios, by contrast, can be staged so that *dis*engagement would have to be the deliberate—and difficult—choice, when it is possible at all. From the start—by design—students are already and unavoidably engaged, already standing *inside* the question or theme or issue. As a result, the energy and focus can be unmatched.

Writing of simulations in particular, Hess (1999) reports,

In various classrooms, I have observed that the same students can be either fascinated or repelled by the social sciences. The difference often seems to come down to whether students find the material to be relevant and stimulating. The difficulty of the material does not seem to matter nearly as much as its vividness. I have found simulations to be the one consistently effective tool for sparking student interest. (p. 1)

In his book *Playing Politics*, political scientist Tobin Grant (2004) says very much the same for political science because, "like card games and sports, politics is something that makes the most sense if it is actually played, not just talked about" (p. vii). This book argues that game-like simulations and other active-learning scenarios can be much more widely applied (Asal & Blake, 2006).

Built-Ins Are Powerful but Unobtrusive

Scenarios can readily be designed to respond to a variety of specific needs and special situations. For example, the usually vexing issue of unequal participation can easily be addressed. Scenarios can be set up to equalize or otherwise rearrange participation patterns (McIntosh, 2001). If students are working a problem in groups, for example, one devilishly simple solution is to put the most assertive or talkative students in the same one or two groups, so that students in other groups have to step up to leadership in their own. If the group work is later cashed out in class, the instructor can be sure to allocate equal time to each group's report, or maybe sometimes "accidentally" run out the clock before overly vocal groups get to report out at all.

If nothing else, some sort of mediator or judge can be tasked with regulating how much or how long other participants speak. This will be totally natural, even necessary, if it is a structural part of the scenario; for example, a courtroom trial in which a variety of participants must speak. Again, a role-play designed around a sequence of different encounters can automatically distribute participation in desired ways. "The structure of a scenario can have a huge impact on who speaks," reports my colleague and co-teacher Anthony (Tony) Crider, citing a classic Reacting to the Past game.

> In the Trial of Galileo game, the scene bounces around from day to day. One day the speeches are moderated by professors in the Collegio Romano. Later, Prince Cesi invites guests to perform skits at his palace party. Eventually, cardinals select their new Pope in the Sistine Chapel. (A. Crider, personal communication, 2017)

The usual problems seem so recalcitrant, I think, partly because we simply take for granted the formats that generate them, in particular the open-format, all-purpose, opinion-based discussion. Thinking in terms of alternative scenarios immediately opens up a wider range of options that can be designed to structure different dynamics into the situation from the start. Considering the problem of underpreparation, for example, teachers who need to motivate students to do more thorough research for their positions on contentious issues can simply set up a scenario in which students know that their factual claims will be subject to public scrutiny: role-playing some sort of trial or public hearing, for example. The teacher need do nothing more. After one or two public dismantlings of underresearched cases, quality improves dramatically (DiCicco, 2014).

A day's scenario might be quite unpredictable at times. This tends to intrigue students in its own right (Langer, 1997). It also motivates far better preparation. In a lecture-based pedagogy, no preparation is really necessary, however much it might benefit learning. Students know they are never going to be on the spot. By contrast, in courses that use a variety of scenarios, students quickly learn that they need to be ready for anything. The usual artful dodging will visibly fail. Pettenger and colleagues (2014) quote a student debriefing one of their climate-change negotiation simulations: "If I didn't research something, another state would bring up the issue" (p. 503). As Reacting to the Past's founder Mark Carnes (2014) puts it about another scenario, "No one can fake a sermon in defense of Anne Hutchinson's theology" (p. 142). Everyone will know immediately if you are not prepared. But such a defense is exactly the sort of thing students soon realize that they will likely have to produce—and more or less on the spot. The only way is to be ready!

Scenarios Promote Highly Particularized Learning

Scenarios and simulations put students into specific situations. Some may be invented for the nonce, but typically, as we've already seen, they are modeled on real-world situations such as a courtroom trial, running a hospital ward, climate negotiations, National Security Council meetings, or the Model UN (Goodnough, 2006). Likewise, the Case Method and PBL are based on real, specific problems (Kreber, 2001). As Ruth Clark (2013) puts it in her classic book on scenario-based e-learning, scenarios thoroughly "contextualize learning" (p. 13; see also Sorin, Errington, Ireland, Nickson, & Caltabiano, 2012).

Students can study the UN all they like, for instance, but until they are actually within it and trying to work it, they will not have a real feel for it or any investment in it (McIntosh, 2001). At one Model UN session I co-ran, multiple teams were incensed by the veto power of the Big Five on the Security Council. This puzzled the novice instructors—after all, it was in the readings, and students had been told about it in lecture. Apparently all of that had gone by without notice—one more random and irrelevant fact—until at the eleventh hour our particularly obstreperous French delegation was vetoing hard-crafted resolutions right and left. *Then* the students noticed. They demanded, "They can *do* that?" and started poring over every word of the UN Charter to see how they could change it. Now they probably know the Charter better than their teachers do.

Students Catch Fire

Scenarios can truly *catch fire*, in the striking phrase of Teagle Foundation President Robert Connor (Heiland, 2011). Teachers who adapt the role-playing models report that their students, used to disengagement, become "instantly passionate" (Auman, 2011, p. 158). There can be "delightful, fitful, episodic, explosive collages of simultaneous 'happenings'" (Postman & Weingartner, 1971/2009, p. 28; see also Bonwell & Eison, 1991).

Carnes (2014) recounts the peevish roommate of one of his students who complains bitterly about his class because her roommate became so engrossed in the historical role-plays. He unexpectedly meets the roommate at lunch after some of his students commandeer him to pick his brains one day as he is on his way to a meeting. The roommate, at the table too, starts to rant at him:

> My second week in college, Katy and I were in our dorm room. There's a knock on the door. I answer it. They're Athenians, they say, come to see Katy. Next thing, they're hanging out. "Athens this, Socrates that"—all night! Next night, same thing. Then they show up on the weekend. . . . October comes and they're gone. Then some Confucians show up. More of the same. Then November and it's the Puritans. I can't even eat a meal without them (Carnes, 2014, p. 182)

At first Carnes thinks the roommate is teasing, but he soon realizes there is no irony in her voice. In the end, she hisses, "You stole my roommate!" and stalks off.

The roommate (never named) speaks from hurt. She had rather different expectations of the social life of college. Still, unintentionally but utterly eloquently, she testifies to the electricity of real engagement. Katy no doubt started off with exactly the same expectations as she did. Yet suddenly, unexpectedly, college has caught fire. Every night in her dorm room, Katy and her classmates find themselves in the midst of living history, replaying and remaking it themselves. Someone knocks on the door and it's not just some fellow college student wanting to shoot the breeze or the bull, but Athenians, Confucians, or God knows who, and the fate of Socrates or Galileo or South Africa is in their hands, all over again. Even on the weekends and at meals, they can't get enough of it. All that dry, old, dead stuff is insistent and alive. It matters, and she is in the middle of it. What a gift! Underneath, I suspect, the roommate's anger is really jealousy.

Some of Carnes's veterans, long graduated and on the road, write to him that they burst into tears upon encountering the Boston grave of John Winthrop (from the Hutchinson game) or the places Socrates once haunted. They hadn't fully realized, so to speak, that those figures were actually dead. And in truth they *weren't* dead for them, not after they had wrestled with them, or *been* them, as part of one of his classes. Even years later, the fire never quite goes out.

Satisfaction Is High All Around

Positive reports are nearly universal in the active learning literature. Students in PBL courses consistently report high levels of satisfaction with scenario-based work (Maitland, 1997; O'Neill & Hung, 2010; Schwartz, 1997).

Zeeman and Lotriet (2013) cite their students' reports of deep enjoyment of the new course and conclude that "the introduction of performance practice to teach these dramas brought a whole new dimension to teaching and learning in the course" (p. 179). Costello and Brunner (2008) report that "students respond positively to all aspects of the empowered classroom" (p. 63), especially extensive use of problems in class, role-playing by both instructor and students, and well-structured collaborative work. Writing of Model UN simulations in a widely cited review article, McIntosh (2001) reports that "the excitement generated . . . can be a key for opening the world to students who might otherwise have drifted through the mandatory introduction to international relations" (p. 269). Writing of trading game simulations, Takahashi and Saito (2011) report that "students concentrate fully on, and become deeply obsessed with, the thrilling nature of the game" (p. 406). Pettenger and colleagues (2014) report that students from a range of institutions role-playing an international climate-change negotiation regularly ask for longer simulations and more demanding preparation. Even the novelty and unpredictability of scenarios proves intriguing (Langer, 1997), especially when different scenarios overlap different methods, themes, designs, and time scales (Gettinger & Walter, 2012; Dahlgren, Fenwick, & Hopwood, 2016).

Teachers also catch the students' energy, excitement, and general satisfaction. Auman (2011) writes, "One of the main benefits of [using a simulation game to teach psychology] was how dramatically it changed *my* engagement on the class" (p. 159; emphasis added). It's no surprise that active, immersive, and thoroughly dynamic pedagogy, taken up with gusto by students, can be deeply rewarding for teachers as well (Carnes, 2014; Diamond & Christensen, 2005; Stevens, 2015; Viachopoulos & Makri, 2017). For example, Schwartz (1997) notes with amazement that most of his students and, as he emphasizes, every single one of the graduate tutors, rate his PBL course design extremely highly, in what used to be a listless, large-lecture clinical biochemistry course. Remember too that in designing our scenarios, we have effective design options to build in desired features and address or forestall potential problems, as well as the capacity to design in what energizes *us*.

Why Not Teach by Staging?

Of course, readers will also have concerns and objections—reservations about or even objections to Teaching by Staging. These need to be considered at the start and answered at least in an initial way. Broader answers will emerge as we continue.

I'm Not Theatrical

It may seem that Teaching as Staging requires teachers to become theatrical, although many teachers have neither the training nor inclination for such a role. Actually, however, the teacher does not need to be theatrical (Diamond & Christensen, 2005). Scenarios can be set up to run themselves. For example, Carnes (2014) writes of moving his seat farther and farther back in his role-playing classrooms until the students more or less "forget that I am even there" (p. 34). He certainly sets the scenes and arbitrates and advises behind them, but apparently he rarely or ever puts himself *in* the scene.

For my own part, I often do put myself into the scene, especially in the impromptu scenarios. I like the greater control this kind of involvement offers—the chance to more deftly shape and prompt the energy. Besides, apparently I *am* somewhat theatrical. Much more on this will emerge throughout this book. The point here is that greater involvement is only one of many possible ways.

More importantly, many scenarios are not necessarily theatrical at all, for anyone. Problems (as in PBL), cases, debates, or other kinds of simulations do not require any kind of acting skills, although they sometimes can be enhanced by them. Scenarios can be driven by many other dynamics besides the interaction of roles. Again, the chapters to follow offer many more and varied examples.

Lectures Can Be Just as Dramatic

No, they can't. It is true that the play of ideas can be thrilling, even at the usual measured pace (Burgan, 2006), at least to us lifelong academics. Still, intellectual drama is not at all as evident to most students, even with a good exposition, and first-rate expositions, let alone skillfully dramatic ones, are not exactly common either.

Moreover, even the top-notch lecture is still only a pale echo of what students may experience working within even a half-decent scenario or simulation. Think of the Model UN experience briefly narrated earlier, or Carnes's student Katy's utter immersion in Reacting work, in lunchrooms, midnight dorm sessions, as well as classes, where Carnes (2014) speaks of moments of "heart-stopping intensity" (p. 5). McIntosh (2001), writing of Model UN simulations, reports that "there is energy in a . . . simulation that can't be matched in even the best lectures . . . For all the importance of reading and hearing about International Relations, nothing matches the experience of *doing* it" (p. 275).

It is not just that scenarios are typically more dramatic. They are also *differently* dramatic. It is not as though the lecturer is simply replaced by a few students in some kind of set-piece that also may be dramatic or undramatic in much the same ways. In the typical scenario, again, *everyone* is engaged and implicated. It is a profoundly different dynamic. No one participant necessarily drives the work; it unfolds in unpredictable ways shaped by all the participants.

Chapter 7 describes a simulation in my co-taught Life in the Universe class when a scouting party from a future human deep-space exploratory mission finally landed on an alien planet—a completely remade classroom—and proceeded to entirely miss, and half wreck, the forest-shaping hive-mind intelligence already there, the entire class, in two groups, having worked in secret for half the term to prepare for this encounter. The aftermath was a week of impassioned debriefing to understand what happened (Crider & Weston, 2012). A lecture at this level of intensity is simply not possible. If somehow it were, it would kill the lecturer on the spot.

Not All Students Are Theatrical

Sometimes students need to be theatrical in role-plays and the like. At least some students need to take on the roles and step up to participation in general. Some students may worry that they are no more up to it than many teachers.

Some are, some aren't. There are those who will find their voice and niche in more dramatic roles. In general, however, recent studies show that a wide range of theatrical techniques, including Improv methods, are "extremely effective in the live classroom" (Berk & Trieber, 2009, p. 33) and across a wide range of fields, from management and business education to the humanities, without requiring much initial skill. According to Berk and Trieber's (2009) summary of an impressive range of studies,

> when improvisation is reformatted into small-group collaborative learning activities in a learner-centered environment, it can be a powerful teaching tool. Research evidence demonstrates that it can promote spontaneity, intuition, interactivity, inductive discovery, attentive listening, nonverbal communication, ad-libbing, role-playing, risk-taking, team building, creativity, and critical thinking. (p. 30; see also Spolin, 1986)

Not everyone is inclined toward Improv either, of course, although it is worth noting that the chief demographic for Improv as a cultural phenomenon is the Net Generation—that is, basically, our students (Carlson, 2005; Junco & Mastrodicasa, 2007). Again, however, not everyone needs to step into any kind of acting. Those less inclined will find ways to play supportive roles, and because everyone understands that acting is not really the point, in my experience it works out.

Again, moreover, many scenarios are not necessarily theatrical at all. Working through problems, cases, or other kinds of simulations does not require acting skills. Being a thoughtful individual, being willing to take some initiative and work well with others, and being open to the unexpected are quite enough.

Doesn't Staging Require Small Classes?

Most of my own classes are small (30-ish students), and many of the methods described here are tailored to that size. But scenarios can work at much larger scales too. There is a growing and encouraging literature on scenario-based methods in large-class settings (Donham, Schmieg, & Allen, 2001; Hmelo-Silver, 2000; Shipman & Duch, 2001; Takahashi & Saito, 2011; Tormey & Henchy, 2008). Even hundreds of students can easily take active parts in scenarios when multiple groups are organized to take them on, in parts or in parallel, with feedback formats that require that they stay on task without supervision. At Elon, Model UN is run on purpose as a big simulation with multiple sections taking part. Indeed, it cannot work any other way. The largest Model UNs involve *thousands* of students (Crossley-Frolick, 2010). Asal and Blake (2006) note that more participants can actually make it easier to model complex interactions. Such large-scale coordinated simulations can be extremely exciting by virtue of their sheer size (McIntosh, 2001). Small classes can't come close.

It Won't Work for Every Subject

True. Neither will any single pedagogy. Again, I do not always teach by staging either. Plenty of class meetings and sometimes whole courses may need to run in other ways. I argue that a *primarily* scenario-based pedagogy can and does work well in *many* class settings, including many settings where currently it is rare or not even imagined at all. However, do not mistake this for the argument that teaching should only or always be conceived as staging. Why suppose that any single method would work for all subjects on all occasions?

Ironically, in practice, this objection often seems to be an excuse to continue to lecture, rather than consider any other pedagogy even occasionally. Even apart from anything that might be said in favor of another pedagogy, why would lecturing, of all things, be the default backup across all fields, types of topics, or course objectives—as if it were somehow unproblematic while all other pedagogies need to exhaustively prove themselves by different and perhaps unattainable standards? "It won't work for every subject," indeed. To paraphrase a contemporary bumper sticker about capital punishment in

Texas, I'll believe that this objection is serious when people start using it to jettison the lecture.

Education Isn't Fun and Games—What About Learning?

This objection, though baldly and confidently put, in fact calls upon certain deep assumptions about teaching and learning that are also, arguably, deeply problematic. Moreover, what happens in staged scenarios, fun or not, obviously *can* be learning. Again, numerous studies show that even by traditional measures of information retention, students learn as much or almost as much using scenarios and simulations as they do by being served up the information in lectures (Boud & Feletti, 1997; Carnes, 2014; Krain & Lantis, 2006; Viachopoulos & Makri, 2017). At the same time, through the simulation or scenario they are building a range of additional skills and understandings that traditional education ignores or diminishes—many of them directly connected to the "fun" aspects, such as role-playing and collaborative casework (Crossley-Frolick, 2010; Dittmer, 2013; McIntosh, 2001). Other writers laud scenario-based participatory learning for the "transformative learning and collective action" (Kumrai, Chauhan, & Hoy, 2011, p. 525) to which it can lead. There is even good evidence that active learning, particularly through simulation and role-play, leads to more optimistic and positive attitudes toward the world at large (Bernstein & Meizlish, 2003; Krain & Shadle, 2006).

It should go without saying that active learning *is* learning. One of my aims in this book is to show how spectacular and full of life—ebullience, electricity, intensity, joy—it can be. If it does not look like the stereotypes, maybe for this very reason, why is that not to the (immense) discredit of the stereotypes?

"Fun" is a polemical little word, anyway, hinting at passive, spectator-like enjoyment. Yet that is emphatically *not* what scenarios and simulations enable or require. They're typically demanding and edgy—that is why they work. As one of my students put it, the fun is more like skydiving than sunbathing. No one is Snapchatting or daydreaming on the way down.

Most aspirationally, we might speak of complete engagement or "flow" (Heiland, 2011). In psychologist Mihaly Csikszentmihalyi's (1996) germinal formulation, flow is "an almost effortless, yet highly focused state of consciousness" (p. 110). It is a deeply enjoyable mode of engagement and experience that, in short, "can help shape particularly *intense* forms of student engagement in learning" (Heiland, 2011, p. 116, emphasis added; see also Dee Fink's [2003] account in his aptly titled *Creating Significant Learning Experiences*). Carnes (2014) points out that although long educational tradition excludes games from classrooms and any kind of seriousness at all, they too make for marked flow in this sense and therefore can be extremely effective teaching tools. Games engage "aspects of the self relating to emotion, mischievous subversion, social engagement, and creative disorder" (Carnes, 2014, p. 13; see also Huizinga, 1950).

Why is any kind of enjoyment automatically supposed to be a sure sign that learning has flown out the window? A very short answer lies in traditional philosophies of human nature, from Plato's to Freud's, that conceive of humans, and especially young humans, as instinctively prone to slide back into animality. Fun is therefore a sign of regression. Properly engaged, however, and viewed anew, the craving for *activity*—and, for that matter, "mischievous subversion, social engagement, and creative disorder"—might not be a distraction or an impediment at all, but more like the condition of learning itself. Rather than treating subversion, engagement, and the like as weaknesses of human nature to be resolutely put down by self-discipline or external control, we might take them as a lovely sign of how curious and supple the mind and body really are. School should *meet* that eagerness, not set itself up against it and then take the inevitable resistance as a sign that the screws must be tightened even further.

These are very large subjects. The point here can only be that fun and games might be just what education needs. To some extent, our own attitudes can make it so. If a classroom game seems like mere fun and a day off, is it because the instructor makes it so? McIntosh (2001) notes, "[w]hether students actually learn about the world or merely treat the [scenario] as just another game *depends on the approach taken by the instructor*" (p. 270, emphasis added).

I Refuse to Pander to Students' Need to Be Entertained

"Entertainment," like "fun," is a weasel word. Carnes's student Katy is utterly engaged in her Reacting to the past class, but surely it is not "entertainment." If anything, the passive absorption of lecturing is more like entertainment, even or especially when spiced up with videos and the like, as now widely recommended by lecturing's latter-day defenders. Contrast that to the high energy and activation of Improv theater, for example. As just noted, Improv and other such methods fit the current generation of socially oriented, multitasking digital natives, with their rapid switches of attention, social attunement, random humor, and the like (Berk & Trieber, 2009; Carlson, 2005). The mode of engagement is intense as well as media-centric. Highhandedly dis(mis)sing it as mere "entertainment" misses its high energy and pedagogical potential.

No class should pander in the sense that it plays to student prejudices or laziness. Teachers take justifiable pride in challenging students, in the sense that our classes are both demanding and perhaps provocative and unsettling as well. Yet this is exactly what Teaching by Staging does—in fact, I would argue it does so par excellence. It requires engagement; it calls on and heightens a certain tension and even risk; and at its most unusual and entertaining, like role-playing, it may actually be the most powerfully transformative. Carnes (2014) cites an underground student guide from Smith College advising students against taking a Reacting course on the grounds that it is so compelling that "it tricks you into doing more work than all your other courses combined" (p. 6). There you have it—from the horses' mouths.

There Is Too Much to Cover

Chapter 2 argues, among other things, that "coverage" is largely an illusion. Just because we *say* something to students—even tell them repeatedly—does not mean that they understand it, know it, or even remember it much beyond the class period. Composition professor E. Shelley Reid (2004) argues that we need—deliberately, publicly, and collectively—to focus on what she calls *uncoverage*:

> to emphasize discoveries that lead to long-term learning over immediate competencies. That is, we need to conceive of [our courses] . . . as an intellectual engagement rather than an inoculation, as practice in a way of encountering the world rather than mastery of skills or facts, as preparation for a lifetime of thinking like a teacher . . . . Exploratory, inquiry-driven, reflective study . . . should be set out as a first priority in our curricula. (p. 16)

Harland (2002) says much the same thing: "The accumulation of a vast body of temporarily-held knowledge is probably [!?] less important to students than helping them develop independence and lifelong learning skills" (p. 13). Reid (2004) even argues, "Aiming for coverage as a primary goal can undermine all of our other goals" (p. 17).

By the end of our courses, we naturally want students to have learned specific things, and typically a lot of them. Yet as counterintuitive as it may seem, lecturing on the content is neither the only nor the best way to reach this end. Even the simplest "flipped" classroom, for instance—staged or not—gives students the content for reading and exploration outside of class, leaving class time for explaining, exploring, and applying it (Bergmann & Sams, 2012; Mazur, 1997). Again, the problems and cases in PBL can be structured so as to produce just as knowledgeable but far more collaborative, creative, and widely competent students in the end (Hmelo-Silver, 2000).

Scenarios Take Too Much Preparation Time

A verity in the pedagogical literature seems to be that, in McIntosh's (2001) words, "active learning of all types requires more time from instructors and students" (p. 270). For its practitioners, this is taken to be a necessary although sometimes steep price to pay for active learning's many advantages (Lean, Moizer Towler, & Abbey, 2006; Pettenger et al., 2014).

I am sure that this can often be true, especially when a teacher transitions into this new pedagogy. Staging certain kinds of scenarios can require elaborate preparatory work. In general, however, at least in my experience compared with my colleagues', preparation time for Teaching as Staging is not notably longer than preparation for lecturing. Often, I have to admit, it is notably shorter—sometimes almost embarrassingly so. Of course there are the usual demands on preparation. We must carefully review the readings, like any teacher regardless of pedagogy. We must think up and think through the scenario. We must prepare handouts, secure and prepare the necessary spaces, arrange the props if any, and so on. All of this takes time. Nonetheless, at least in my experience, it takes markedly less time than to prepare a decent lecture on the same subject.

Staging may *seem* to take more time because the preparatory work is public and visible. Teachers typically prepare lectures out of public view—at home, at night, or in their offices—whereas the teacher who is always rearranging chairs and tweaking worksheets and costumes looks busy much of the time. I often look very busy at school. Off duty, though, time is much freer.

What About Assessment?

What about tests? Scenario-based teaching still aims, in part, for particular knowledge in the end, so a scenario-based teacher can still use standard testing if desired. Again, I have suggested that a wider range of skills are also promoted in scenario-based teaching, and many of these too can be evaluated. In fact, such assessment practices are already well developed across a wide range of scenario-based pedagogies and disciplines (Bernstein & Meizlish, 2003; Burgess & Taylor, 2000; Duch & Groh, 2001; Lovie-Kitchen, 2001; Maitland, 1997; Pellegrino, Lee, & D'Erizans, 2012).

A colleague who uses simulation games to teach educational psychology—setting students up to model a school board debate about whether to institute a developmentally based moral education program, for example—still uses a full range of traditional assessments, such as position papers, peer review, reflection papers, class participation, and even quizzes (Auman, 2011; see also Raghallaigh & Cunniffe, 2013). Model UN teachers may assess students by their participation as well as through reflective essays (Obendorf & Randerson, 2013). Usually there are awards and prizes for teamwork and best delegate at Model UN conferences as well. Bernstein and Meizlish (2003) make extensive use of student activity journals to grade their simulation of the budget process in the U.S. House of Representatives, noting that "journals of active students were almost always qualitatively differently from those of inactive students" (p. 201).

Auman (2011) also mentions grading student productions for mock media campaigns, along with position papers they produce for their roles in the simulation. Inside a simulation based on the French Revolution, Carnes grades student contributions to the revolutionary newspapers that daily make their appearances. In the Life in the Universe courses I have taught with Tony Crider, students ended up expressing their understandings of the perils and possibilities of extraterrestrial contacts partly *as* extraterrestrials (more on this in Chapter 7) and in forms such as mythologies, art works, manifestos, and even an in-group wiki. Tony and I would sometimes respond in kind—that is, inside the scenario as well. Of course we and our students also stepped out of those roles, returning to our own persons, as part of the summative and reflective work—but work of either sort, inside or out, can be graded. This kind of grading can even be, mirabile dictu, thoroughly enjoyable.

It's Risky!

Lecturing can *look* successful even if absolutely no one is listening. All it takes is for everyone to be quiet. Staging scenarios, by contrast, makes everyone partly responsible for their success. Students have to respond, take it up, and look sharp. But maybe they won't. Some days, maybe no one wants to step forward. Quietness then can mean visible and uncomfortable failure. A class may respond in unexpected ways that do not coalesce, or it may fail to solve a problem or pull off a role-play, ending in frustration. Blank stares, automatic passive resistance, the expectation that at the end of the day you will really just lecture so that students can absorb or not as they please—all of this can be uncomfortably evident.

Teachers can manage the risks to some extent. We can use more scaffolded or naturally engaging scenarios, and we can plan to call first on students who we know are game and ready. If a scenario is truly failing, we can also just call it off and try something else next time. Still, there are tradeoffs. We only want to modulate the risk so far, because the risk itself also brings many of the advantages of teaching by staging. Box 1.2 gives a bit more of the rationale, and I return to this theme in some detail in Chapter 6.

Some of my colleagues complain of students' unwillingness to take risks. Students are too self-protective, they say. Why aren't they more willing to venture guesses and new hypotheses, try a position or role on for size, or step out and step up? The answer to this question, I think, is that *we* rarely take serious (or any) risks either. Perhaps only when we professors manifestly cast ourselves into this kind of uncertainty and exposure, as an act of joyful trust and a visible condition of greater mastery, can we justly ask students to do the same.

BOX 1.2
Hidden Possibilities

I've cited Mark Carnes's (2014) experience of student reactions to his Reacting to the Past games, such as the student who angrily accused him of "stealing her roommate" because her roommate became so utterly absorbed in defending Socrates or prosecuting Anne Hutchinson that every knock on her dorm room door probably meant another group of Reactors coming to relive and remake history. Another story (he has many) is of an African American student from Brooklyn, playing a Ming emperor in another game, who has to go home with a fever but then begs her mother to let her come back because, she pleads, "my people need me." When her mother asks who her people might be, she replies, half in delirium, the Chinese people, of course—her subjects. Her mother immediately hauls her off to the emergency room.

Most professors would die for a hint of that level of student engagement. Worse, I am afraid, some actually deny that it is even possible. Carnes (2014) reports, astonishingly but tellingly, that some professors to whom he has recounted such stories simply refuse to believe them.

Those professors have never seen such things in their own classes, so in a sense they disbelieve on the best of grounds. Yet how deep a resignation and hurt there also is in that denial! They have stopped believing in students'—and their own—possibilities, and this disbelief has consequences: They do not create settings in which any such further possibilities can emerge. Thus they *wouldn't* see such things in their classes because they do not make the space for them in the first place. Their disbelief becomes self-certifying, a tight little circle of disappointment from which neither students nor professor can escape.

In teaching, as in life, you often can't know what is possible unless you make space for it to emerge. Our profession calls for a certain venturesomeness. Thus, Teaching as Staging invites students to take an active part in shaping their classes, show their stuff, and enrich the ongoing interaction in ways that only they can. Capacities then show up that you would never have suspected. "The more I empower students, the more they accomplish things of which they did not think they were capable," says one teacher (Sandy, 1998, pp. 49–50). "It can be a challenge," writes McIntosh (2001), "to learn to let go of the center stage while maintaining a structured environment, but the rewards are worth the effort. Student talents come to the surface that would remain hidden in a more conventional format" (p. 275).

It is, in part, an act of trust. We need to co-empower students, or let go of the center stage, before we know what students will make of that power and stage. And we need to make that space up front, so to speak, without knowing how students will take them up (Weston, 1996a; 2004). There will be failures, too—for one thing because students rarely believe that they are capable of such things either. Creating the spaces that call them forth is part of the risk and the edge for everyone—and paradoxically and, yes, beautifully, a condition of their emergence.

This Book

This book aims to lay out a conceptual and practical framework for Teaching as Staging and to ground it with illustrative and sometimes provocative narrative, from both the existing literature and my own practice. The present chapter has sketched the basic idea of Teaching as Staging and its attractions along with some objections and responses.

Chapter 2 carries on with a critical look at Teaching as Telling and Teaching as Guiding, contrasting them both with Teaching as Staging. Lecturing comes in for a thoroughly bad rap—mercifully brief, at least. Next I applaud the usual motives of "student-centered teaching," but argue that the idea overreacts to the repudiation of "teacher-centered teaching," and moreover misconceives and understates what teachers who try to be student-centered actually do. Often they would do much better to conceive of themselves as stage-setters, or so I will try to show. Beyond teacher-centered teaching and student-centered teaching, in short, we can begin to catch a glimpse of something else: *scenario*-centered teaching.

Chapters 3 through 5 develop the model in detail. Chapter 3 elaborates the notion of scenario as used in this book and then works through an extended example of a scenario tailored to a single class session. Chapter 4 takes up the archetype of the impresario. Chapter 5 continues by outlining the main dimensions of pedagogical scenarios, broadly speaking, and then outlines three main but non-exclusive families of scenarios, which I label Step-Right-Ins, Task Groups, and Role-Plays. Main features and representative examples—at least somewhat familiar extant contemporary pedagogies—are offered for each.

Chapters 6 through 8 offer illustrative narratives from my own practice by way of filling in the picture. Chapter 6 illustrates shorter and daily kinds of scenarios. Chapter 7 narrates some of my adventures in role-playing, for example role-plays on a variety of scales from my Environmental Ethics class, and the alien-contact simulation, already briefly mentioned, from my co-taught Life in the Universe classes. Chapter 8 continues with whole-course scenarios, including an ethics class design in which part of the chief work of the class is to explicitly constitute itself as an ethical community, and my Philosophy of Education course in which every educational philosophy is taught using its own favored pedagogy—a scenario of scenarios, as it were. Chapter 9 concludes with a brief look at some sample classes "under the open skies."

CODA
No Judgment!

It is no news that teaching today is often highly constrained and pressured (Hockings, 2005). Many professors lack institutional support for or even administrative comprehension of anything other than lecturing, and they have little enough support for anything more than perfunctory attention even to that. Sometimes they—we!—are impossibly constrained by huge classes; increasingly heavy teaching loads; massive pressures toward "coverage" from administrative and certificatory mandates; the available textbooks; disciplinary self-understandings (Reid, 2004); and even such simple things as desks bolted to the floor, room schedulers unwilling to meet or even invite your room requests, and janitorial mandates such as the default desk arrangement in most classrooms.

I know. I have been there, too, although for most of my professional life I have been freer than many in these ways (although it has taken work). To be clear, then, nothing in this book is meant to impugn teachers whose room for anything venturesome has been thoroughly closed down or off in these ways. On the contrary, you might even consider its normative import, such as it is, to go in the other direction. By offering a sketch of the possibilities for teaching that go far beyond not only the norm for many professors but also in a sharply different direction from even the idealized norm for today's best-established and most privileged faculty members, this book might give us some basis for a more systematic critique of the whole system as it stands.

Finally, though, I feel compelled to push the edge even here. Often there is more space in seemingly stuck situations than it may seem at first. We justly bemoan large class sizes, for example, which of course create huge constraints, but even so, we may also consider ways in which large classes create new opportunities and advantages. As suggested earlier, scenarios such as Model UN enactments actually require large numbers of students to be effective. A beleaguered teacher may try other strategies, too, such as seeking out more supportive cohorts already teaching in innovative and maybe even scenario-centered ways in their institution and beyond.

All too often, the more creative or possibilistic kinds of thinking are closed down by the reigning culture of complaint, and in this we are all implicated to some extent (Senge, 1992; Weston, 2004). In the end, this book is a plea—or, perhaps more aptly put, this book hopes to be an intervention—for a culture of radical pedagogical possibility.

2

NEITHER SAGE NOR GUIDE

To make our way deliberately and systematically into Teaching as Staging, we require a somewhat fuller account and a sharper critique of the familiar alternatives. We can be expeditious. The main aim is to undergird the move to a new model, and in many ways the best arguments for it are its positive virtues. Still, scenario-centered teaching develops naturally out of an understanding of the limits and difficulties of the default pedagogies, and these are steps we must briefly retrace first.

Teaching as Telling

To put it only a little baldly, the function of the lecture is to transmit information from teacher to students. Naturally then, on this model, teaching is *telling*. All of the familiar features of school follow directly from this starting point.

Teacher-Centered Teaching

From this viewpoint, teachers are positioned as authorities in relation to students by virtue of having something important to tell students. At the college level in particular, what qualifies teachers—traditionally almost their sole qualification—is their knowledge of a field. They possess the information that needs to be passed on. Ideally, students come to them receptive to it, and teaching is simply the act of passing information on. Teaching is supposed to be the easy part—everyone knows how to tell people things, after all—and acquiring the information the hard part, certainly the only part that gets any attention in most graduate programs even today.

Correlatively, we are invited to conceive information as something that comes in pieces: in discrete bits or bytes, and therefore it seems even more natural to break down subjects into subtopics and these in turn into yet smaller sets of information, which can then be nicely organized into conveyable units, like courses—that is, literally, rounds through the usual topics—as well as into textbooks and their canonical chapters, and ultimately of course into lecture programs. Meanwhile, retention is also easily testable. How many pieces do the students retain? There is a clear and quantitative model for testing, in short, that fits perfectly with everything from the SATs and all their cousins to in-class quizzes.

Lecturing has massive inertia in today's colleges and universities. It is still by far the most common teaching method, across all disciplines, all class sizes, and all institution types, and at rates that have changed little since the 1950s (Bligh, 2000; Gardiner, 2000; Lammers & Murphy, 2002). Faculty and students alike regularly identify lecturing with college teaching as such. It also offers massive ego boosts to professors (Abrahamson, 1997; Evans & Boy, 1996). Who wouldn't want to be considered a fount of wisdom, reverently attended to by crowds of young people eager for guidance? Multiple critics have pointed out that such authority-centered schooling is also a natural preparation for hierarchy-based workplaces, and that this preparation was originally unabashed and by design (De Graaf & Miersen, 2005; Gatto, 2002, 2009).

Physically, lecturing is built into the layout and design of the majority of our classrooms, for example with fixed desks meant for one frontal focus of attention. Online education, the latest thing, is actually more of the same: still lectures, but to 50,000 students rather than 50. Passive absorbency remains the insistent *implicit curriculum* (Giroux & Penna, 1983) of our own training and self-expectations as teachers. Nearly all of today's college-level faculty, after all, were primarily lectured to themselves. Students often expect the same thing: you're not really in college unless and until you've had to suffer through lectures. This by itself often creates an overwhelming undertow toward the lecture norm for teachers trying to work themselves toward alternative pedagogies (Schwartz, 1997; Evans & Boy, 1996; Miflin & Price, 2001).

No Support in the Data

Of course lecturing often *looks* good, given the usual assumptions about teaching. Lecturers lay out material in connected, articulate, maybe even clever and entertaining ways, and students quietly write the information down in their notebooks. Many students do manage to retain enough of this information at least to go on to the next course. Bligh's (2000) well-known work offers a measured, if backhanded, endorsement of the effectiveness of lectures. For some subjects, he reports, it is at least no more ineffective than the other usual methods.

Yet in general, even judged solely by information retention, the results are utterly abysmal. A few studies have suggested retention as high as half a lecture's information content, but rates of 20% or less are the norm (Blackburn, Pellino, Boberg, & O'Connell, 1980; Bonwell & Eison, 1991; Burke & Ray, 2008; Davis & Alexander, 1977; Gustav, 1969; McLeish, 1968; Milton, Pollio, & Eison, 1986). Astonishingly, this is true even for immediate retests. One study found that retention of information from lectures starts at about 35% for information introduced early on and declines precipitously after about 25 to 30 minutes. Eventually it falls into the single digits. From whole chunks of lectures, sometimes nothing at all may be retained (Burns, 1985).

I do not know how even a 50% retention rate could be considered a success. Isn't it already a kind of disaster? The other half of the carefully structured lecture, presumably essential information too, is just to be written off from the start? And again, this is under the best possible conditions.

It is not a matter of bad lecturing. The data suggest massive content loss even in the best transmission. Of course technique helps a little. With some quick activity to wake people up, such as Buzz Groups (talk to your neighbor for a minute) or just the chance to get up and stretch, retention improves, a little. However, it quickly drops into the bargain basement again, this time to stay (Middendorf & Kalish, 1996). There seems to be little or no data on retention across multiple lectures back to back, although this is the actual student school-day experience at many institutions. Maybe we just don't want to know.

According to "the largest and most comprehensive meta-analysis of undergraduate STEM education published to date,"

> To test the hypothesis that lecturing maximizes learning and course performance, we meta-analyzed 225 studies that reported data on examination scores or failure rates when comparing student performance in undergraduate science, technology, engineering, and mathematics (STEM) courses under traditional lecturing versus active learning. The effect sizes indicate that on average, student performance on examinations and concept inventories increased by 0.47 [standard deviations] under active learning ($n =$ 158 studies), and that the odds ratio for failing was 1.95 under traditional lecturing ($n = 67$ studies). These results indicate that . . . students in classes with traditional lecturing were 1.5 times more likely to fail than were students in classes with active learning. Heterogeneity analyses indicated that both results hold across the STEM disciplines, that active learning increases scores on concept inventories more than on course examinations, and that active learning appears effective across all class sizes. (Freeman et al., 2014, p. 8410)

These results, conclude the authors in their cautious and understated voices, "raise questions about the continued use of traditional lecturing as a control in research studies, and support active learning as the preferred, empirically validated teaching practice in regular classrooms" (also Freeman et al., 2014, p. 8410). Note also that this is in the STEM fields, where traditional lecture models have the strongest hold (Bajak, 2014).

Students do pass the tests—at least most of them do—and of course the tests are keyed to the lecture method and content and presuppose different enough retention failure to get a normal curve of grades (Christenson, Reschly, & Wylie, 2012). Large amounts of pure information may even remain in short-term memory for a few days or weeks, maybe until the end of the class if the final is cumulative, but not necessarily much after that (Evans & Boy, 1996). An advisee of one of my colleagues reported to him that she'd taken a medieval history class a year or so earlier, but when asked what she remembered about medieval history, she could think of nothing at all. From an entire course, which she'd passed with a creditable grade, too, the only thing she remembered was that the cover of her textbook was green.

Teaching Students to Think—Not

Moreover, all of this is still only to interrogate lecturing solely by its own standard: information retention as judged by discrete-item tests. Advocates of active learning do not mainly argue that active learning is better than passive learning for the sake of retaining information so conceived. More accurate is to say that the critics have an entirely different model of the human being, and consequently of learning and its goals.

Critics characterize lecturing as a "filling station model" (Gardiner, 2000, p. 121) of teaching or, in Paolo Freire's (1970) classic terms, as a *banking* model of education. Knowledge, Freire claims, is pictured as a kind of currency that lecturers deposit into students' accounts. Students' knowledge accounts, of course, are initially supposed to be empty. They have nothing to offer themselves on the subject, or at best a tiny bit of knowledge, probably poorly organized and conceived, and probably coupled with much more chaff. In these terms, the presupposed model of teaching is once again the one-way transmission of specific content from what is sometimes also labeled the *jug*—the teacher, brimming with well-organized knowledge—to the *mugs*, students, all too aware of their own emptiness but (one hopes) thirsting to be filled.

In Freirean terms, by contrast, teaching's proper aim is to help students become actors and subjects in their own rights, not passive absorbers or mere objects in the educational process. Critical dialogue, rooted in the experiences that students already bring to education, rather than merely acquire through it, is a key means to education as "the practice of freedom" (hooks, 1994). For others, the key premise is the active mind: naturally exploratory, curious, and, therefore, yes, even restive. The teacher's challenge is to embrace and harness that activity and give it order, direction, organization, and maybe inspiration as well (Barkley, 2010; Barr & Tagg, 1995).

In these critics' view, the inescapable root of the problem is the essence of the model of Teaching as Telling itself: that it is *telling* in the first place. Information is understood as given, both in the sense that it is literally given by the authority-professor to students but also, symbolically mirroring the structure of the lecture itself, in the sense that it is established, finished, and not to be questioned. Knowledge is not for the learner to challenge but to receive, to deposit. There is no openness in it, no question, no *process* (Margetson, 1997). Especially if the lecture is well organized and clear—that is, precisely if it is a good lecture by the usual standards—and even if the lecturer takes pains to trace the twists and turns of the development of the knowledge being presented, still a proper lecture should and will lay the story out so that the final result seems only fitting and natural. The uncertainty, struggle, incompleteness, confusion, and dead-ends that characterize students' work as well as our own—and in fact characterize all real thinking—will not come into view without enormous artfulness by the lecturer, and even then the students will mostly be waiting, by habit long ingrained by all their other lectures, for the next factoid to write down in their notebooks.

No wonder that, according to yet another study, students from lecture courses show no appreciable gains in independent or critical thinking skills. Summarizing more studies:

> Regardless of the quality of the lectures, students were lost confronting a real problem, were unable or unwilling to question anything the teacher or textbook said, and remained superficial, competitive, and unconnected to their own learning. (Hockings, 2005, pp. 313–314; see also Crawford, Gordon, Nicholas, & Prosser, 1998; Trigwell, Prosser, & Taylor, 1999)

The words actually hurt. To put it simply, the fundamental concern is that lecturing does not, and by nature *cannot*, teach students to think. If anything, it teaches them *not* to think (Box 2.1). Shockingly, but in a sense also quite obviously, the implicit curriculum of lecturing seems to run exactly counter to what we say (and, no question, surely mean) we want to teach.

BOX 2.1
Burgan's Case for Lecturing

A widely cited 2006 essay by the American Association of University Professors' Mary Burgan offers one of the few unapologetic defenses of lecturing I have been able to find. Burgan holds that lecturing's chief value is that it exposes students to lecturers' "passionate display of erudition" (Burgan, 2006, p. 30; see also Bent, 1970; Saarinen & Slotte, 2006). Students do not want to work through their classmates' unfounded and offhand opinions, she claims, nor even have to develop or foreground their own views, when they can simply take in the vastly better informed and developed views of the masters. Let them learn how to think by watching expert minds at work. Their own thinking can come later.

Burgan points out that students regularly pay fantastic admission fees to experience the basically one-way transmission of musical or theatrical performances. Similarly, she suggests, in its lecturers "the academy too offers students the thrill of being together at an extraordinary event, the public display of daring and dazzling intellectual expertise" (p. 34). But the analogy doesn't hold. Students don't go to rock concerts multiple times every day, nor do rock concerts require homework, nor are students even studying rock music. Burgan has here a sterling argument not for any kind of everyday pedagogy, but for the very occasional—and perhaps uniquely skillful—eminent visiting scholar.

To come to the point another way, let's imagine that we were somehow designing formats from scratch by which to display "daring and dazzling intellectual expertise." Surely we would not even look twice at lecture as such a format. Not when few actual lecturers will be either daring or dazzling, by the law of averages if nothing else. Not when even certifiable experts are often notoriously poor lecturers to boot (with all due respect to both, they are different skills). Not when genuine mastery, as just argued, is far more open-ended, far less thoroughly defended or definitively structured, far more exploratory, and, yes, far more improvisational than the nicely organized and definitive kinds of information presentation than lectures are designed to offer (Amundsen, Saroyan, & Frankman, 1996).

Students do not actually see a lecturer's mind *at work* at all. Again, as Margetson (1997) points out, they see expert *conclusions*, not *processes*. "Work" is precisely what they do not and arguably cannot see.

As her argument reaches its rhetorical climax, Burgan insists that many of the foundational ideas of natural science, as well as many other subjects, "cannot really be learned without a substantial amount of direct exposition" (p. 33)—that is, lecture. She then goes on, seemingly as an offhand and rather sarcastic illustration of this point, to claim that "No faculty member can 'guide' an ordinary student into familiarity with the Periodic Table" (p. 33). Her reference is to Dmitri Mendeleev's great contribution: a way of organizing all the chemical elements by unique atomic number into a single table, displaying systematic relationships between the known elements, and predicting specific but then still-undiscovered elements from the structure of the table (Scerri, 2006).

Burgan offers no argument for this claim. Apparently it strikes her as so obvious that it needs no argument. Probably she also could have picked a dozen other examples that would have served her point as well. Yet the periodic table is the example she did pick, and there is a certain honor in following through with that example. For here is the striking thing: there are in fact a wide range of games and simulations that allow students to learn the periodic table in ways very different than "direct exposition."

Numerous online simulations are available from sources as diverse as the National Aeronautics and Space Administration, the Royal Society of Chemistry, California State University, and others. Some are even designed for middle schoolers. Interactive periodic tables allow students to (safely!) test all manner of chemical reactions and display the underlying physical structures in ways that they can in turn explore and manipulate (Diener & Moore, 2011). Games and creative writing assignments have been developed to, yes, guide younger students into understanding the nature and interactive potentials of different elements (Burke, 1995; Corcoran & Allen, 1994), and there are ingenious ways of introducing older students to the underlying logic of the periodic table, even as simple as giving them only the logic—the bare structure—for them to fill in on their own (Cherif, Adams, & Cannon, 1997).

A game co-developed by my Elon colleague Dan Wright (Wright & Mitchell, n.d.), actually sets up students to *reinvent* the periodic table, although in a simplified way, using a set of cards much like Mendeleev himself used (Scerri, 2006), and building in, if desired, some of the uncertainties and false clues that afflicted Mendeleev's own data (Mlodinow, 2015). Going still further, Olivares, Merino, and Quiroz (2013) challenge their students to design *new* periodic tables, which must accomplish the same fairly technical purposes as the standard one but in some original way. This lovely approach not only teaches students Mendeleev's table but also highlights the possibility of alternative formulations even of such basics—again, the possibility, indeed necessity, of creativity in science.

(*Continues*)

Box 2.1 *(Continued)*

Clearly Burgan never even looked. Such is the spell cast by Teaching as Telling that she apparently did not consider such alternative pedagogies even possible. Yet they are not just eminently possible, many of them already exist, and they may well be superior to what she calls "direct exposition." To adapt a remark I made earlier about Model UN, the difference is between being told about Mendeleev and *becoming* Mendeleev—if students, as in Wright's game, reinvent the periodic table themselves. Then it no longer seems a random and "given" arrangement of elements, but an elegant and powerful way of comprehending and relating the whole of the chemical elements. Even more deeply, students who learn scientific basics this way are offered a glimpse of science as a synthetic process that they, too, can take part in—radically different from the message of simply presenting those basics as finished, factual products only to be accepted and memorized. They enact science itself in a different key—and, among other things, get a major boost as knowers in their own eyes.

Lecturing Presumed

Of course, it will immediately be said that even everyday lectures can be improved (Bligh, 2000; Middendorf & Kalish, 1996; Harrington & Zakrajsek, 2017). Bows toward more active methods are possible, such as brief group work or buzz groups. Video, PowerPoint, and the like can be used to illustrate and make key points more vivid. When certain administrators and businesses imagined taking lecturing onto the Internet in a big way through massive open online courses (MOOCs), their presentations began aspiring to cinema-quality pacing and visuals. The MOOC movement seems have gone into a tailspin recently, but at least it made it clear that the production values of lecturers' visual aids can be, and in some places are being, immensely improved.

I'd rather attend that sort of lecture, too—if I had to go at all. The curious thing, however, is that the entire discussion still simply presumes lecturing. We are encouraged to ask how visual media can augment and improve lecture delivery, and to contemplate all sorts of creative and cinematic possibilities, while classrooms everywhere are still built as lecture halls, now with lots of built-in media. But who thinks that movie theaters are active learning environments? Why don't we ask how online or other forms of computer-based interaction might *take the place* of lecturing instead? Why don't we think creatively about how contemporary visual and other media might enable pedagogies that are different *in kind* and not merely technologically veneered versions of the same old deeply problematic thing?

Summarizing the benefits of active learning, some sources actually list as the very first benefit "giving students a break from the regularity (and potential ennui) of consistent lecturing" (e.g., Sasley, 2010, p. 63). Of course, Sasley goes on to mention a few other benefits, such as, well, better learning across the board, developing analytical skills, problem-solving, teamwork, personal responsibility, creativity, and so on. But when the sheer relief of even an occasional break from lectures still definitively trumps all of these other compelling advantages, we are in a parlous state indeed.

On another front, it may seem that we are finally moving beyond the lecture model by "flipping the classroom"—inverting the usual relation between content delivery and practice-style homework. In the flipped or inverted model, the practice is done in class, with instructor guidance, while the content delivery is presented by textbook (the old way) or recorded lectures, posted online, read or viewed by students prior to class (Bergmann & Sams, 2012; Mazur, 1997).

"Flipping" lectures does not eliminate them, however; it only relocates them. Students now have to view lectures on their own in advance: still one authority figure talking, "covering" the subject. Flipping has the advantage that students can set their own pace, fast-forwarding through material they (think they) understand and repeating parts they don't. In class, the instructor does not have to go over the basics that students are already supposed to have studied. But again, why "present" that "material" in a lecture format in the first place? Even the traditional reading homework in a standard written textbook would allow students much freer pace-setting, and that is still assuming that traditionally parsed or instructor-assigned material is necessary in the first place.

Way back in 1899, John Dewey was advocating using class meeting times for active, teacher-guided application of material that students could approach beforehand on their own (Dewey, 1899/1959). Still, again, one might also go much further in the same direction; for example, by setting up scenarios and projects in which students and not mainly the teacher also select and prepare the necessary background material, without any lecturing at any point. The scandal, as it were, is that the concept of flipping, as presently approached, still explicitly and emphatically preserves the standard elements, just in reverse order. Again, again, again: What if those elements need to be rethought?

Teaching as Guiding

Dewey (1897/1959) held that the only truly satisfying and effective pedagogy is one that joins a flow that already exists in learners' and communities' lives, engaging and expanding on their vital interests, rather than trying to

oppose those flows and establish (impose, enforce, etc.) some other supposedly more proper interests and activities in their stead.

> The child's own instincts and powers furnish the material and give the
> starting point for all education. Save as the efforts of the educator connect
> with some activity which the child is carrying on of his own initiative inde-
> pendent of the educator, education becomes reduced to a pressure from
> without. It may, indeed, give certain external results, but cannot truly be
> called educative. (Dewey, 1897/1959, p. 20).

Dewey (1897/1959) writes of children here, but exactly the same point
applies to college students and indeed to learners at every age.

In short, there is another way. Already implicit in the critique of Teaching
as Telling is a different and indeed opposite conception of teaching. From
purveyor of information and the room's center and source of authority and
discipline, a Deweyan teacher is transformed into students' ally; partner; or,
in King's (1993) iconic label, a Guide on the Side—"on the side" because
the main action is now the student's. Rather than the traditional teacher-
centered pedagogy—in King's (1993) equally punchy label, the Sage on
the Stage—the alternative is insistently and proudly centered on students.
Their energies drive the process, their interests motivate it, and their experiences *fund* it, to use another lovely although curiously dated Deweyan
term, and their experiences are what the process ultimately reconstructs.
Learning, as Dewey (1938) conceives it in *Experience and Education*, is the
reconstruction of students' experience through critical reflection.

Student-centered teaching promotes active learning, as introduced in
Chapter 1. It is built on students "doing things and thinking about the things
they are doing" (Bonwell & Eison, 1991, p. 5; Felder & Brent, 2009). In this
model, naturally, teachers take their cues and material from students, whose
energies manifestly drive the action (Hertel & Millis, 2002). The pendulum
swings. Students must actively engage, putting forward ideas or actions, so
that the teacher can usefully *re*-act and help them reshape, rethink, and elaborate their thinking and action, constructing and reconstructing knowledge
and skill as they go.

In the Guide model, the teacher can also be considered a kind of coach
(Evans & Boy, 1996; Sandy, 1998)—another powerful and familiar guiding metaphor. No one would coach by talking endlessly at player-learners
who are required to remain still and passive in the process. On the contrary,
the players are intensely active. The coach teaches by helping them reshape
their activity. This is obviously true in sports, but arguably it is also true of
academic skills such as writing or thinking. Here, too, student activity is,

or should be, constant and primary. It should drive all the action. Thus the professor moves, as McIntosh (2001) puts it,

> beyond the traditional roles of lecturer and evaluator in a classroom to become facilitator and coach within a learning community. It can be a challenge to learn to let go of the center stage while maintaining a structured environment, but the rewards are worth the effort. Student talents come to the surface that would remain hidden in a more conventional format. (p. 276)

Coaches of sports teams know the satisfaction that can come from stepping back in this way, although personally it can be hard. Students step *forward*. That is one of the great attractions of *not* being at the "center," of living and learning alongside young people, helping them go further on their own.

Getting Out of the Way?

The Guide model is problematic too, I will argue. Indeed, perhaps not surprisingly, its problems are the reflex of the problems with the Sage model just considered.

If the problem with the model of Teaching as Telling is that it makes the teacher highly active and the students passive and reactive, then it seems logical and obvious that the solution is to reverse the valences: to make the *students* highly active and put the *teacher* into a more reactive and sidelined role. I am sure that this is why Donald Finkel's (2000) classic book about innovative teaching methods, for example, is titled *Teaching With Your Mouth Shut*. Read his account carefully, though, and you quickly realize that Finkel does not "shut up" at all. He just insistently raises questions rather than answering them. He models "think-alouds"—talking through the process of thinking—rather than presenting finished thoughts. Indeed, as if he were quite aware of the passivity his title suggests, he devotes wide swaths of his book to extensive accounts of what he *does* do as a teacher, much of which involves his mouth wide open, even when he is explaining, at some length, why he isn't otherwise talking very much.

Nonetheless, Finkel, or anyway his publisher, titled his book in a way that reflects a striking animus against any lead by the teacher at all. In such hands, the Guide model seems to me to promote a role for teachers that is too reactive and passive (Watson, 2012). Finkel's (2000) laudable mandate to "get the teacher out of the *middle*" (pp. 103–104, emphasis added) seems to slide all too readily into getting the teacher out of the *way*, as Postman and Weingartner (1971/2009) put it explicitly in their iconic book, *Teaching as a Subversive Activity*. Finkel (2000) says he wants, sometimes at least, to get the teacher "out the *door*" (pp. 126 & 131, emphasis added). Any notable activity by the teacher as such becomes suspect (Watson, 2012). Postman and Weingartner seem to demand an approach so single-mindedly student-centered that teachers are deliberately and systematically disempowered at every turn. If good teaching is a subversive activity, apparently first and fore-most what it must aim to do is subvert *itself.*

The assumption seems to be that activity in the classroom is a zero-sum tradeoff. That is, there can be only a finite, limited, fixed amount of activity, so that what one side gains, the other must proportionally lose. In even cruder terms, sometimes it seems to be supposed that we must be *either* teacher-centered *or* student-centered. Each "center" is supposed to exclude the other. Thus, my Guide-inspired colleagues regularly regret that they "talk too much" in their classes. If activity in the classroom is really a zero-sum tradeoff, then any teacher activity at all is indeed a defeat or failure (Bergmann, 1981). Only on such an assumption does it become so natural to conclude that to reject a wholly teacher-centered pedagogy requires us automatically to make ourselves wholly student-centered. Even in the much less radical pedagogical literature, however, this is a common inference (Jones, 2007).

And no question: It is easily possible to talk too much. In fact, though, surely this is not because the best thing would be for the professor never to talk at all. Nor is this what my colleagues really mean, any more than Finkel (2000) did. The hope is to talk *differently,* or stage the whole discussion with different dynamics, which, I argue, is likely to be far more active than any kind of circumspect, reactive, and halfway-out-the-door guide.

More Than Guiding

Teachers do not need to get out of the way at all. They need to *make* the way. On a more realistic and inviting conception, we remember that teachers often need to be mobilizers and activators of student energies. "Activity" in the classroom is not in fact a zero-sum tradeoff. We must also highlight and develop a distinctive kind of activity, even deft and energetic leadership, on the teacher's part.

King (1993) says of her Guides on the Side model that, "all he did was structure the situation to allow [certain lines of student questioning] to happen" (p. 33), and later, about another teacher, that she "unobtrusively arranges the context and facilitates the process," for example by giving differ-ent students only pieces of a larger integrated set of information and requir-ing them to teach it to others in groups so that they may "assemble the jigsaw puzzle" together (p. 34). On the surface, it may look as though these teachers are doing virtually nothing, only assisting students and responding to whatever bubbles up from their interaction and activity. Yet I argue that this misses a crucial dimension of the teachers' activities—so crucial that we have to marvel at the power of the Guide model to thoroughly obscure what is really going on.

The other teacher created the "puzzle" in the first place, which surely took a great deal of work and careful thought. Then she divided it into functional pieces and orchestrated the class so that puzzle solving could take place in an effective and unimpeded way. This teacher's *pro*activity as well as *pre*activity is essential here. It takes imagination and serious legwork to create such a project in the first place.

Here, obviously, both students *and* teacher are active, and each side's activity presupposes and completes the other's. The same is true in King's first example. To "structure the situation" so that it unfolds in the most revealing and useful ways, as King says of the first teacher's work, takes a high and skillful degree of orchestration, scenario-setting, and staging, and hardly so modest (why ever say that "all he did" was this?) or even necessarily so unobtrusive either. Once again, this is not at all a merely reactive teacher. He does not do anything like just "get out of the way." On the contrary, his work takes great skill and an unusual kind of self-possession. Something much more vital is going on.

In an influential paper, Barr and Tagg (1995) argue that teachers must become "designers of learning *environments*" (p. 24). Finkel (2000) echoes the phrase: "The teacher's job is to shape the environment in a manner conducive to learning" (p. 8). To do any of this is, however, is essentially to orchestrate class activities (for another and especially influential example, see Box 2.2) as well as structure the physical or virtual settings that support them. That is the intended "learning environment." It is markedly a more aspirational and active role than mere guiding on the side. Not just Guiding, certainly not Saging, but . . . Staging.

BOX 2.2
Teaching as Orchestration: How Dewey's Laboratory School Taught History

In Dewey's Laboratory School at the University of Chicago, middle schoolers were introduced to nineteenth-century U.S. history by trying to card cotton—to separate out the seeds (Dewey, 1899/1959). Quickly, the children "worked out for themselves," in Dewey's typical phrase, how difficult it is, and thereupon began to understand, in their very hands as it were, something of the deadening daily routine of plantation slavery as well as the transformative effect of the cotton gin. Then they actually invented and built their own primitive gins—and spinning wheels

(Continues)

Box 2.2 (*Continued*)

and looms—learning in the same way about making textiles and basic machines in general. Then it was on to the Industrial Revolution.

How compelling this unfolding work must have been for those children! From the point of view of on-the-ground pedagogy, meanwhile, what is striking about this example, like those mentioned previously, is how thoroughly active the teachers must be to ensure that the activity unfolds and flows in the most productive ways. The students certainly did "work out" all manner of things for themselves. At the same time, however, their teachers and support staff orchestrated the unfolding situation and set the class off on this track. Immense preparatory vision and legwork were required so that the unginned cotton and the materials to make looms, clothes, and all the rest appeared at just the right times. Someone had to know the history inside and out, as well as how to sequence it into the class's workshops and discussions.

Dewey makes it clear, in addition, that the students in this kind of activity are also happily and consistently active, that the class has repeated electric moments, and that along the way the students pick up a variety of other useful skills. They even ended up making some of their own clothes. They became proto-inventors: actually (re)inventing the loom, for one thing. Personally, every time I read this account I wish I were back in middle school with them—so different was my own education.

Only as a result of this kind of work, maybe, as the class's exploration actually unfolds, might some of the teachers sit back a bit and look a little like Guides on the Side in the actual event. Once in a while, they might even satisfy Finkel and step out the door. But this is only the *last* step—or, more accurately, just the *next* step—and by no means the teachers' whole contribution. Again, we need a model of teaching that gives teachers' *orchestration* full credit and attention.

Rethinking the Coaching Analogy

Usually the point of the coaching analogy is to underline the student-centered nature of teaching and learning on the Guide model. The players play the game, after all, whereas the coach advises from the sidelines. What better or clearer model for Guides on the Side?

But the coach's role during a game is not an appropriate analogy to the teacher's work. The coaching analogy specifically fails to recognize how actively a coach orchestrates a team's *training*. During practice, the coach is not "on the side" at all. There is no waiting for players to take their own initiative. On the contrary, the coach is in the middle of things, running drills, practicing plays, and intensively working specific skills as well as whole-field or whole-court awareness. The coach plans and sets up the drills, watches the pacing, works with each player individually, and critiques and inspires the team as a whole—not to mention often hauling water and driving the team bus, which are not as merely ancillary as one might think. Logistics and setup of all sorts are keys to the work.

Of course there is a continuum. Sometimes the coach really is just a guide, carefully observing the players' moves and advising them one on one about specific improvements and keeping track of how they do. At the other end of the continuum, however, especially when coaches interact with the whole team, they go much further, for example, by setting up unexpected and edgy challenges to hone their players' attention and other skills. (For another telling example of both, see Box 2.3.) Sometimes this is literally staging, again. My children's coaches often played with the players too, when it came to mock games, which were sometimes set up with unusual or especially challenging scenarios, such as two live balls on the field at once. Always moving the edge out a little further . . .

BOX 2.3

A Real Coach–Teacher

Leon (Lee) Silver was a California Institute of Technology (CalTech) geologist who coached the Apollo astronauts to read the lay of the land so that in their brief lunar excursions—humanity's first chance, as it were—they could recognize the best samples for geologists back home, eventually including, with Apollo 15, the famous "Genesis Rock."

Silver's method? Dress rehearsals for the real thing. The astronauts suited up and made their way over wild lunar-type landscapes, prospecting in just the way they would when they got to Moon. These rehearsals were entirely real in their own ways.

> Traverses—or the routes over which the crews would pass—were carefully thought out in advance. The crews worked from maps exactly like those to be carried on the actual missions, and there were assigned stations along the traverse, each station with its required tasks, each to be reached by a time specified in advance. (Bain & Hershey, 1971, pp. 7–8)

Moreover, within this activity, Silver did not merely comment or react on some kind of sideline, but was insistently in the astronauts' faces. They would clamber around the desert or Rio Grande valleys in their bulky mock spacesuits, eyeing the landscape through their visors, chipping

(Continues)

Box 2.3 (*Continued*)

rocks with little hammers. Silver danced around them unencumbered, critiquing and exhorting all the while. Later they would re-walk, suit-free, the entire traverse to talk through what they had seen—and see what they missed. Then, back at another traverse.

This was coaching, to be sure, but it certainly was not on any kind of "side." Even in these rehearsals, the astronauts were doing the work, of course, but Silver's actual way of carrying on was much more than the kind of reactive and student-driven guiding pictured by the usual Guide on the Side model. He set up the whole scene, constantly acted the gadfly and provocateur, and never let up.

As Bain and Hershey (1971) state, "To Silver, an interesting and attractive environment is the difference between a productive or unproductive learning experience. . . . All of this is calculated to promote student enthusiasm and momentum" (p. 8). I take *environment* here to refer to not only the physical setting but also the scenario into which Silver put his trainees. Strikingly, there also seemed to be a kind of game afoot:

> Of course, good teachers have always known this, and Silver carries a reputation as a good teacher. Astronauts, however, present a special case. For one thing, they are disciplined achievers who labor mightily as long as they feel a sense of accomplishment. Then, too, they are mature, gifted, and sophisticated and must be approached on an individual level. In a very important way, effective training becomes a game of finding keys to unlock interests, curiosity, and responses. Silver clearly prefers to describe it as creative instruction. He also clearly enjoys the test of wits. (Bain & Hershey, 1971, pp. 8, 10)

Eventually, the astronauts reported, Silver got into their heads as well. It was only when his crews finally got to the moon that he was really just on the sidelines—again, only that was like the actual game in the coaching analogy—and even then there he was in the control room, talking geology over a quarter million miles, advising and supporting as only he was in a position to do.

There is a real coach–teacher for you! And what would it be like to teach in Silver's way—all of it, from creating the analogues to traverses to matching wits with students—in a college classroom?

Envisioning Teaching as Staging

In my career as a teacher, I only gradually came to understand how active I was becoming in ways like those just outlined. Long before I had worked out an alternative model, it was stories like Silver's or like Dewey's middle school teachers that made my heart sing and inspired my next classroom ventures. Only slowly, and no thanks at all to my official Guide on the Side aspirations, did I come to realize that this was my characteristic mode of teaching: to set up scenarios within which I might *then* guide or coach students. I was coming to see both what profound necessities and opportunities we have as teachers to activate and orchestrate a class's energies, especially to organize students' work around captivating and dynamic scenes that they can enter readily and that bring all of us together to a higher level of energy, intrigue, and fruitfulness. Students can (mostly) run the show, yes—once there is a show ready and waiting for them to enter and run in the first place.

Finally I came to see that I needed an alternative general model of teaching. Its basic elements are already present in the terms and conceptions that have emerged out of the critiques sketched earlier and the experiences and models that prompted them. The idea of Teaching as Staging is a way to describe the kinds of orchestration, setup, and behind-the-scenes activity that energize and shape actual class work so that in the event—and only then—the teacher may (may!) step largely aside, or (better!) step *in* along with students. Let me close this chapter with a first bare sketch of the basic contrasts.

Contrasting Centers

Teaching as Telling is single-mindedly teacher-centered. Teachers possess the knowledge that must be transmitted, unilaterally, to students. In terms of its object or vehicle, Teaching as Telling could be called a knowledge-centered vision of education.

Teaching as Guiding is paradigmatically student-centered. Practically, students' interests drive the process. In Deweyan terms, again, their ongoing reconstruction of their own experience is supposed to drive the process. In terms of its object or vehicle, Teaching as Guiding could be called an experience-centered vision of education.

Teaching as Staging calls centrally on student engagement and activity, and so of course it is student-centered too. Still, such teachers do not wait for students to take the initiative. They do not merely facilitate the action on students' terms. Instead, their model is *also* teacher-centered, indeed profoundly and proactively, because the teacher's able staging of well-chosen scenarios is the primary means of engaging and structuring students' action in the first place. The center is neither primarily in the teacher nor primarily in the students but is shared by all, albeit in different ways.

Such a classroom could be called *multi*-centered. It might seem that if everyone is a "center," the notion of centers loses its meaning, but I think it actually applies with greater force. It evokes a certain quality of attention or consideration that should be extended to everyone (Birch, 1993). Moreover, if we cast our eyes beyond the teacher-student scale, such a classroom actually does have a specific focus. There is a specific vehicle of the shared work. This is the scenario. Teaching here is *scenario*-centered.

Who Is Active and How?

Teaching as Telling not only presupposes student passivity but also typically enforces it, by everything from the rules and expectations of classroom decorum (*students* "shut up") to the sheer layout of the lecture hall or typical classroom. Teaching as Guiding, I've suggested, runs the risk of overreacting in the other direction, setting up a kind of teacher passivity or reactivity that, when actually enacted, may be frustrating all around.

Teaching as Staging, like Teaching as Guiding, calls centrally on student engagement and activity. In Teaching as Staging in particular, however, the aim is to bring everyone into the activity—specifically by *activating* students around certain designed experiences or "environments" they thereupon enter, scenarios preplanned by the *pro*active as well as *co*-active teacher. Part of the key is the setup, again, and the teacher is the stage-setter in different modes, from creating role-plays to rearranging the desks. Well-chosen scenarios, ably and deftly staged, are essential to engage and structure students' action in the first place.

Learning this way is certainly not passive, but even to call it "active" seems understated. Scenarios may evoke intense student activity (Fink, 2003). Students get to be a bit hyperactive, too. I will try to show that, and how, such teachers may also put themselves into the thick of things as they actually unfold "on stage" when the action is rolling—not just proactive but at times actually a bit hyperactive themselves.

What Is a Teacher?

We could also tell the story from the point of view of the role-archetype of the teacher. The teacher who tells is, again, what King labels the "Sage," with all the action "on the Stage." Here teaching is a performance, a one-person show. The sage *presumes* student engagement, or at least attendance, and such teachers orchestrate only their own performances—for that is all that counts.

Guiding *awaits* student engagement— it's from "the side," remember— and is supposed to orchestrate nothing at all, working only with the dynamics already in play for students.

By contrast, Teaching as Staging *orchestrates* or *provokes* engagement. Scenarios may be edgy and unexpected, and as we soon shall see, students may find themselves in the midst of them before they know it. Scenarios are designed to be urgent, impatient, impolite, and demanding.

Here the teacher's role can be altogether more ambitious, canny, and designing than in either the Sage or Guide models. At the least, again, this kind of teacher is at the center of the work and the planning, with the fundamental aim of mobilizing or activating student energies, and to do so they have to mobilize themselves in turn.

Is there also an archetype for this role? I believe there is: again, it is the literal stager of theatrical events. As I will elaborate especially in Chapter 4, we can think of the teacher who stages scenarios as a kind of impresario. Conceiving and crystallizing the role of the teacher, then, we may move from Sage on the Stage, past Guide on the Side, to *Impresario with a Scenario.*

A summary of the styles discussed in this chapter is shown in Table 2.1.

TABLE 2.1
The Contrasts Summarized

	Students primarily . . .	*Teacher primarily . . .*	*Learning oriented and driven by . . .*
Teaching as Telling	Passive	Active	Established knowledge
Teaching as Guiding	Active	Reactive	Students' existing experience
Teaching as Staging	Activated	Co-/Proactive	Scenarios

3

SCENARIOS

The stage is a state of mind, not any specific location.

—David Sedaris (1997)

K ey to Teaching as Staging is the concept of the *scenario*. This chapter fleshes the concept out and then illustrates it in detail in a sample one-class pedagogical design.

The Concept of a Scenario

Etymologically and originally, a *scenario* was a brief synopsis of an event or a series of scenes or events posted backstage in a theatrical production to guide the performers and stagehands. The practice originated in the commedia dell'arte form that developed in Italian carnivals in the seventeenth century, where the action was mostly by professional actors playing stock figures. Always improvisational, the form evolved into masked political satire in late eighteenth-century France, sometimes politically so edgy that Napoleon even banned it in 1797 (Palleschi, 2005). By then the scenario had become a detailed outline of actors' entrances and exits and a step-by-step outline of the plot, which was pinned up backstage for ready and hurried consultation by the performers and stagehands. The pinned-up version was also called *canovaccio* in Italian—literally, "what's on the canvas," because it was actually pinned to the back of the stage curtains.

Today we speak broadly of *scenarios* in the sense of a scene or setting, as in "The scenario is a hundred thousand years ago as you step from your time machine" or "The scenario is your first encounter with the love of your life." Vocabulary.com's account is broader still:

A scenario is a specific possibility. To plan on playing with a bunch of bear cubs is a scenario—a dumb one, but still a scenario . . . .

When people are wondering what to do, they think of different scenarios. Moving to a big city is one scenario—moving to a tiny town is another. A football team has to plan for many scenarios, like the starting quarterback being injured. The government plans for hundreds of scenarios, such as natural disasters and attacks by terrorists. In literature, a scenario can mean a summing up of what's going on—what the situation is. A scenario is similar to a situation, but a scenario hasn't happened yet and might not happen at all. (Vocabulary.com, 2015)

Scenarios in this sense are used in strategic thinking and planning by businesses and other organizations as well as governments. They may be useful in planning scientific experiments or medical treatments. Notice also that scenarios even in this broad sense have a dramatic structure. A story about playing with a bunch of bear cubs will go somewhere, have an overall shape, and some sort of closure. Imagine it as a scene in Improv theater, for example. In that case it will probably go somewhere hilarious and unexpected—Joining the circus? Becoming honey gourmets?—but still it will be a logical development from the original situation.

Scenarios as Dynamically Structured Situations

Working our way toward more formal definitions, we might start with *situation* as the generic concept (Box 3.1).

BOX 3.1
Defining a *Situation*

A *situation* is some happening or state of affairs.

A scenario, then, will be a situation *structured* in certain ways (Box 3.2). Maybe it is a courtroom or other sort of trial, maybe it is a marriage or a murder mystery or a scientific investigation, or maybe it is some version of these adapted to a classroom.

BOX 3.2
Defining a *Structured Situation*

A *structured situation* is some kind of happening or state of affairs organized on a pattern known to all and at least partially revealed at the start, although it may become more evident or detailed as the situation unfolds.

In particular, a structured situation's unfolding pattern may be *dynamic* in the sense that it tends to deepen and develop through a series of changes driven by an internal logic or built-in progression (Box 3.3). At the same time, its outcomes typically remain open-ended. Participants in the unfolding situation shape and reshape it as they go along. A trial goes through known stages until it reaches a verdict, for example, but that verdict is up to the judge or jury. A marriage changes and evolves over time. An exploratory expedition sets off with a plan but repeatedly adapts to the unexpected as it goes along.

BOX 3.3
Defining a *Dynamically Structured Situation*

A *dynamically structured situation* is a structured situation in which structure progressively develops or unfolds following an inner logic that orients but does not completely determine the direction of the situation's movement or final resolution.

Teaching as Staging, then, is the attempt to bring dynamic situations to life in the classroom (Box 3.4).

BOX 3.4
Defining a *Scenario*

Pedagogically speaking, a *scenario* is a dynamically structured situation enacted in a specific setting, such as a classroom.

In short, the aim of Teaching as Staging is to place oneself and one's students within well-designed scenarios and then let the scenario do its work, or, as our definition in Chapter 1 put it, let the dynamics of the situation itself frame and drive most of the action and learning that follow.

Readers in college pedagogy will know that the notion of scenarios is already part of the discussion. For one thing, although the term is seldom explicitly defined, a wide variety of kinds of simulations and problems are called *scenarios* in the literature (Asal & Blake, 2006; Burgess & Taylor, 2000; Dahlgren et al., 2016; Harland, 2002; Hertel & Millis, 2002; McDaniel, 2000; Obendorf & Randerson, 2013). When ethical problems are put before engineering students in a role-play format, for example, what is called a scenario may be a short description of hypothetical personalized conflict around issues of stem cell research or nanotechnology (e.g., Loui, 2009).

In Ruth Clark's (2013) influential guidebook *Scenario-Based e-Learning*, a *learning scenario* is defined as a "work-realistic assignment or challenge, which in turn responds to reflect the learner's choices" (pp. 5–6). Among Clark's paradigms are challenges such as diagnosing the problem with a car that won't start, in a training program for automotive technicians, or dealing with a variety of challenges as a wedding adviser. Each of these is a *dynamically structured situation*, in the terms just defined, which is precisely what makes them programmable to "respond to reflect the learner's choices." Novice auto technicians confronted with a dead battery, for example, can try out different diagnostic strategies, get results, and make new tests, later also comparing their decision trees with those of an expert. The e-learning basis makes the scenarios interactive, flexible, immediate with feedback, easily adjustable, and widely accessible.

Clark's (2013) range of paradigms is confined by the web-based modality within which she works. For our purposes, however, there is no reason to restrict pedagogical scenarios to workplace applications. A scenario might be a car with a dead battery, but it might equally well be a theological conundrum, a biological experiment, or some historical encounter that students are replaying. Scenarios of these broader kinds do not lend themselves so readily to computer-based programs, but they are certainly still scenarios. The dynamic is no less a problem-based type of learning. It is just that on-the-spot teachers are essential to them—on-the-spot improvisers, of all sorts, within a latter-day canovaccio.

Scenarios Are Structured but Not Scripts

Pedagogically, then, scenarios are far more than general discussion topics or theoretical problems. They are patterns or designs for specific, structured, interactive engagement. In this sense, they are indeed *possibilities*, to return to Vocabulary.com's (2015) definition, but specifically possibilities that embody a *process*. They open up a logically unfolding set of thoughts or suggest a dramatic situation that can be entered into and worked out, rather than only confronted in one step, so to speak, as a situation that is static and "given," allowing only one or a few responses to a set question. Instead there is an unfolding drama, a curiosity only gradually answered, and thus an excitement in them too.

Remember again that the original canovaccios were not scripts but only outlines of the stage setting and the action. The actors had a great deal of leeway in their actual dialogue and movements. That was understood to be part of their craft, their art. It was also a canny political adaptation. The canovaccio was kept deliberately vague, left to the improvisation of the actor, partly as means of foiling censorship. The authorities could not reliably know or control what was unwritten or censor or censure dialogue that was mostly improvised on stage.

Still, the scene was meant to go somewhere specific, with specific steps along the way. The aim of the canovaccio was to coordinate all the participants' actions around that structure or outline. In that way, although scenarios may call on much improvisation, they are typically more defined than scenes in Improv theater today. Improv enactments may morph in many directions and veer off into something that ends up totally different than the starting point. That radical kind of openness is the very point of Improv. *Scenarios*, by contrast, in the sense that I want to use the term here, invite something more like role-playing. The roles establish certain directions and patterns, although how the role is enacted may still be quite open.

Another simple paradigm of a dynamically structured situation would be a scenario in which a decision needs to be made in a well-defined time frame according to rules that are also fairly stringent and already well known. Think of a criminal trial with its well-defined roles and procedures. Attorneys for the opposing sides make opening statements; testimony is called forth and challenged, first by the prosecution and then the defense. Then there are closing statements, the judge's charge to the jury, jury deliberations, and a decision. These roles and procedures give structure to the situation and define specific roles within it. The whole scene is systematically and deliberately headed toward a verdict, although again that verdict itself may be open.

Scenarios, then, for our purposes, are both fairly tightly structured and open-ended. They likely have steps, roles, and some kind of inner logical or dramatic structure, although the full structure may not be evident at first. Part of the intrigue, in fact, may be the gradual emergence of that compelling logic or structure, including outright surprises along the way. Yet the actual enactment, as well as the final outcome, will remain for the participants to determine together.

Scenarios Progressively Unfold

Again, Clark (2013) defines a *learning scenario* as a "work-realistic assignment or challenge, which in turn responds to reflect the learner's choices," adding that they naturally evolve into "progressively more complex experiences" (pp. 5–6). This addition is useful and indeed essential for our purposes as well.

In Clark's (2013) programmed learning scenarios, students' initial choices have consequences that make their own demands for further information gathering and choices. Maybe would-be auto mechanics learn general test patterns for dead car batteries. This enables them to make finer and finer distinctions between possible causes, as the source of the trouble is progressively narrowed down and localized, calling in turn for the use of more specialized diagnostic and repair equipment, all tracked and later displayed by the program and compared to an expert's procedure. The same works for planning a wedding or treating a sick child. In each case, "progressively more complex experiences" are built into the *situation,* and therefore the learning program.

Or again, in a court case, evidence must be used and must stand up to critical scrutiny. Otherwise the judge may summarily dismiss the case or the jury quickly reject it. Because the accused is assumed innocent until proven guilty, there is a formal presumption within which the trial proceeds: The burden of proof is on the prosecution or the party that brings the action. There may also be initially hidden but extremely telling features of the evidence, which structured critical scrutiny should uncover in time. At first it may appear that there are multiple witnesses, for example, but on careful examination perhaps it turns out that only one person was in a position to actually see the alleged crime. What if all the other supposed witnesses got their confidence about it from X, and X is demonstrably a chronic liar with a clear motive for lying in this case besides?

Of course, a mock trial, just like a real trial, might end in conviction anyway. Justice can miscarry. Nonetheless, we can still say that "progressively more complex experiences" are thoroughly built into this situation. The normal course of such a trial should progressively uncover the flimsiness of the evidence, and the result will likely be acquittal. Its inner logic, not necessarily evident at first but waiting to be uncovered and gradually, will have its effect—which is why such trials, again either staged or real, can be so dramatic.

Philosophers call this sort of progressively more complex experience a *dialectical* process—a term we will find useful at many points in this book. There is a fair amount of disagreement about the exact nature of dialectics, but commonly recognized elements include some kind of back and forth between recognizably distinct stages of thought, each developing in response to the inadequacy, incompleteness, or contradiction of previous views (O'Connor, 2004). The experience is "progressively more complex" in the more exact sense that it is progressively better developed, more thoughtfully worked out, responsive to more issues or points of view, and in general more worked *through* toward better-resolved conclusions and understandings—again, all driven by what is progressively better recognized to be the implicit demands of the situation itself.

Thus we may also define *scenarios* in dialectical terms (Box 3.5):

BOX 3.5
Defining a *Scenario* in Dialectic Terms

Pedagogically speaking, a *scenario* is a dialectically structured situation enacted in a specific setting, such as a classroom.

Scenarios and Simulations

Simulation is also a familiar term in the pedagogical literature. Hertel and Millis (2002) define *educational simulations* as "sequential decision-making classroom events in which students fulfill assigned roles to manage discipline-specific tasks within an environment that models reality according to guidelines provided by the instructor" (p. 15). This definition may be too narrow for some simulations—assigned roles may not be necessary, for example, and not all simulations may be so discipline-specific—but we can certainly embrace the general notion of a specific model that students can enter, with assigned tasks and some sequencing of the group's engagement. Blecha and Haynes (2017) give helpful examples:

> When students are assigned roles as buyers and sellers of some good and asked to strike deals to exchange the good, they are learning about market behavior by simulating a market. When students take on the roles of party delegates to a political convention and run the model convention, they are learning about the election process by simulating a political convention.

So understood, simulations are clearly a kind of scenario. Just as our definition has it, they are dynamically structured situations enacted in a teaching context. Many have a dialectical structure as well. Markets have formal structures defined by functions of prices, by buyer and seller choices, and more broadly by current property law and practices of various incarnations such as stock exchanges. Political conventions have their own underlying structures, rules, and protocols. Both are constantly in movement, through well-defined stages, as determined by these structures and toward certain ends.

Hertel and Millis (2002) use the terms *simulation* and *scenario* interchangeably (see also Dahlgren et al., 2016) and even sometimes write of *simulation scenarios*, but the terms are not interchangeable in my usage. All simulations are scenarios, in the sense I use here, but not all scenarios are simulations. For one thing, the concept of a simulation implies that there is some specific aspect of reality that the simulation simulates (Asal & Blake, 2006; Lean et al., 2006). Scenarios, however, may be the actual problem itself, not merely a simulation of it. An unknown type of object, for example, may show up in what I call a Step-Right-In scenario at the start of a Critical

Thinking class session. Students have to figure out what the object is. This is not *simulating* anything else—it is a Sherlock Holmesian challenge in its own right.

I suppose that an impromptu in-class talk show could be said to simulate a real on-air talk show, but really only in the sense that it may use some of the same props, such as a microphone and stage lights. It only models something else in a superficial sense. In fact, I would say, it *is* a talk show in its own right—not a simulation, again, but definitely a scenario. Likewise, student Model UN conferences are in one sense quite exactly simulations—they aim to teach students, from the inside, about the UN and how it operates—but at the same time they can be considered deliberative assemblies on world issues in their own right. In fact it seems to me quite enlivening and optimistic to take them as such.

Even more clearly, when my Elon colleagues' Senior Seminar students in Environmental Studies spend their term researching and preparing draft Environmental Impact Statements (EISs) for local projects, they are not merely *simulating* EIS preparation. They are actually preparing one, and they have to present and defend it publicly, often with real stakeholders present, as well (MacFall, 2012).

A Sample One-Class Scenario

I teach an advanced General Studies course on Marx, Darwin, and Freud—a sort of intellectual history course with a very compressed manifest. Yet we do not just look at each figure's thought fully developed. My design aims for an element of drama or, again, dialectic—"progressively more complex thinking," indeed. Thus, we approach Darwin, for one, as his thinking developed, beginning with his voyage on the *Beagle* and especially his visit to the Galapagos Islands.

For purposes of a first extended example of a pedagogical scenario in action, let us picture this moment—Darwin's epiphany—as a classroom scenario. Later chapters will look at a variety of scenarios from a multitude of courses and contexts, but I think it is wise to explicate the concept first with a single case. For a sample topic, then, I have tried to pick something suitably illustrative that is accessible to most college teachers but at the same times fairly high-level, lest anyone still think that staging scenarios is only for fun days in introductory classes. Teaching as Staging is just as much—or even more—for the really serious stuff.

Darwin's Epiphany: The Setting

The young Darwin was a firm believer in the fixity of species and William Paley's doctrine of "natural theology" (1802/2001). According to natural theology, the exquisite adaptation of the parts of organisms to each other, as well as the adaptation of organisms to each other in larger systems, was a clear and compelling sign of the hand of God everywhere. Paley's favorite analogy of the theory was how human artifacts such as pocket watches, an impressive technology indeed for the times, showed sure signs of a maker, in this case human, with discernible characteristics. The natural world, then, is like a huge artifact. Its exquisite and thorough going order also suggests an artificer equal to the task, and moreover, wonderfully, something of the mind of that great Artificer can be known from the order we can observe.

Paley's theology invited just the sort of exploration and chronicling of the natural world that the naturalists of the next generation undertook. Darwin came to the Galapagos Islands first and foremost as a careful observer, collecting specimens of exotic species as well as extensive geological observations to send back to the museums and eager scientific societies of England. He only spent a month or so there, coming and also leaving more or less a Paleyan. Yet his experience there, as well as elsewhere on his three-year voyage around the world, led him eventually and inexorably to a radically different view of the origin of species. This is our theme.

The backstory includes the natural setting as well. The Galapagos Islands are relatively young, only about three to five million years old. In his narrative in The Voyage of the Beagle (1845/2001), Darwin notes that there are still volcanic cones everywhere one looks, some still active, and many aboriginal lava flows visible. Whatever processes led to the existence of species there must have happened very recently in geological time.

Certain observations then take on special importance. One is the number of unique species. Indeed, Darwin writes, "considering the small size of the islands, we feel the more astonished at the number of their aboriginal beings" (1845/2001, p. 69), meaning by "aboriginal beings" species that might seem to have originated locally because they are found nowhere else in the world. Indeed, Darwin visited a number of far-out ocean islands—Hawaii, for example—and found the same surprising plenitude of aboriginal species on all of them.

In contrast, these species may be unique but their genera are not. They remain related to types of species—larger families of lifeforms—on nearby continents. For example, the famous Galapagos finches are found nowhere else in the world, yet they are still a kind of finch, obviously, and there are other kinds of finches everywhere, particularly in the nearby Americas. As Darwin (1845/2001) puts it,

> Most of the organic productions [of these islands] are aboriginal creations, found nowhere else . . . yet all show a marked relationship with those of America, though separated from that continent by an open space of ocean, between 500 and 600 miles in width. (p. 69)

The same is true of the aboriginal species worldwide. Although isolated islands may have relatively similar physical environments to other isolated islands worldwide, their aboriginal species typically do not resemble other isolated islands' aboriginal species. Instead they show a "marked relationship," as Darwin puts it, with other species on the closest continents. What might a naturalist make of that?

Finally, the *mix* of species on the Galapagos, like other ocean islands, is also distinctive. Typically there are few large or even moderate-sized land animals, such as the grazers (goats, deer, etc.) found in profusion on the continents, although the islands may have ample grazing habitat. In the Galapagos, the tortoises are actually the grazers: lumbering, inefficient, not particularly well adapted to the role, but there they are. Again, is this a clue? To what?

Darwin's Epiphany: The Argument

The key pedagogical challenge is to help students see how these specific and sometimes sharp observations led Darwin in the end to utterly overthrow the Paleyan view and embrace evolution, or what he calls "descent with modification" instead. Leading up to the session I am about to describe, I ask the class to read Darwin's (1859/2001) summary of his argument at the end of *On the Origin of Species*. The expectation is not that they fully understand it, but rather that they can use it as a point of reference in the work they are about to do.

They begin to see that the argument, at its core, is a comparison of predictions. Darwin systematically compares "special creation" and "descent with modification" as explanatory accounts of the existing patterns of species and their distribution in places such as the Galapagos. In turns out that the two views make sharply different predictions—and these predictions can be tested. Creation comes out wanting, whereas the striking but seemingly otherwise unlikely features of species distribution in places such as the Galapagos are exactly what an evolutionary view would predict.

On a creationist view, the species mix on islands such as the Galapagos, as everywhere else, was determined by God, who of course could have populated them exactly as He chose. There are no physical constraints. God *could* have created just the species mix we see. A priori, however, there is no reason that He would. He might more plausibly have created the same mix of species that we see on nearby continents, including, for example, the usual well-adapted grazers (goats and the like—much better than tortoises) and the usual finches. Why create 13 entirely unique species of finch instead, each scrabbling out a bare existence on 1 or 2 lonely islands to boot? And stick tortoises in places they clearly do not belong?

Or the Creator might have made the species mix the same as on other similar isolated islands worldwide. After all, many such islands have very similar geologies and climates. But we don't see this pattern either. Instead, each set of islands has its own peculiar species mixes, usually with a number of families of species missing, with its aboriginal species (again) resembling related species on nearby continents while differing significantly from other isolated islands'.

"Such facts," Darwin (1859/2001) insists, "are utterly inexplicable on the theory of independent acts of creation" (p. 168). His alternative explanation is now familiar and radically different in kind from Paley's. It is simple, stark, and wholly natural, and it predicts exactly what we see. New islands everywhere will be colonized by species from nearby continents—more specifically, by those species that can get there—which then adapt and are modified into new species by the new environment's opportunities (e.g., lots of different kinds of finch food, especially seeds) and the lack of many of the usual competitors (such as other grazers, which normally would outcompete tortoises on land).

To us, perhaps, this explanation may seem no more than common sense, but it certainly did not in Darwin's time. It would take him more than 20 years to work out the mechanisms and even just advance his theory in public. In class, of course, we can fast-forward. But this is still a key point to stop and explore, and in the class it is our first step into Darwin.

Staging a Scenario-Based Class

These themes don't just seem ready-made for lecture, they seem to necessitate it. A lecture could review Darwin's key texts, unfold the argument, demonstrate Darwin's reasoning, repeating the key points to drive them home. An enterprising Sage on the Stage might project some pictures of endemic Galapagos species, even following up with Darwin's famous chart of the finch beaks to illustrate the "gradation and diversity of structure in one small, intimately related group of birds" (Darwin, 1859/2001, p. 71). No question: the inherent drama and detail in the argument would take such a lecture a long way.

A good Guide on the Side, meanwhile, might ask some students to read key passages from Darwin out loud and then ask them to restate the argument in their own words, carefully and step-by-step. This teacher could guide the class to frame more general formulations of the basic argument, making the session a broad-based class conversation that periodically includes Darwin's voice as well through his text, perhaps opening the question at the end of whether this is a fully persuasive argument and why or why not. Once again, it can be done, and done well.

Yet the last chapter was not kind to either Teaching as Telling or as Guiding. We ended with the promise of an alternative. Still, the best argument—and certainly the most practical argument—against settling for one of these default pedagogies would be to lay out a fully fleshed alternative that is seriously more attractive, more active, and more *co*-active. We now have the conceptual infrastructure of scenarios sketched in the first part of this chapter to help as well. How might a teacher put it to use?

Designing the Scenario
Such a teacher's aim, remember, is to make the inner logic or dynamic of the argument at the very same time the driving drama of the classroom interaction itself, albeit perhaps in a simplified or streamlined form. We must start by distilling the fundamental point—the central argument—as tightly as possible. In this case, as we have said, it is the contrast and conflict of two different predictions for the species mix on isolated oceanic islands such as the Galapagos.

What might it take to stage this literally as a *scene*? To do so, we need to actualize the contrast of the two different predictions in some concrete form that students can readily inhabit. What suggests itself is essentially a version of the basic opposition just laid out. Specifically, each prediction might be *actually constructed*, by the students themselves in real time, as a populated island, with the two different predictions being generated by different processes. The dynamic can then be managed so that students bring the two predictions/islands into contrast with each other. The culminating step would then be to consider which prediction actually fits the species mix we see on such islands. Thus the scene would, quite precisely, "progressively unfold."

Notice that we have already and quickly come to the stage of actual class-session design. To stage such a process, we might discern four steps. First, two separate groups of students would need to generate their predictions, using creationist or evolutionary frameworks respectively. Second, the groups need to come back together and put their predictions side by side. Third, they need to compare and contrast them, explaining and exploring the reasoning behind them. Fourth and finally, both can be compared to actual islands, notably the Galapagos as Darwin encountered them.

Four Acts, so to say. Let us look at the possible staging of each in more detail.

Act 1: Populating Two Islands

The class is gathered for the day. Copies of *On the Origin of Species* (Darwin, 1859/2001) are on the tables—his first appearance. I might start by mentioning that when Darwin embarked on his fateful circumnavigation on the *Beagle*, he was all of 22 years old—basically the same age as the students. Our book cover shows the classic photo of him as an old man with a long beard and implacable look. The class walks in to see projected portraits of the young, eager, open Darwin, the one who scrambled so fatefully onto the Galapagos shores in 1835 in what was still a completely different world.

The room is already equipped with a workspace, or several, depending on the size of the class. Tables are pushed together, each with markers and a poster-sized sticky pad. I offer a brief greeting and introduction—brief because I seek a sense of urgency, and there is much to do—and then I simply say that we are beginning with a project, 20 minutes or so of focused group work. Some groups will go to a separate space. I say no more about it. I do not want the students to think too much about what other groups are doing. Anyway the class is quite used to this sort of thing by now.

We quickly form into groups of 6 or so: 4 groups, say, for a class of 25. I keep 2 groups in the classroom and send the other 2 to an adjoining room or other workspace already set up the same way. Each set of groups has an instruction handout that gives them an immediate orientation and tasks (Handouts 3.1 and 3.2). Then, to work!

The instruction sheets tell each group that their job is to populate an isolated and at present unpopulated oceanic island near the equator. Their job is to decide on the types of species that will be present—also those that will definitely *not* be present. The aim is to generate the kinds of predictions Darwin compares and get the students thinking inside one of the models.

The two groups in one room act as God. Congratulations, I say. Your job is to populate the islands given a Paleyan understanding of creation. The God groups' prompts include questions such as the following:

- What would be Your main considerations about what species to create on Your island and the habitats You give them?
- Would You create new, unique species or stick with species You also used elsewhere? Why? (What is Your track record in Your creative work generally?)
- Would it matter to You what lifeforms You've put on nearby continents? Why or why not?

HANDOUT 3.1

Sample Instruction Sheet: Creationist Perspective

Creation 101: The Island Project

You are the Creator God. Congratulations.

Imagine an oceanic island rather like one of the Galapagos or Hawaii. In Your land-making phase, you created it way off in the ocean, not very close to any continental landmass, though of course it is connected to the larger Earth by wind, ocean currents, weather, and so on. It has the usual collection of potential habitats: deep water, shallow water, shorelines with sand, warm and fertile inland areas (as You'll recall, it is equatorial, though quite temperate, being in the middle of the ocean), also hills and mountains.

We are going to focus on one aspect of Your creative endeavors right now—how You will stock Your island with life: plants and especially animals. Of course, being God, You can populate it exactly as You wish: any way is possible. Remember, though, that especially according to William Paley's natural theological picture, You are a comprehensible, orderly, and good Creator. Creation as we know it elsewhere has an orderly and sensible pattern, so surely this should be true also on faraway islands. You don't want to confuse or mislead the inquiring minds of Your creations.

Work out a rough idea of what types of plants and animals You'd be most likely to stock Your island with, what their distribution would be, and how they would or would not relate to similar species elsewhere in the world.

Here are a few questions to consider:

- What would be Your main considerations about what species to create on your island, and where you create them?
- Would You create new, unique species, or stick with species You also used elsewhere? Why?
- Would it matter to You what lifeforms You've put on nearby continents? Why or why not?
- Likewise, would it matter to You how You stocked similar habitats on various continents or on other islands elsewhere in the world? Why or why not? If so, what detectable empirical difference would it make?
- Are there any lifeforms that would definitely not be present in Your plan? Is there any reason that You would exclude large numbers of possible lifeforms (well stocked elsewhere, let's suppose)? Or would the range and variety of island lifeforms be more or less the same as other places, islands or not?

Please draw some kind of depiction—schematic, it doesn't have to be representational—of the islands and their lifeforms as You'd create them.

HANDOUT 3.2
Sample Instruction Sheet: Evolution Perspective

Evolution 101: The Island Project

You represent Evolution. Congratulations.

We are going to focus on one aspect of your species-building endeavors right now: how evolution would determine the lifeforms that stock certain oceanic islands.

Imagine an oceanic island rather like one of the Galapagos or Hawaii. It is not very close to any continental landmass, though of course it is connected to the larger Earth by wind, ocean currents, weather, and so on. Since the Earth is a dynamic system, it will be understood that it is a fairly new island—formed initially by volcanoes that rose out of the sea over "hotspots" under moving tectonic plates. (Remember that the Galapagos are only three million to five million years old, and they started out as bare, dry lava.) It has the usual collection of potential habitats: deep water, shallow water, shorelines with sand, warm and fertile inland areas (as you'll recall, it is equatorial, though quite temperate, being in the middle of the ocean), also hills and mountains.

Given this condition and your understanding of evolution, what kinds of lifeforms (plants and especially animals) do you predict would come to inhabit your island at present, what would be their distribution, and how would they or would not relate to similar species elsewhere in the world?

The following are a few questions to consider:

- Does it matter that your island is geologically new? Why? How?
- Are there any constraints on what original species you have to work with? Why? What constraints? What difference do they make?
- Would you predict that your island would have new, unique species, or species also found elsewhere? Why?
- Would it matter what lifeforms have evolved on nearby continents? Why or why not?
- Likewise, would it matter what lifeforms stock similar habitats on various continents or on other islands elsewhere in the world? Why or why not? If so, what detectable empirical difference would it make?
- Would the range and variety of island lifeforms be more or less the same as other places, islands or not?

Please draw some kind of depiction—schematic, it doesn't have to be representational—of the islands and their lifeforms as you would predict them.

The other room's groups are the evolutionists. I congratulate them too. They have parallel but different questions:

- Does it matter that your island is geologically new? Why? How?
- Are there any constraints on what original species you have to work with? Why? What constraints? What difference do they make?
- Will your island have new, unique species or species also found elsewhere? Why?
- Would it matter to you what lifeforms have evolved on nearby continents? Why or why not?

Once the groups are set up in their separate spaces, I bounce between them to ensure that the students understand the assignment and to prompt them to begin making connections. Maybe even insistently. *Would* it matter what lifeforms are on nearby continents, for example? Why? To the evolutionists, for example, I ask: How are the progenitor species going to get to their isolated islands? They have to be able to cross open ocean, right? What kinds of species can do so, at least occasionally? Which cannot? What are the implications for the population of your island?

However, this kind of question does not come up at all for God, who can bring forth any species anywhere with the mere snap of His fingers. So what kinds of considerations might be on God's mind? Students who ask how we could possibly presume to know how God might think can be reminded that, at least on Paley's conception, it is key to God's great artisanship that it be comprehensible—precisely that it be recognizable, knowable. Consistency and "track record" matter. This thought may be provocative or energizing to some students. At any rate, for the moment, I say, let's play Paley's game.

I ask the groups to draw their islands with a representative complement of species. That is the point of providing them with colored markers along with sticky posters. I emphasize that artistic quality is not the aim for the drawing, just clarity. In addition, there is a form or spreadsheet for reporting predicted species mix in a readily compared format, listing types of land animals, aquatic animals, and possibly trees and other plants.

Act 2: Reporting Back
The next step is to bring the groups back together to display and explain their predictions. They come back into the shared space intrigued by their world-making work and curious about the work of others. Sometimes they do something dramatic. One time the God groups came back into the classroom playing the "Heavens Are Telling" theme from Haydn's oratorio

"Creation." An evolution group meeting in the nearby philosophy suite had some students who knew about my file drawer full of costumes: Some came in wearing animal masks.

This is fun, but not just that: It also reminds us what is at stake. The levity sharpens the serious work. In Telling mode, the teacher could of course make the point that all of natural theology is at stake right here. It is far better for the students to make the same recognition concretely by parading in playing Haydn. They themselves highlighted the stakes. For it's true: all the beauty of Paley's and Haydn's world is about come crashing down.

At this point, each side's instruction sheets are also shared with the other group. No more mystery about what the other set of groups was doing. Every student can thus begin to enter into both ways of thinking, as explained and applied by their fellows.

At first we just ask questions and note the most general features of each island. On both views, for example, we should expect that specific natural environments will be populated by well-adapted organisms. This is why the famous finches are not by themselves some kind of proof of evolution—a common misconception. A considerate or even merely efficient Artificer would certainly make species well adapted to their niches. Evolution predicts the same for other reasons: Less adapted varieties do not survive. The telling differences are going to be deeper and more subtle.

Act 3: Sharpening the Contrasts
Now we can explicitly highlight and explore the divergences, with the two sets of sticky posters side by side on the board or wall.

Usually the Creation group has a good complement of the usual animals. Why not? God has His usual broad palette, and there is the usual selection of niches: plenty of nice upland grasslands, for example, for grazers. There is no problem about their ancestors originally getting to the islands from somewhere else: God just snaps His fingers and they are there. Moreover, a benevolent Creator would see no profit in making creatures or plants ill-fitted to their habitats. So there are no awkward tortoise grazers, for example: let them stay in the waters where they can swim with grace and speed. Tortoises on land are ludicrously slow and clumsy.

For their parts, though, the evolutionists have had to work only with the types of animals that can get to the islands on their own from somewhere else—by flying, swimming, or floating. Now students begin to understand why tortoises might be the grazers in places such as the Galapagos. They have seen for themselves that the usual grazer species simply cannot get there. No goat can cross 600 miles of open ocean on its own. Indeed, of all mammal species, the primordial Galapagos had only a single species of small rat. It makes sense. Yet the consequence is that the species mix will be dramatically and tellingly different.

The evolutionists' island will not have humans either, considering how late and uncertainly humans came on the scene. Creation groups, in contrast, might put humans on the islands from the beginning, too. Why not? If the whole world is made for "man," why create tropical paradises but leave them empty of the only species that really counts? The last time I ran this exercise, however, one Creation group considered but decided against humans in the end. We're too apt to go bad, they said, and disrupt the tropical Eden—although obviously original sin doesn't seem to have prevented the Creator from putting humans most everywhere else.

Regardless of which way one goes with the theology, the choice itself helps to highlight the underlying dynamic of creationist thinking. Populating the world could be considered a moral as well as an aesthetic sort of project and, indeed, precisely a *choice*. That now begins to appear a distinctive and radical conception in itself. And the mechanics of natural dispersion do not come up at all.

Down the list of questions the divergences continue. Would isolated islands tend to have distinctive species—that is, unique to themselves, even compared to very similar environments elsewhere? Creationism would say no. Surely God would paint with the same palette everywhere. Why waste massive creative efforts on tiny, never-seen, out-of-the-way places, with repeated extinctions along the way? But evolution says yes. Between randomly different pioneer species and genetic drift since their first arrival, isolated populations naturally diverge from each other and the species norm, and they could diverge in a wider variety of directions. Or again, would it matter what lifeforms inhabit nearby continental masses as opposed to continents farther away? It wouldn't matter at all to God, but does matter, hugely, to evolution—because where else are the pioneers going to come from?

Act 4: And Now for the Facts

By now it is evident to both groups that the two modes of thinking could hardly be more different, in both their premises and their consequences. Finally, we can ask which prediction fits the facts of actual isolated oceanic islands. The answer is that what we see on isolated islands worldwide lines up with the evolutionary predictions and contrary to the creationist ones.

Of course this answer is no surprise. The students have read their Darwin, and many prominent examples—the unique finches, the upland tortoises, and so on—already figure prominently in Acts 2 and 3. Yet there is still a satisfying drama in returning to the question now. Now might be a good time for that Galapagos slideshow or a tour of the flora and fauna of some of the world's other isolated islands. Still more to the point, a review of the relevant texts might be instructive. Now the students can come up for breath. They can see their work on the board or walls around them. Darwin's epiphany is now vividly before them. They have, beautifully and decisively, recreated it themselves.

Denouement

Soon after returning to England, Darwin wrote *The Voyage of the Beagle*, primarily as a popular travelogue. Yet even then, he showed a few hints of his emerging new view. Speaking of the Galapagos, he writes:

> Seeing this gradation and diversity of structure in one small, intimately related group of birds, one might really fancy that from an original paucity of birds in this archipelago, one species has been taken and modified for different ends. (Darwin 1845/2001, p. 71)

It would take a couple of decades more and, famously, a prompt from Alfred Russell Wallace to come out and argue it full bore. In On *the Origin of Species*, finally, Darwin is explicit:

> On [the] view of migration, with subsequent modification, we can see why oceanic islands should be inhabited by few species, but of these, that many should be peculiar. We can clearly see why those animals which cannot cross wide spaces of ocean, as frogs and terrestrial mammals, should not inhabit oceanic islands; and why, on the other hand, new and peculiar species of bats, which can traverse the ocean, should so often be found on islands far distant from any continent. Such facts as the presence of peculiar species of bats, and the absence of all other mammals, on oceanic islands, are utterly inexplicable on the theory of independent acts of creation . . .
>
> [And again], it is a rule of high generality that the inhabitants of each area are related to the inhabitants of the nearest source whence immigrants might have been derived. We see this in nearly all the plants and animals of the Galapagos archipelago, of Juan Fernandez, and of the other American islands being related in the most striking manner to the plants and animals of the neighboring American mainland; and those of the Cape de Verde archipelago and other African islands to the African mainland . . . [T]hese facts receive no explanation on the theory of creation. (Darwin 1859/2001, p. 168)

Students can now see that in both paragraphs, the last lines are key to the logic: "Such facts . . . are utterly inexplicable on the theory of independent acts of creation" and "These facts receive no explanation on the theory of creation." Darwin clearly intends to be comparing a theory that works to a theory that does not. Creationism is actually an empirical theory, on this view—at least it was then, in its Paleyan form—and the argument is that it spectacularly fails the test of experience (Kitcher, 2006).

In my classes, Darwin himself—me, or sometimes a colleague, in a bit of costume—has even been known to show up to drive the last nail home. He will read the class these very texts, the words back in his own mouth at last, and make these very points. This may seem only a kind of playfulness, perhaps, and the students will certainly enjoy it, but it can be a powerful moment as well. Darwin is able to speak in his own voice, as it were: Students can actually imagine that here, right in front of them, is the person who blazed the intellectual trail we have just recapitulated. Other times, I just ask some students to read the key passages out loud ("With expression!" I insist). The words become that much more vivid and powerful.

The dialectical drama continues, of course, and more scenarios of different sorts follow. After the Galapagos moment we take up the theory of evolution proper, and I try to set up the students to essentially reinvent and rearticulate it. Spelling out the actual mechanics is harder than they think, and the usual partial understandings ("species adapt") often get in the way. Things then calm down for a few days as students assimilate and discuss more of *On the Origin of Species* (Darwin, 1859/2001) and later works and begin to take Darwinian thinking in their own directions. Near the end of the Darwin section, I may invite a "Young Earth" creationist—also a PhD biochemist at a nearby leading pharmaceutical firm—to visit and make his argument, driven by his unshakeable faith but scientific and detailed in its actual arguments. Students are typically unpersuaded, but are certainly provoked to explore contemporary Darwinian responses. In another iteration of the course, we concluded the Darwin portion by role-playing a Reacting to the Past game based on the 1999 Kansas School Board debate over teaching intelligent design in the public schools.

Still, this particular scenario remains the class's key dramatic and dialectical launch into Darwin. In the last chapter, I quoted Dewey's description of the children in his laboratory school who "worked out for themselves" the world-historical as well as the mechanical character of cotton gins, for example. So it is here: Within the frame of the scenario, students work out for themselves the Darwinian paradigm shift. They rediscover, of course in a very abbreviated and simplified way, his argument for the necessity and power of an evolutionary perspective. There is no need for another, more teacherly or traditional kind of summary or debrief—or so I argue in the next chapter—because the students have already done something much more powerful. They have retraced Darwin's intellectual as well as exploratory footsteps themselves. His argument is now their own. The evolutionists have just said the same thing in explaining their island. When they return to Darwin's words, at the end of that decisive day, his words regularly and almost eerily sound like . . . theirs.

CODA
"Someone Is Looking For You"

With Elon astronomer Tony Crider, I co-teach a sophomore honors course we call "Life in the Universe," a wide-angled exploration of contemporary thinking about the possible places of life and intelligence in the universe beyond Earth. One activity early on in our class is another helpful initial example of scenario-based class design in action (Crider & Weston, 2012). I offer it here as a coda to the extended Darwinian example just outlined.

A central theme of our class is the search for extraterrestrial intelligence (SETI). From the beginning, however, SETI faces a seemingly impossible epistemological obstacle. Even before we get to questions about interpreting a possible message from alien intelligences, there is the question of how we would even find them. Where would we look for mail from the stars? Even between us humans, there are multiple modes of communication, from smoke signals to e-mail. Maybe someone is sending us the cosmic equivalent of text messages while we are still primed for snail mail—or tom-toms. We have no idea how a totally alien civilization might attempt to make contact. What kind of medium and channel would they choose? How could senders make themselves evident against the background of constant noise—randomly and naturally generated signals, of which the universe is already full?

We assign our students a classic article on this subject that proposed surprisingly specific answers to these questions. Cocconi and Morrison (1959) proposed to use the medium of radio, as arguably the first and fastest means of interstellar communication a civilization is likely to discover—as, after all, we did. Of the huge range of possible radio frequencies, they proposed to search for signals at the hydrogen line frequency, because a salient feature that would be known to all senders is that hydrogen is the most common element in the universe. For a signal, Cocconi and Morrison (1959) proposed prime number sequences, because as far as we know, prime numbers series can't be generated by any natural processes. Alongside these "alert" signals could be more complex messages.

Cocconi and Morrison's (1959) article occupies less than two dense but momentous pages in *Nature*. The argument is ingenious—if debatable—but in a sense it is also too easy. Students do not get a strong sense of how seemingly impossible an epistemological obstacle SETI really confronts—then or now. It is too easy to sign on to Cocconi and Morrison's answer and consequently follow the path of SETI for the last 60 years. How can we make the problem more vivid, more difficult again—and put students right in the middle of it?

Our answer is a kind of structural analogue to SETI's situation: a different but pedagogically more approachable situation that is entirely real but in which the same rigorous logic nonetheless applies. The aim, once again, is to preserve and accentuate the underlying logic or dialectic of the theme of interest, but to enable it to be staged in a more manageable form. Having introduced the technical possibility of SETI but not yet addressed its epistemological obstacles, therefore, we announce one day, out of the blue, that at that very moment someone is trying to contact this class. "Someone" only knows that this class exists—no other specifics—and that the class will be trying to find them in turn. Which is all that the class knows either. Now make contact, we say.

Silence at first. Some students look at us like we have lost our minds. It is not possible, they finally object, and besides, how do we know that someone really is looking for us? But already some of their peers are beginning to get it. "Isn't this exactly the same type of situation that SETI faces?" they ask. You are not sure there really is someone looking for you, and in any case you know nothing about them except that they may be looking for you and may assume that you are looking for them. Supposing only this, how could you nonetheless find some shared medium (the analogue to radio), some shared channel (the analogue to a certain frequency), and so on, and after all connect? In fact, right now?

I love the moment when the students realize that we are actually serious. Immediately, they also realize that they have a few rather useful hints in that weird little technical article by Cocconi and Morrison that we just asked them to read. Physically confined to the classroom—just as humans are physically confined, for now, to our own solar system—most of our students go to the Internet, just as, they reason, anyone trying to contact a group of today's college students would also do. (Some do other things, such as hang big banners out the classroom windows, for who knows, someone may be casing campus right now looking for signs.) They look for online messages from the "someone," wherever they think he or she might also be seeking out them, as well as leaving their own addresses at every place they also look for them. Indeed, now everyone is racing (we make it a friendly contest among groups, with a small prize), and besides, the search is exciting.

The first time we ran this scenario we had a bet in advance. Tony didn't think it could possibly work. I thought it might. We agreed in any case that the scenario was well worth running and that failure would be at least as instructive as success. In the event, a group of students made contact in 25 minutes, with others close behind. The mystery "someone" that time was my daughter, then a student at Rice University, who, having no way to directly contact our students but knowing that they were an Elon University class, had inserted her Facebook contact information all sorts of places, including in the first line of the university's Wikipedia page. Our students found her within a few minutes of her posting, narrowly ahead of Wikipedia's vandalism-reversion bots.

In the next iteration of this scenario, "someone" was Tony's mother, an Internet user but not adept at it, who kept trying to make contact using Facebook while our students were using more contemporary social media. In many ways, the exercise was even more instructive for the 2 sides having danced by each other, so close yet so far. For, of course, the question is: Why mightn't this be exactly analogous to our situation with aliens? SETI has turned up nothing in 60-odd years, and one of the questions of our course is: What do we make of that? Now it becomes clear that—and how—SETI could fail even if the cosmos is full of other intelligences looking for us, just like Tony's mother. Maybe next time we will try a class of third graders or the like, who may communicate in ways college students would never imagine. We hope they do!

In our first and successful session, we ended the day by Skyping with my daughter to make the "someone" real. She appeared on the classroom's big screen and compared strategies with her age-mates, our students. An unexpectedly dramatic scene, too: She Skyped in from her engineering lab at Rice, a cavernous building full of apparatus and experimenters, looking for all the world like the innards of a giant spaceship. So, indeed, there really *was* someone out there looking for our students, and they found each other, using a tight analogue of classic SETI strategies. And *then* they (re)read Cocconi and Morrison (1959) and understood exactly what they were doing—having just done it, yes, themselves.

4

IMPRESARIOS

*I define teaching as the purposeful creation of situations from which motivated
learners should not be able to escape without learning or developing.*

—John Cowan (1998)

The concept of a scenario came naturally at a certain point in my development beyond Teaching as Guiding. I had finally realized that my characteristic pedagogy was not lecture, and rarely discussion per se, but active in a more systematic and often dramatic way that was also quite tight and dialectical. Scenarios were exactly what I tried to bring into my classes. The idea also was already in play in pedagogical discussions, although I was coming to use the term in a specific and distinctive way.

Still, a scenario is a classroom realization, not a conception of the teacher. Even the notion of Teaching as Staging, useful as it is in contrast to Teaching as Telling or Guiding, still focuses on the activity of staging, and not on the role-archetype of the teacher. What is the teacher if not, or not primarily, a Sage or a Guide? Something was still missing.

At the back on my mind was another thought too. King's cheeky labels are almost cartoons, to be sure, but they are also widely used and helpful at least by way of rough orientation. An almost silly but still significant part of the reason for this is simply that they rhyme. "Sage on the Stage" and "Guide on the Side" are catchy and memorable phrases. Could I make something of the same out of a third way, a vision of a teacher who stages scenarios? But how could there possibly be a suitable role-archetypal term that rhymes with "scenario"?

The Concept of an Impresario

I scanned some online rhyme dictionaries with little hope. But suddenly there it was: not only exactly the right term for the teacher who stages scenarios but also *mirabile dictu*, a rhyme. In a sense, the circle closed at that moment on what eventually became this book. As a teacher my role-archetype is the Impresario. My hopeful entry, in the same mode as King's catchy labels, is the *Impresario with a Scenario*.

Prototypes

It turns out that neither the theatrical link nor the rhyme is an accident. Both terms are Italian and come specifically from the world of Italian theater arts. The term *scenario,* remember, comes from the seventeenth-century Italian commedia dell'arte form. The prototype for the term *impresario* comes from the world of mid-eighteenth-century Italian opera. *Impresa* means an enterprise or an undertaking. Literally, then, in Italian, an impresario is the person who undertakes something.

In the mid-eighteenth century, Italian aristocrats were beginning to buy theaters, and someone was needed to organize the seasons and mount the productions (Rosselli, 1984). Their hired agents therefore came to be called impresarios: the ones who actually gathered together a company or group of actors and musicians—because of course this was below the aristocrats—along with supporting staff, such as set builders, stagehands, and the like, for a specific rehearsal and performance cycle. It required thorough planning and coordination: hiring and rehearsing the orchestra and singers, gathering costumes, planning and creating sets, and even retaining a composer, and with enough lead time to actually produce a new work, because patrons of the time expected operas to be new each season.

Mozart even wrote a musical farce about this role, called *"Der Schauspieldirektor"* (1786)—literally "The Spectacle Director" but usually translated as "The Impresario." Probably the best-known musical and theatrical impresario was the English entrepreneur Richard D'Oyly Carte, who promoted W. S. Gilbert and Arthur Sullivan's famous light operas in the late nineteenth century. Carte sponsored the first Gilbert and Sullivan productions and then entered into a partnership with them to produce more, mounting ever more ambitious performances and traveling shows and even building special theaters just for them. His impresa became the family business and ended up running over a century (Ainger, 2002). The D'Oyly Carte Touring Company sometimes still sees revivals.

Today, even conference organizers or museum curators may be called impresarios when they are especially energetic and engaged in organizing and promoting a conference or show. In the most general sense, then, we may say that an impresario's job is to activate and motivate a group of people: originally actors, musicians, scene builders, and the like, and now a variety of contributors, collaborators, and other charges. The task is to move them from outside the enterprise or endeavor to inside it, to rouse their energies and engage them thoroughly in the joint work. The impresario is the one who holds the big picture, understands how all the parts relate into a whole, makes the vision cohesive, and skillfully realizes it with a particular production or event with the group at hand.

The Teacher as Impresario With a Scenario

The teachers with whom we are concerned do exactly the same kind of thing as a mode of teaching. Their impresas are to specifically activate and motivate their students, moving them inside a class's key enterprise or endeavor to rouse student energies and engage them thoroughly in the joint work. That joint work will usually be a particular production that unfolds in a classroom in the defined period of a class session or over the progress of a course. It is, then, precisely the systematic staging of scenarios (Box 4.1).

BOX 4.1
Definition of *Impresarios With Scenarios*

Impresarios with Scenarios are teachers who primarily teach by staging pedagogical scenarios.

Note that this definition focuses on how a teacher *primarily* teaches. A teacher who occasionally stages scenarios—say, one week of role-play a term—could be called an impresario to that extent, but is clearly not a teacher who conceives the teacher role to be essentially an impresario's. Impresarios *regularly* stage scenarios. It is their chief method, their way of thinking about pedagogy as such, the first and main approach they consider when planning their courses and day-to-day classes. To this extent, we may say that their teaching is neither teacher-centered nor student-centered, although as the last chapter suggested, it draws on and draws in both. At bottom it is *scenario*-centered.

The Theatrical Metaphor

Teaching as Guiding traces itself back in part to Dewey's (1899/1959) theory of learning (Gagnon, 2001). Still, Chapter 2 has already suggested that the actual "design of learning experiences" (Barr & Tagg, 1995, p. 24) requires a specifically strategic and activist kind of teacher—more than a Guide as usually understood. Envisioning the impresario role as a distinct and theatrically minded approach, we can begin to see Teaching as Staging at work in what previously we could only consider especially dynamic and dramatic forms of Guiding.

Recall again the U.S. history module in Dewey's Laboratory School featured in Box 2.2 as an exemplary scenario. There we called the essential work of Dewey's teachers *orchestration*—a nice Deweyan term itself. Synthesizing, organizing, and prearranging were essential to their pedagogy. Again, there is nothing passive or purely reactive about it. Indeed it is notable how compelling and even necessary it seems to be to use musical or theatrical metaphors for this work: composition, production, orchestration, staging.

Teachers of all sorts carefully choose their readings, outline the flow of the course themes, and the like. An impresario–professor adds an eye to dramatic modes of engagement that will be the most irresistibly activating. Just as actors or musicians are drawn into and often captivated by the work being performed, as well as by the company of their fellow performers and the rehearsal and preparation process, so a group of co-journeying learners—a class—may be drawn into and indeed captivated by the work at hand when it is well planned and carried through.

Teaching as an Impresario with a Scenario thus mobilizes its own distinctive kind of energy—something not asked of, or even imagined by, either the Sage on the Stage, totally in control of the one simplified and staid show, or the Guide on the Side, facilitating and mentoring but still circumspectly not just offstage but resolutely staying on the sidelines. In the Impresario with a Scenario model, by design, students and teachers play off each others' energies, unpredictably and often urgently, with the teacher primarily responsible for setting the scene and organizing, focusing, and sustaining the energies of a class in consistently productive ways (Viachopoulos & Makri, 2017).

Also notable in an impresario's orchestration is that much of it is invisible in the final product. The smooth flow of a theatrical production once underway may seem entirely natural, but the smoother it is, the more it probably depends on careful planning and logistical acumen in advance. Likewise, then, the impresario–teacher imagines it all beforehand, sets up the flow of the class to arrive at the critical moment with just the right preparation and tools, down to the level of assigned readings and maybe assigned dramatis personae, and setting up the space, as we shall see, as well as setting the scene and even the pace.

Organizational work is key, too: arranging the whole production for the most efficient process, the greatest ease of flow, the most rewarding use of the largest proportion of time that the participants give to the work, and so that all the energies involved come to crescendo together at just the right time. The teacher's initiative, pre-imagination, and set-up create the essential condition for everything that unfolds. It is no wonder that the usual image of an impresario is of someone with great brio, venturesomeness, and élan. The same can be true of Teaching by Staging. At its best, it is both highly demanding work and hugely rewarding.

Offstage or On

D'Oyly Carte's name is permanently associated with one of the most famous musical theatrical enterprises in history. Yet he was certainly no actor or musician. He remained the business mastermind literally "behind the scenes." There was more than enough work to do there.

Likewise, a well-designed scenario unfolds in a sequential and patterned way mostly on its own. The intention is for students to discover and follow the track mostly by themselves. In the actual event, their teachers may only need to nudge things periodically. This is one reason that such teachers may look superficially like mere guides. I have insisted, however, that even in this they are not passive or reactive at all. Again, after all, they created the tracks in the first place. They are the ones, as it were, who wrote and pinned the canovaccio to the backstage curtains. Thorough-going orchestration is absolutely essential.

In a well-designed scenario, then, the impresario–professor does not have to sustain the process by constant intervention and guidance or control, or have to show up on stage at all. Such a teacher actually can "get out of the way," in a sense, in the unfolding of their scenarios. As Chapter 1 explains, you do not have to be the least bit theatrical to stage scenarios. D'Oyly Carte, in this respect, is the norm.

Still, this is not the whole story. Impresario–professors may also be much more forward. Although many may happily step to the side once the "production" is actually running and let students handle everything, some may also take an energetic role in it. For my own part, I find participation to be an essential part of the enjoyment: playing a cameo role, for example, which typically amuses students too. Other teachers may want to visibly coach on the side—even stopping the action from time to time to add information, give some argument or more careful formulation, for example in a debate scenario, or even rewind and start some crucial part of the action over. In general, as Asal and Blake (2006) note,

> The extent to which an instructor needs to be actively involved in a simulation . . . (other than monitoring the interaction and providing administrative support) depends upon the type of simulation. A simulation with a focus on negotiating a settlement to a problem may not need any instructor

input, while a crisis simulation may require that the instructor play a role by introducing new events to keep the simulation moving forward. (p. 3)

Later chapters offer a wide range of illustrations of these and other ways in which the professor may join or complement the action.

Another point to note is that these considerations only apply to the more genuinely theatrical of pedagogical scenarios. Many others have a less dramatic overall tone and structure. For example, the Darwin example in Chapter 3 is a scenario in which there is a visible and central staging role for the professor throughout the action, although it is not in any serious sense theatrical.

Yet other kinds of scenarios necessarily involve the professor as the central actor: launching a talk show as the host or emcee, for instance, or as the focus of attention in an impersonation. Again, this is optional. Typically a teacher would only stage scenarios of this sort if she or he were inclined to a certain kind of spotlight in the first place. Other times, teachers may take a central role in role-played scenarios, such as judges in mock trials or session chairs in the Model UN, for reasons such as verisimilitude, better control of the pace of the role-play, or fairness to the participants either inside the role-play or in their own persons as students. (More on these and other variations in Chapter 5.) There are tradeoffs here. Students who might have risen to the roles spectacularly too, given the chance, are displaced, and the general presumption in many pedagogical role-plays is against a leading role for the professor for that reason (e.g., in Reacting to the Past: cf. Carnes, 2014; A. Crider, personal communication, 2017). Nonetheless, sometimes I view it as a reasonable or even necessary move.

In any case, the point for now is that impresario–teachers *may* be either behind the scenes or on stage. When on stage, though, their purpose is to help energize and direct the unfolding scenario. They are not the main show. Again, the impresario's fundamental work is to rouse and focus the energy of the class. Indeed, if nothing else, taking a visible role can be a testament to the teacher's own full engagement and willingness to take risks—a provocative and inviting example for students to follow. There are times when we teachers need to take that lead. How can we expect students to jump in with both feet, to take the risks sometimes needed, when we ourselves hold back?

Scene-Setting

Long before the class even meets, impresario–professors conceptualize and prepare their scenarios. *Scene-setting* is their first essential task.

Epitomizing a Theme

The fundamental aim is to find a working representation of the essential process or theme that the class is studying. It needs to be visibly enacted in the classroom, probably in a simplified, symbolic, or structurally analogous form, free from distracting and potentially time-consuming details (Greenblatt, 1981; Hertel & Millis, 2002). We can call this *epitomizing the theme*.

Say a class is reading about the unreliability of eyewitness testimony (Schick & Vaughn, 2014, Chapter 5). To epitomize the theme—to visibly enact it right in the classroom—an impresario–professor would naturally think of staging a brief event in which the class's own eyewitness capacity is put to the test. One day in my Critical Thinking class, therefore, our room is invaded, out of the blue, by a figure armed with a bright red pool noodle sword. I pull out another sword (for what self-respecting teachers don't arm themselves with a pool noodle when preparing for class?), and the intruder and I briefly duel, yelling a few scripted lines before he flees. Then, immediately, there is a survey—What color were the invader's socks? Which of us quoted Shakespeare?—followed by a close look at a surreptitiously recorded video of the actual event.

Here, in short, students' eyewitness experience is engaged before they even know what is happening—like most events about which an eyewitness might later be called to testify—and they can instantly check their accuracy for themselves even as they compare their own results to the general data in the readings. An abstract and surprising theme in the readings becomes vivid and directly relevant. Other themes and questions can also be invoked. For example, the survey has some notable leading questions. Neither I nor the invader quote Shakespeare, actually, but most students report that I did. What do they make of that now?

Many teachers can probably picture themselves staging such a thing. I hope so. It helps to show that, however exotic it may sound in general, Teaching as Staging is an approachable pedagogy day to day. Still, this kind of staging also goes further than teachers typically expect. By the nature of the topic, there is no announcement, no explanation, no warning—none of the usual academic formalities or ponderousness. The intrusion may take all of 20 seconds. Anyone tuned out might even miss it entirely (and often there are students who do—another topic to take up in the debrief).

Immediately after the survey, I show the class a video of what just happened—videotaped by a student confederate. Thus they can instantly check their own survey answers. All of this is happening quickly right around them, on purpose almost too fast to process. Symbolically and practically, then, even (especially) such a quick scenario hints at a distinctive general peda-gogy. This course is about how we ourselves think, it says, and as the course's subjects, we ourselves will be constantly and sometimes unpredictably on the line. Be ready!

Another example. Class debates are a widely used way to induce students to explore contentious issues as well as improve their public speaking and argument skills. Gun control, fake meat, the true causes of the U.S. Civil War—these and many more are real issues well worth exploring in this way. In the hands of a deliberate impresario–professor, debates are likely to be more frequent—and more freighted.

Once again, beyond the specifics of any such debates, the first key point is simply that these are after all *debates*. That is, the most fundamental mes-sage is that there is a body of relevant data, worked-out arguments, critiques, and responses to learn, whatever one's position on the question. In my view, the best way to convey that point is to put students visibly and energetically inside an actual debate from the start.

Again: Epitomize the theme. A more systematic way to say this is that the *best-designed scenario's structure should draw out and draw on the deep struc-ture of the dynamic it is trying to teach.* The aim is to make the structure of the scenario or enactment itself embody the most fundamental lesson. In debates, the lesson is that there are multiple, contending, systematic, and potentially valid points of view involved. Once again, the students enact it in their own persons. They hear it in their own and their classmates' voices, and they see it in their own interactions.

Here are two more illustrations of this key point. The first illustra-tion is a January-term course I sometimes teach that I call "Millennial Imagination." The premise of the course is that there are creative pos-sibilities in even the biggest and seemingly most intractable problems of the age. But I do not simply or even mainly assert this. Instead, the course design quickly gives the students some basic creative and imaginative tools and then sets the students up to repeatedly invent such possibilities them-selves—together, urgently, right in class. *Then* I can make the point explic-itly. Look at what you have done, I say. Right here, together, in the space of 15 minutes, you have come up with genuinely new and radically inventive ideas for dealing with the issue of the day. Remember this and honor it! Never again say, "There is nothing to be done" or that you are not creative enough to think of something new.

This is not sermonizing. I am only pointing out to the students what they have just done. Their own accomplishment epitomizes the theme. My chief contribution in the event is only to highlight that fact—once the right scenario has given them the tools and space to accomplish it.

The second illustration: Chapter 3's "Galapagos moment" scenario rests on a comparison of creationist versus evolutionary predictions for isolated islands. Paleyan creationism, commonsensical and theologically appealing as it may be or have been for his time, is confounded by a peculiar and unexpected species mix in isolated oceanic islands—a mix that turns out to be exactly what an evolutionary view would predict. Accordingly, once again, the proposed scenario sets up a comparison of predictions that the students themselves work out. The key point is not just that students are active, and not even that in this way they quickly get into the details of Darwin's observations, as important as all of this is. The first and foremost point, once again, is that the structure and dynamic of the scenario exactly mirrors the structure and dynamic of the situation they are studying. At the end of the day's session, on the board in front of them, they can see the logic of Darwin's epiphany mapped out by themselves and have found something very similar to Darwin's words coming out of their own mouths to explain it. Epitomizing a theme, indeed!

Activating a Dialectic

Well-designed scenarios *move.* They are not set pieces. They are dynamically structured situations, and their structure progressively develops or unfolds following an inner logic that orients but does not completely determine the direction of the situation's movement or final resolution. Let us call this *activating a dialectic.*

You want the scenario to unfold in illustrative, progressive, and deepening ways, and as far as possible you want it to do this by itself—needing minimal teacher intervention or visible stage direction during the event. As students prepare their arguments for debate and engage each other, for example, they naturally also learn the details, strengths, and weaknesses of each position. In both anticipation and enactment, then, the actual staged confrontation, with its built-in rounds of critique and rebuttal, will powerfully bring out the strong and weak points of their arguments as well as the need to consciously make a case, attending to audience and voice and constantly adjusting and responding to the arguments of others.

In short, entering and sustaining a well-planned debate activates a dialectic. The desired flow should be the default condition. Students would have to resist to stop it, rather than they or the teacher having to mobilize to make it happen in the first place.

Likewise, in the Darwinian scenario, the deep structure of the situation is the comparison of two predictions. Thus, again, by design, students generate two distinct predictions from two radically different theories of the origin of species. The class has to apply two broad explanatory frameworks to a special case, and mostly on their own. This work then automatically and urgently sets them up to move further: to compare the two predictions to each other and test them by comparison to actual observations.

Everything comes alive. What might have seemed to be mere histories of random curiosities mean something vital again. They're back with Darwin on the *Beagle* and the Galapagos shores. Quite exact logic comes into play, too. How might tortoises have become grazers? Why would it matter that the Galapagos's famous finches are finches, after all—American birds, that is, rather than some family of birds more typical of continents farther away? The students have to get into backstory, and the backstory is, well, a story— indeed, a drama!

Mobilizing the Work Together

In support of epitomizing key themes and activating the dialectic, the scene set by a scenario should seem natural to the students and organic to the class, and of course it should also be manageable in the time frames available—although maybe just barely. Topically, scenarios must integrate and unfold in an artful and effective way within the larger flow of the course. They must be grounded in the work done so far, be usefully revealing or provocative in the event, and issue in specific results and understandings that can be reinvoked in discussions to come. Often they will need to be simplified to highlight central features and pare away inessentials (Greenblatt, 1981).

Deft design is essential for desired interaction patterns. The contemporary pedagogical literature is helpful for this purpose. For example, well-known Cooperative Learning models aim to structure "positive interdependence" into students' classroom interactions (Johnson, Johnson, & Holubec, 2008; Kagan, 1992; Millis, 2014; Millis & Cottell, 1998; Ross & Smythe, 1995). The aim is not just student activity but thorough-going collaboration— constructive work that is necessarily with each other. In Jigsaw Group tasks, for example, students in a small group have their own piece of vital information that their group needs to solve some problem. In Numbered Heads Together (Kagan, 1992), the teacher randomly calls on one member of a group to answer for all, so there is a premium on the group being sure that everyone is up to speed on the answer—very different than the usual premium on individually knowing the answer.

Deliberate redesign of classroom interaction patterns toward cooperative and generative patterns is vital work. Thinking in terms of scene-setting can take it to another level, however, giving the teacher a broader and more powerful framework within which to work. Kagan's Numbered Heads Together, for example, is still essentially a competence-oriented drill. It may naturally lead the participants to attend to their classmates' expertise, but that is *all* it does. Designing a whole scenario, by contrast, gives the teacher a chance to build in "positive interdependence" in a far richer and truly more positive way.

Rather than simply structuring interdependent groups to teach themselves the material, for example, an impresario–professor would be more apt to embed the entire interdependence in some dramatic context. Consider again a Model UN simulation. Student teams represent different countries' delegations to a Security Council or General Assembly meeting. Each member specializes in some set of issues, often taking part in separate UN subcommittees as well as being available, at quite literally a moment's notice, when crisis erupts—as everyone knows it will—to help shape the delegation's response under pressure. Everyone must be at the top of their game or your country will fall flat in front of, well, the world. Here, then, the deep structure recreates the same positive interdependence as Numbered Heads Together, but without the workaday aridity of a method that could apply to any subject whatever or the stilted air of obviously manipulated interactions. Instead, the scenario is real and compelling in its own right. The United States is about to bomb Syria again, and you are Iran, a key Syrian ally. Your whole team must work out a response together, and right now. Unavoidably, deeply, and visibly, you count on each other. That is *real* "heads together." Groups' mutual dependence flows organically from the subject. Students learn the material better, as they demonstrably do in any kind of cooperative classrooms—*and* they are utterly absorbed and excited (McIntosh, 2001).

Consider your other interactional goals in the same way. For example, if part of your aim in an argumentation or critical thinking class is to prompt students to engage in larger arguments beyond the class, then to epitomize the theme, an impresario–professor would actually engage such arguments in and with the class. Students can write letters to the editor or make submissions to online forums, although these methods typically do not allow for much useful feedback or interaction. A scenario devised by my colleague Ann Cahill goes much further. Cahill sets up student panels to recruit their own argumentative adversaries from beyond the walls and prepare them and bring them into her classes to conduct constructive arguments/dialogues with them (Cahill & Bloch-Schulman, 2012). Student groups are tasked with selecting a topic, deciding a group position on it, and then finding an appropriate outside person to come in and argue the opposite.

The results are real debates with real stakes and real people, who moreover are extremely knowledgeable on their topics. Students have to be thoroughly prepared to hold up their end—again publicly and on the spot. Sometimes the visitors have to be briefed and reminded to maintain dialogue and not give speeches—a delicate but useful task for students to master too. The debates tend to be civil and intriguing, and the guests are often surprisingly hard to answer. And, of course, they are real. The novelty of new voices, the difficulty of finding a way to respect argument together, and learning how to respectfully shift someone from speechifying to interaction are all key lessons and skills of the class, and captivating to watch in action.

Stage-Setting

Impresario–professors are not only scene-setters but also *stage*-setters. The physical classroom layout is to be arranged for maximal effect in support of the scenario of the day. Every classroom has various possible layouts that physically, symbolically, and even acoustically shape what happens in it. Try to stage energetic small-discussion groups in a room set up for lecturing, with all the seats fastened to the floor and facing forward. You know what will—or, more to the point, won't—happen. It may be possible, but at best only barely and awkwardly.

The "Sage on the Stage" label reminds us that even "Saging" is staged, indeed with a vengeance. Sages usually just presume the staging—it may even be beneath notice, left to architects, desk manufacturers, and janitors. But try lecturing in a room set up for small-group interactions, with no clear center or raised dias or podium or special lighting, and maybe with students facing each other (not you!) in moveable and comfortable chairs and with shared work surfaces. How will it go? Circled chairs or desks send another, very different message. No chairs at all (imagine that!), another.

Teachers with theatrical minds pay attention to such features almost as if they were on a proscenium. They intentionally create settings that support and sustain the interaction patterns they seek. We do not want to constantly be fighting our classrooms. We want the layout of the room to create the most supportive possible "choice architecture" (Thaler & Sunstein, 2008).

Layout and Space

For active, student-centered classrooms, whether in kindergarten or graduate school, teachers can set up seats or worktables in groups among which the teacher circulates. For lively classroom debates, two rows of chairs can face each other. Discussion-based classes call for chairs or desks arranged in a circle. For a talk show, studio-style seating with a broad aisle or two through the chairs is ideal, evoking the feel of real TV studios (a few spotlights, maybe with splayed-out extension cords and the like for even more realism, also help) and also, not accidentally, facilitating the emcee's movement through the whole audience. Every student is visibly within the mic's reach at all times.

When students walk into a room divided into two sets of chairs facing each other, they already know what is about to happen. Likewise, when they walk into a roomful of tables with three or four chairs each, by the time they sit down, they are already in workgroups—no need for elaborately counting off or rearranging them into teams. When they are given a project, work can start even before official class time begins. Think, too, of the effect when further students enter the room. They can see that the train is practically leaving the station already. Quickly they find a seat and jump in. Again, merely to take a seat in such a classroom is already to take a stand or join a project—to make yourself a part of something ongoing and demanding.

We may briefly invoke another aspect of Model UNs as a further example. Model UN teachers such as Obendorf and Randerson (2013) actually arrange to use local government meeting chambers (on the weekends) for Model UN sessions, and they report that "the use of a formal horseshoe-styled debating chamber . . . adds immeasurably to the student experience. Convening in such a venue contributes to the seriousness with which the students approach the proceedings" (p. 357). They add the "purpose-built debating chamber, equipped with microphone and large-screen closed-circuit video projection of delegates as they address the chamber, facilitates discussion" (p. 357). It increases the drama and raises the stakes. (Box 4.2 offers another example.)

Because scenarios are partly embedded in room layouts, in short, part of the work of impresario–teachers is to use this kind of stage setting to maximum effect: to signal, enable, and promote the kinds of interactions for which they aim. As Sasley (2010) notes, again in regard to Model UN spaces,

> In trying to highlight the importance of intra-group discussion as a contributing factor to international outcomes, I found it more useful to put students in their own physical space. . . . This gave the simulation a more realistic cast. . . . [It] allowed each group to be as open and honest about their options as they wished, since they did not have to worry about other groups overhearing their deliberations and thus giving away their position. Having students meet in their own rooms also heightens the sense of reality, since they are alone as a group. (p. 68)

BOX 4.2
Where Matters!

In a recent note, my colleague and sometime co-teacher Tony Crider speaks specifically to the question of space in his Reacting to the Past experience.

Out of sheer convenience, the majority of my scenarios take place in the classroom assigned by the university's registrar. However, when time and space permit, we go elsewhere. Our oldest auditorium (built in 1924) fills in for the Smithsonian's Baird Auditorium as students restage astronomy's Great Debate of 1920. In the Trial of Galileo game, a nearby bar serves as Prince Cesi's palace, and the campus chapel becomes the Sistine Chapel. The change in location provides a different ambience that has a notable impact on the students' performances. The acoustics of the chapel alone are enough to demand more reverence to the student playing the lead Cardinal Bellarmine. In our simulations of human-alien contact, having students construct and inhabit their own alien worlds (in an overly heated classroom, in a darkened black box theater, on a rooftop) was a critical part of the experience. The new spaces allow for an added sense of liminality for the students.

One surprisingly simple aspect could be done easily and for many courses. Have two separate rooms booked for a single scenario. . . . Only the weavers can go into the public house to have a beer in the Rage Against the Machine game (Reacting to the Past). Only cardinals can enter the Sistine Chapel for the Conclave in the Trial of Galileo. In my experience, the tone of verbal engagement and the students engaged can change drastically by pulling some of them into such mini-scenarios.

In the Darwin scenario, remember, it was critical that the two different types of groups populated their islands out of earshot of each other. Contrasts only came at the next step. Symbolically, then, the separate physical spaces make it clear that two quite separate kinds of thinking are in play, while dramatically, the uncertainty of the contrast to come also heightened the intrigue.

Other Room Preparations

Even so simple a thing as placing markers and sticky posters on student work-tables or on the walls in advance helps set a certain kind of stage. Students walk into a project whose shape is already called forth by the room. Class may never officially start at all—or we may come to a plenary session much later—but the work can be tightly and insistently structured all the same.

Playing music as the class gathers also can energize and sometimes even give some direction to the shared work before it officially begins. My students like bluegrass for its typically rousing tempos, and we are, after all, in bluegrass country. Classical pieces vary the offerings. Historically oriented classes can begin with period music. Students walk into the first day of my Modern Philosophy class (Descartes to Kant, roughly 1600–1800) to the strains of Monteverdi's 1610 *Magnificat*, which Descartes likely heard in his youth. As we proceed in that introductory session we come to the last act of Mozart's *Don Giovanni* (1787), an utterly different kind of piece in multiple ways, and the obvious question—what happened?—becomes my first way to frame the central question of the whole course. Philosophically too, what happened? Likewise, the eerie strains of whalesong, unexplained at first, may greet classes that take up themes of communication with aliens, including seeming aliens right here on Earth.

Much else in the physical setting can also be arranged to nudge the desired work of the class. Vary the light. Make it brighter or darker on different days, maybe, or in different parts of the room or at different times during the class. Use lamps or spotlights to create focused central spaces. The uniform and general bright lighting of classrooms is useful in its way, but often impairs the focus that a scenario may require.

There's clothing. Even the hint of a costume can invoke the author of a reading or some stock character in a dramatic way—and license the impersonator to take on the role: a different way of speaking, perhaps a more insistent or outré perspective. In Model UN conferences, students are required to dress in formal business attire or in the national dress of their assigned country, adding to the formal sense of the occasion (Obendorf & Randerson, 2013). A gorilla has even been known to visit my and sometimes my colleagues' classrooms when we read Daniel Quinn's *Ishmael*—that is, Quinn's Ishmael himself. (More on impersonation in Chapter 6.)

Food can be part of stage-setting too. If nothing else, it is especially helpful for classes in time slots when students (and teachers) are likely to get hungry. People don't think or work well when depleted or too aware of their stomachs. Crackers, apples, popcorn, lemonade, even hot cider work well, if you can manage it. Considerateness with food is much appreciated by students and a boost to the work. If there are a lot of students, they can easily be organized to manage most of the food themselves. Regularly, on their own initiatives, my student groups bake cookies for each other.

Food serves some scenarios directly as well. The smells of spices from around the world—curry, galangal, saffron, adobo, sometimes with actual food—always enlivened my Global Experience first-year seminars at Elon. How can we feelingly speak of other places in the world while everything we smell and taste reflects the familiar locality or bland and purified air? Some of my environmental studies classes have been able to meet at the University Farm, where we get special dispensation to pick and eat vegetables right off the plants. Often some of my students are among the farm managers. Most of the rest, like most Americans, have no experience of eating so directly from the Earth. Not even washed! Once again it is not just that the food is nourishing. Picking and eating it right from the fields is thought-provoking and symbolizes and nourishes, so to say, the key themes of the course itself.

Pace-Setting

Goldsmith (2009) defines *pacing* as

> the rhythm and timing of classroom activities or units, which includes the way time is allocated to each classroom component and the process of how one decides that it is the right moment to change to another activity [or] sub-activity. (p. 33)

Just as every producer carefully considers the overall flow of time through a production, so such pacing must be another prime focus, along with scene and stage, for the impresario–professor. How the scene/class opens; the tempo and order in which things unfold from there; how the flow of the period comes to closure and sets up the next—all of this takes artful planning and execution (Greenblatt, 1981; Hohti, 2016). Given the pedagogical literature's general tendency to hold itself aloof from anything smacking of the theatrical, maybe it is not surprising that these are not widely treated topics, but in my view such considerations are nonetheless crucial.

Opening

Often the most effective play or story begins in the middle of things, not from some logical beginning, or with some especially dramatic event. Almost never do they begin with an exhaustive or didactic explanation of what is about to come. I believe there is a lesson here. At the least, might it not give us pause that this insistently linear didacticism is instead the academic norm (Costello & Brunner, 2008)?

Of course, sometimes some preexplanation is necessary in scenario-based teaching, for example if the scenario is especially elaborate in a way that requires student preparation. Still, an exhaustive or apologetic explanation up front can completely deanimate a scenario. For my own part, at least,

I prefer to err on the side of too little rather than too much. Let students scramble to keep up. It keeps them intrigued and on their toes.

In the Darwin scenario, for example, students are almost immediately sent off to their creation or evolution groups to populate their islands. I prefer the groups not to think much about the other group's standpoint—even to fully process that there *is* another standpoint—until they have already made their predictions. This is literally to start right in the middle of things. They know already that things are going to happen, but they will find out *what* things only in due time.

In other sessions, I might use some immediately engaging but smaller problems or exercises primarily as a warm-up—these are labeled Step-Right-Ins in Chapter 5. Students walk into the room, and there it is already waiting for them. Maybe it is on a handout I give them with a few words of greeting, or it is a project already set up on worktables. Other times I use literal warm-ups, such as quick exercises borrowed from Improv theater workshops (Berk & Trieber, 2009; Newton, 1998). In the Waldorf schools where my Philosophy of Education students and I observe, teachers begin with rhythmic or harmonic exercises, like drumming or round-singing, to gather and focus students' minds for the main lesson of the day, which follows immediately. I have tried these, too, although I have found that my college students are rarely as good at them as Waldorf second graders. We try to learn.

Pace-setting can begin well before the official start time of the class (Lang, 2015; Newberry, 2013). Typically, the impresario–teacher needs to be in the room anyway, setting the stage: rearranging the furniture or setting up the lighting or projector. Ask students who show up early to help. Talk to them. A few minutes later, and still well before the official start time, set them some warm-up work like that just outlined. The effect—once again, very much intended—is that when the rest of the students enter the room, they enter a *live* space in which things are already happening. Such a class does not need to be jump-started from a dead stop only once the clock is running. Indeed, sometimes there is no moment when class suddenly "begins." It may be 10 or even 20 minutes into the official class period before I or a student moderator call the class into plenary session. A few times, more or less on purpose, we may never do so at all. We all get a sense of walking into a live, relational, working *pace* as well as space.

Flow

Teachers are used to thinking about how much time to devote to specific themes, discussions, and activities, fitting it all into a class period. On the next level, we might consider how all of these pieces can be set up to flow seamlessly and energetically into each other—with the tight pacing of, well, real drama. Why not, when the action or ideas often really *are* dramatic? More generally, we want the period to have a sense of coherent movement and connection, rather than leaving a topic half-discussed, say, sidetracked into details, or having to stop in the middle of whatever we are doing when the clock runs out.

Burns and Gentry (1998) argue that a degree of tension, or what they call "tension to learn" (p. 133), is essential to the design of simulations and scenarios. This may sound abstract, and surely has many dimensions, but one useful and easily achievable kind of tension simply lies in the pacing. Used deftly, varied tempos can create and sustain intense engagement and excitement by themselves. We might also plan the shape of the period to offer a certain complementarity. Maybe an abstract or a difficult theme is introduced, illustrated, and then quickly applied, but with a judicious break or two in between depending on the length of the period. Long or late classes might have snack breaks as well.

Quick pacing—or, more broadly, projects or challenges with a certain urgency—is a compelling way of keeping students on task and the work genuinely enjoyable and satisfying. Maybe there is only a short work time to produce a result to report back, although then the aftermath, analysis, and reconsideration can take a more reflective pace. However, as Asal and Blake (2006) point out, sometimes it may be useful to stop the action entirely in a scenario to reflect on what is happening and being learned. Frame the previous work explicitly as a scenario—step out of it for a time—and then step back. I may even rewind and replay some of the action, perhaps nudging it in a different direction the second (or third) time. Other times a more leisurely tempo, reinforced by other props such as food, symbolically and practically makes the space for slower reflection. In any case, obviously, whatever scenario is mounted should be realizable in the time frame available and should not just *fit* but naturally *flow*.

Closing

Dramatic closure is satisfying if the scenario itself has been dramatic. When we have pulled off a talk show, for example, I may close with a little emcee patter and music and call for some play-acted audience applause. The message is that this was not just a class but a *happening*. And now the show is over. Typically, moreover, that's it for the day. Class is over. We never actually step out of the day's scenario into something more familiarly academic.

The pedagogical literature takes it as almost axiomatic that debriefing a scenario, usually in great detail, is necessary before learning (all too often, it's said, *any* learning) has certifiably taken place (e.g., Dahlgren et al., 2016; Hertel & Millis, 2002; Sasley, 2010). Sometimes this is surely true, especially when things have not gone as expected, or are complicated, or have unclear strategies. Yet the envisioned debrief usually sounds much like a reversion to the default modes: that is, telling students what they (should have) learned, or guiding a discussion about it. I argue that this kind of debrief can profoundly undercut a scenario in the end, reprioritizing traditional methods by reasserting them as the frame within which everything else must be processed and validated.

Consider the island-populating scenario once again. Fundamentally, it seems to me that recapitulating Darwin's experience and his resultant epiphany already is the learning. No more Telling or Guiding is needed. The scenario essentially and already *is* to retrace Darwin's intellectual and exploratory footsteps. The results are already posted on the walls or boards. We've had to articulate and argue the main points to compare the two sets of predictions to each other and to the actual facts. Perhaps we could end with a brief celebratory recapitulation—or not—but this recapitulation is unlikely to look like the "well-orchestrated debriefing" that Hertel and Millis (2002, p. 21) explicitly require. Rather, I claim that the day's learning is already accomplished, thoroughly and engagingly and right before our eyes, too— but we need to have the eyes to see it as such.

Sometimes, yes, a formal debrief is crucial even in my scenarios. My Philosophy of Education class is a case in point (more on it in Chapter 7), but it is also somewhat of a special case among my designs, because its mechanics require an explicit shift between staged pedagogical enactments and joint analysis of those enactments. Or again, some scenarios may involve a number of actions by different parties that may not be known to all the other students, for example, or if known, not fully understood. These may need to be revisited and explained at the end—students will be curious, and more learning will be involved. In the Darwin scenario, notice, this work is built into Acts 2 and 3 of the scenario.

Teachers who feel the need to be more didactic might try impersonating Darwin, starting by using or reading his own words and then elaborating in dialogue as necessary. Even if you do go in for systematic articulation and analysis of a scenario after its enactment, in other words, it does not have to look like a normal class. From that realization, however, it is once again only a small step to realizing that a scenario might well be planned to embed or build in its own debrief from the beginning.

My advice is simply to make the closure dramatic and decisive. Once you are relieved of the nagging feeling that at least at the end you should play teacher, many more possibilities open up. In certain role-plays, for example, especially if the roles have been challenging emotionally or otherwise, you might set up students to ritually divest themselves of them—to give them back. If some simulation has reached an official resolution, some ceremonial presentation of that resolution may be in order, such as a communiqué from the winning side, a mock press conference—staying in roles—or a "sense of the meeting" statement quickly drafted by the appropriate group and posted on the class website. Note again that most of these forms of closure also offer ways to of consolidate and repeat the results of the class's work, but they certainly do not represent any form of Teaching as Telling.

CODA
What an Impresario With a Scenario Is *Not* (Necessarily)

There are some notable alternative pedagogies that are somewhat theatrical in character and some that at least sometimes use scenarios. I would like to end this introduction of the impresario–professor with a brief clarifying contrast to these.

Professor as Performer

One persistent misconception is that an impresario–professor is basically a professor who is theatrical or dramatic. I have been at pains to point out already, by contrast, that an impresario is the one who *mounts* the show, which is quite another thing from acting in it—although one also well might. The primary work of an Impresario with a Scenario, again, is to stage engaging and instructive scenarios. It does not take a theatrical personality or performance to do so.

Conversely, theatrical professors might not be impresarios. Brandeis professor Lyn Felman (2001), for one striking example, describes her pedagogy as a combination of a one-woman interactive theater show and a college lecture. She dresses up in gender-bending or overexpressive ways, gets outrageous from the stage, and calls on students regardless of whether they volunteer. The results sound like classes that are intense and transformative indeed. Still, the drama is centered on Felman and her behavior. It is mediated and catalyzed by her. I have no complaint about that—hers is just a different model. Again, though, an impresario–professor is not mainly a *performer*–professor. Although impresario–professors may also perform and even be the center of attention in a few cases, they do not aim to be the stars of the show. Ultimately, in Teaching as Staging, it is the scenario that does the real work.

Occasional Impresarios

Some teachers may use just one or two scenarios in an otherwise conventional class. Even some teachers who mount ambitious Model UN scenarios, for instance, still speak of them as only "a useful adjunct to more traditional teaching methods" (McIntosh, 2001, p. 274).

For any number of reasons a teacher may choose to teach this way. Certainly there are classes and teachers for which it is appropriate. Still, we can now at least see the possibility of something more radical. An Impresario with a Scenario, as conceived here, is not simply a teacher who uses scenarios from time to time. To embrace an impresario role is to make the staging of scenarios your chief and regular teaching method. Even more than that, it is to reconceive your role as a teacher as, above all, a mobilizer and organizer of class energies. Staged scenarios are more apt to simply *be* the course, not adjuncts to it or a mere occasional technique (Carnes, 2014). *Lecture* is more apt to be the "adjunct" pedagogy—if such a professor still lectures at all.

"Edu-Prop Theatre"

Alex Fancy (1999) has written and co-performs an actual play in which a disenchanted lecturer is interrupted by certain students who end up transforming the teacher–student interaction. Inspired partly by the so-called "theater of cruelty," which aims to engage audiences by first making them uncomfortable (Artaud, 1988), Fancy uses this "edu-prop theatre (p. 95)," as he calls it, to prompt discussion after the performance with his audiences, usually professors at teaching conferences. Within the play, moreover, students actually reimagine the teacher in an impresario sort of direction, leading one of them to say that

> this teacher we are talking about is like a director in a theatre. Directors have to get the actors excited about a script, maybe they act out bits of it themselves, and they become spectators so that their students can assume the role of actor. (Fancy, 1999, p. 114)

The fictitious professor is displaced from his lectern and ends up moving through and around the audience, sometimes more seen than heard. In a nice touch, the student actors stay in role to moderate the discussion after the scripted part has ended.

I applaud Fancy's courage in staging this drama before an audience of professors. Theater of cruelty, indeed. Still, this kind of staging is extremely limited in contrast to the work of the impresario–teacher as pictured in this book. For one thing, most strikingly, Fancy's production is apparently only staged for professors, or at best mixed groups of faculty and students at special workshops. That is, ironically, teaching "like a director in a theatre" does not seem to be part of Fancy's actual classroom method or to be intended to invite classroom emulation or applications by others. Moreover, it is all scripted, and the drama is introduced and apparently didactically explained to the audience in advance, which (again) is not at all how an actual director in a theater would operate.

Fancy's production seems to stop, intriguingly and frustratingly, on the verge of something much more powerful. By scripting the three students in the play for actors who begin interspersed with the audience, he brilliantly and deliberately fudges the boundary between a production being staged *for* the audience and something being staged *with* them, so much so that sometimes members of the audience even join in before the scripted part is over. Surprise, unpredictability, and discomfort emerge in his play, but at the same time they seem to be confined by and to it. Fancy (1999) writes that his object is to "illustrate how drama can be used in faculty development" (p. 97). But why not do so in actual teaching? Why not use such powerful drama, unexpectedly emerging and also perhaps much more open-ended, in our *classes*?

Theater of the Oppressed

Augusto Boal's (2000) Theater of the Oppressed is an interactive exploration of oppressive situations—say, an employer mistreating an employee or transparent media misinformation—in which the observers make suggestions about alternative responses to the situation, which the actors then act out (Boal, 2000). Audience members might also tap out the initial actors and act out alternatives themselves, either way becoming what Boal calls *spect-actors* (see also Stevens, 2015; Wardrip-Fruin & Montfort, 2003).

As far as I know, the Theater of the Oppressed has rarely been used as a school pedagogy. Yet it may be much more suggestive for the impresario's purposes than Felman's or Fancy's methods. It is theatrical but in an entirely different mode, with wide participation built in and an intent to empower and transform the participants. There is a strong inner dynamic and even dialectic as well. The initial problem drives the action within a readily grasped format, but without being scripted. Trying different approaches and replaying interactions and outcomes within the scenario can be empowering and revealing in nonpolitical contexts as well (Hertel & Millis, 2002).

Still, Theater of the Oppressed is probably too episodic and too political to be the best overall model for the impresario–professor's theatricality. Generally, it does not compellingly carry students ever deeper into a subject but remains focused on immediate problematic situations. Sometimes that is necessary. At best, however, it is still only one among a variety of participatory dramatic scenarios that an impresario–professor might use.

One-Style Impresarios

Beyond the occasional impresario are professors who might use one particular kind of scenario extensively in their classes, but no other. Many might even be said to wholeheartedly embrace Teaching as Staging, except that it is essentially just one type of staging, one type of scenario. For example, some professors and programs run whole courses using only PBL or Reacting to the Past games (Carnes, 2014).

There are undeniable advantages to sticking to one type of scenario. Students get well adjusted to them, for one thing. Rapidly shifting types of scenarios sometimes can lead to adjustment issues and confusion. Teachers get used to and expert at a few known scenario-types as well. The main types also have extensive and largely separate practitioner literatures, inviting and supporting specialization.

Yet the general conception of the teacher as an Impresario with a Scenario is more inclusive, open-ended, and informed by the sense that there is a very wide range of types of scenarios and methods of staging them in classes. Any teacher will (must) work with some subset of these. Still, there are advantages, in fact arguably great advantages, in developing and staging a wide range of different types of scenarios.

Most obviously, different types of scenarios fit different themes and topics. An all-Reacting to the Past class will not run 10-minute role-plays or impromptu talk shows or take up problem-based challenges in small task groups—the only scenario is lengthy and full-on. Chapter 5 discusses a range of different types of scenarios in detail. Why restrict yourself?

Many of the prominent types of scenarios have their own practitioner literatures and support communities, and certainly these can be helpful. Still, I have already suggested (and the next chapter will argue) that they needlessly separate or silo themselves from each other. Impresario–professors might better connect these practitioner communities or synthesize and adapt them creatively to their own needs and preferences. For my part, although I have been informed and inspired by Reacting to the Past games and Model UN simulations, and I co-teach an adventurous course with a leading Reacting teacher, I have rarely run such games or simulations according to the official models. Instead, I (we) have run forward-looking Reacting-like adaptations, inspired by other models, as emerges in Chapter 7, as well as small-scale adaptations of Model UN formats of various sorts, again inspired by other models and the needs of particular courses (e.g., melding Model UN formats with the Council of All Beings model) (Bragg & Rosenhek, 1998). There is much more possibility and room to move between and beyond the official models.

5

DIMENSIONS AND FAMILIES OF SCENARIOS

Chapter 4 elaborates three main desiderata in the design of scenarios: to epitomize some theme, to activate engagement and a dialectic, and to shape and mobilize constructive work together. All of these can be achieved in a variety of ways as different characteristics and features of scenarios shift. The following are 12 crucial dimensions along which scenarios may vary.

Scale

How *big* is the scenario or simulation? How much time and work does it require, and on what schedule? Some scenarios may be quick events or "happenings" and may occupy a short part of a single class period. Others may be the armature of an entire course—or any scale in between (DiCicco, 2014).

Urgency

Is speed of the essence? Some scenarios can be quite fast-paced and urgent. They may be highly time pressured by design or necessity. Others may take more preparation. A certain deliberateness may even be part of the intended point.

Readiness of Entry

How readily is the scenario entered? Will students understand it, at least well enough for starters, with little or no lead-in explanation, or will they need to be introduced to it prior to entering it? With how much detail?

Surprise

There is a certain intrigue in a class when students know that the unexpected will happen. Also, students tend to come better prepared. When surprises are common, they quickly realize that poor preparation can seldom hide. Therefore they need to be ready for anything. Life is like that too, after all. Problems or challenges typically do not come to us announced and predefined. Often it is up to us to define (even notice) them in the first place.

However, more depth is possible in a scenario where students can prepare in advance for its specific challenges. It is also possible to do both, of course, embedding surprises within a broadly preannounced scenario.

Competition

Is there a competitive element? For example, does the scenario pit individual students or student teams against each other to find the fastest or best answer, win a debate, or the like?

There may be low-level competition in side-by-side work when groups tackle an absorbing problem to arrive at potentially different answers, perhaps with a vote between group proposals in the end. Or the scenario may be a simulation where everyone understands that the main point is to understand a competitive process, whatever the outcome for their team. When we are beginning to get a grip on Marx's theory of the stages of capitalism, for example, my Marx class may play Bertell Ollman's simulation game Class Struggle. Both sides do their best, but everyone knows from which direction the storm is coming, and even the capitalist team revels, or at least understands, when the proletarians and their minor-class allies come over the barricades at the end.

Other times there may be straight-out competition with real stakes (Dittmer, 2015). Reacting to the Past games, for example, have definite winners and losers, with possible (albeit small) consequences for grades as well. Carnes (2014) argues that the competitiveness of games increases the commitment and energy levels. He also claims that the game aspect is perceived as "subversive," as he puts it, of the supposed seriousness of college. Students need something a little crazy and edgy, he says, citing studies suggesting that as many as three-quarters of college students play video or online games every single day and the prevalence of campus games such as Humans Versus Zombies. "The whole concept is so wrong-minded," he says, "that students find it irresistible" (Carnes, 2014, p. 59).

Group or Individual?

Is the scenario or simulation primarily to be taken up by students individually, in small groups, or by the class as whole?

Role Differentiation

Are students asked to play individually different roles? In a role-playing game, typically they are. The dynamic between different roles drives the action. In a small working group, by contrast, all members might simply share the group's overall task, although here, alternatively, individual students might be assigned or assign themselves different roles, such as idea generator, devil's advocate, and the like. If the topic is contending positions on some issue, then students might be assigned or assign themselves to the different positions.

Role Depth

If roles are differentiated, how exact (and exacting) are they? Just being a note-taker or group negotiator is one thing, whereas channeling a specific historical or contemporary figure is quite another. One differentiation between scenarios and simulations lies here: A scenario is a general scene, whereas a simulation is usually a more exact reproduction (Hertel & Millis, 2002).

Drama

Is there a dramatic dimension? Is there some occasion for acting or impersonation? For example are there specific roles that might invite the use of accents or a bit of costuming? Is the scenario built on some kind of encounter or opposition, maybe with an unpredictable outcome, keeping everyone on the edge of their seats? Reacting to the Past scenarios replay historical encounters or decision points, with the outcome once again "to be determined." Other kinds of scenarios are problems or cases that pose intriguing and difficult challenges but do not call for any form of dramatic engagement.

How Problem-Driven?

Problems may vary in their degree of generality and specification. They may be as specific and front-and-center as a clock that has to be built from a collection of parts without instructions, or as general as resolving a multifaceted intellectual crisis or comparing two empirical predictions with each other and with the actual facts. However, a restaged historical encounter or a talk show may be much less specifically problem-driven.

Steps and Stages

Does the scenario or simulation unfold in one step or many? Sometimes just staging a scene is mostly the point, such as a talk show or a debate in which different sides simply offer their views, although these may be cross-examined and challenged by the emcee or other students. A more involved debate, though, might move through phases, as in formal debate. A comparison of predictions, as in the Darwin scenario, will have natural logical steps. Idea generation may only be the first stage in a longer process in which, say, small groups prepare a proposal or position for presentation and perhaps join in debate in a later, whole-group meeting, whose charge will ultimately be to choose between them. More staging and planning are required if there are multiple steps, but multiple steps also can build in drama and uncertainty.

Dialectical Stringency

Scenarios and simulations may vary in how stringent and specifically directed is their logic. Some will only be going one place. Others may have a demanding inner logic but still allow development in more than one direction. Still others may have a less demanding inner logic and consequently remain still more open-ended.

Different families of scenarios are defined by different ensembles of choices along each of these dimensions. The rest of this chapter explores three such families of pedagogical scenarios. Some are familiar, and some are unfamiliar, at least conceived in the way I will propose. Either way, I have found myself using these types of scenarios extensively, as have other teachers, often widely enough that there is a detailed and helpful literature on which we can draw.

Step-Right-Ins

Let us call the first family of scenarios *Step-Right-Ins* (Box 5.1).

BOX 5.1
Defining *Step-Right-Ins*

A *Step-Right-In* is a typically small-scale, problem-driven scenario that is readily entered while still fairly challenging for its short time frame.

Key Features

The label *Step-Right-In* is meant to capture an element of invitingness and degree of urgency, and especially readiness of entry. Considering the 12 dimensions distinguished earlier, we can give a more detailed characterization in Table 5.1.

TABLE 5.1
Step-Right-Ins

Dimension	Step-Right-Ins
Scale	small
Urgency	high
Readiness of entry	high
Surprise	yes
Group	any
Competitive	maybe
Role differentiated	unlikely
Role depth	unlikely
Drama	possible
Problem driven	yes
Steps and stages	unlikely
Dialectical stringency	low to moderate

Step-Right-Ins are used to immediately focus a group's energies; that is why starting with them, as students indeed walk right in, is so helpful. To step into the room is also to step right into the work. This is also why Step-Right-Ins are typically small scale, urgent, and brief—so that the class can move to other kinds of work, building on and seguing from them. Their function is largely to get students engaged, focused, and flowing (Heiland, 2011).

Note some other dimensions typically *not* present in Step-Right-Ins. Normally there is little time for role differentiation, or therefore for role depth, although an exception might be if a class has been studying a certain role or set of roles, so that students can take them on without much preparation. Step-Right-Ins are probably not competitive, either; there isn't time. Steps and stages are unlikely for the same reason. Step-Right-Ins trade dialectical layering for manageability on tight schedules, although a well-designed puzzle question might, all the same, require several distinct steps to reach an answer.

Exemplars

A Step-Right-In may be as simple as a quick warm-up, like a quick Internet news search or a logic puzzle that students tackle by themselves or in pairs.

Perhaps they are simply asked for good questions—a fine way to open a class that might then undertake to answer them. Astronomer Peter Newbury projects the "Astronomy Picture of the Day"—an Internet feature—in his classroom before each class, with two questions always posed for students as they come in: *What do you notice? What do you wonder?* To teachers, he adds:

> This is another opportunity for you to give students practice interpreting graphs/diagrams/photographs; give them practice talking about your field; create an opportunity for . . . students to contribute to the class, rather than being spectators; and learn what . . . students are thinking about— that's critical if you want to build new knowledge on existing knowledge. (Newbury, 2013)

Discussion of the day's image can start out informally with a few students before class officially begins, and then expand to the whole class as more students enter, naturally segueing into whatever topic is next on the agenda.

This may seem no more than a fun class opener, and in the hands of some professors it might be. But it can also be a genuine and powerful scenario in precisely the terms we have been using in this book. It is not a small thing that every day Newbury's students walk into their classroom and immediately find themselves off somewhere in space. Of course—this is Astronomy class! From a staging point of view I would think it helps if the image is large and the room otherwise fairly dark. It ought to *feel* like space too.

Moreover, the invited reaction is not just a brief moment of awe, although surely that is appropriate too. Coupled with Newbury's two questions, these images also activate an insistent dialectic. "What *is* this image?" students have to ask themselves and each other. We're no longer on Earth, but where *are* we? How can we figure it out? And what does this image make us want to know?

Of course, it should also be clear that this simple kind of Step-Right-In can be used with a range of subjects. Imagine walking into your classroom daily to some fragment of grand opera, a quick window into the futures market in Japan, or a news story from Al Jazeera about Zimbabwe. Newbury's questions apply here just as well: What do you notice? What do you wonder?

In engineering classes, a classic Step-Right-In is the challenge to build a device to protect an egg from breaking when it is dropped onto a hard surface (NASA, n.d.). Materials are typically limited. Each student group may find itself with an actual egg and maybe a little cardboard, some paper, a paperclip or several, and some tape. The instructor says that in 15 minutes, their eggs go out the window. Again, it is a small but urgent and fairly difficult challenge, it is immediately understandable and engaging, and it also ends with the application of an exacting criterion. Either the egg breaks or it survives.

A more systematic Step-Right-In would be some kind of class debate, as Chapter 3 suggests. Perhaps they are literally "step-right-ins" in the sense that I might stand in the hallway or outside my class building, buttonholing my students on their way in, quickly ascertaining their views on the topic of the day and assigning them to a seat on one side or the other inside the room. These days I am almost like a carnival barker: *Step right in!* indeed. Sometimes others besides my students also join in.

Inside, they find the room already abuzz. Even if I don't preassign seating, I may just set up two sets of chairs with large labels for each side. Again, just to take a seat in such a room is already to take a position. This is "choice architecture" par excellence: deliberate classroom layout with student engagement already built in. Students unavoidably step into something specific and soon to be demanding.

If the students can be expected to have mastered the topic enough to pull it off, debate can start right away. Or they might get 5 or 10 intense minutes to prepare. Perhaps they have a handout with prompts, an appreciated head start that also affords the teacher a chance to give the class well-organized and punchy notes that without the debate would not be assimilated half as well, if at all. Now students eagerly pore over them—and those of the other side, if they can get them. In one way, this is not so different from what many lecturers already do: lay out a set of arguments and consider their strengths and weaknesses and various criticisms and possible responses. The difference that makes all the difference is that in a debate so staged, the *students* are the ones immediately stepping into and making and replaying the arguments. With gusto! Box 5.2 offers another example.

BOX 5.2
Rethinking the First Day of Class

For another sort of exemplary Step-Right-In, I would like to draw on a recent article in *Teaching in Higher Education* on the subject of the first day of class. The authors "support an . . . approach to the first day . . . designed to immediately engage students in the course through activities designed intentionally to accomplish more than introducing students to the scholarly objectives of the class" (Anderson, Mcguire, & Cory, 2011, p. 293)—quite unlike the standard approach to first days of classes. In the terms of this book, Anderson and colleagues offer a Step-Right-In approach to the course as a whole.

(Continues)

Box 5.2 (*Continued*)

"The tone for the entire semester can be set within that first class session" (p. 294), Anderson and colleagues (2011) declare. Indeed, surely the tone for the entire semester is set within the first class session of almost any class—it's just that we rarely notice that effect when the usual norms are taken for granted. If our first days do not invite students to step right in to the course from the very start, though, isn't it an entirely predictable result that they are less likely to step right in later either? What if we invited them into the course in a different spirit, making the most of the surprise factor, too?

> Several researchers have examined first-day activities designed to do more than distribute the syllabus and discuss course policies. These techniques were deliberate in their objective to immediately bring students into the essence and heart of the class. (Anderson, Mcguire, & Cory, 2011, p. 296)

Their framing is exact. *Immediately bring[ing] students into the essence and heart of the class* is precisely what a first-day Step-Right-In can and should aim to do.

Anderson and colleagues (2011) cite sterling purveyors of such an approach, such as a University of South Carolina sociology professor who opens his class on the sociology of deviance by setting up one of his graduate students, unknown to his undergraduate class, to create low-level disruptions during class—basically, staging in-class deviance. Students react in a variety of ways, mostly uncomfortable. The professor then makes those very reactions the subject of intensive first-day discussion . . . right out of the gate, as it were, aiming to "excite students," as he puts it, "through unexpected activities that promote their participation, collaboration, and wonderment" (Higgins, 2001, p. 2). True, this could be done on any day of the class, in principle, and I'd be all for that, too. There is no reason to stop after the first day. Yet it is a stroke of genius to start on the very first day—stepping right in, indeed.

Task Groups

Many teachers use group work in many ways and for many purposes. We consider Task Groups here specifically in the context of scenario-based teaching (Box 5.3).

BOX 5.3
Defining *Task Groups*

Task Groups take on scenarios that are typically problem focused, fairly accessible and urgent, structured for cooperative effort by a small group, and may be difficult enough, as well as embedded enough in the main dialectic of the course, to require moderate amounts of time.

Key Features

Again considering the 12 dimensions distinguished at the start of the chapter, we can give a more detailed characterization of Task Groups as follows in Table 5.2.

TABLE 5.2
Task Groups

Dimension	Task Groups
Scale	medium
Urgency	fairly high
Readiness of entry	high
Surprise	maybe
Group	small-group
Competitive	likely
Role differentiated	unlikely
Role depth	unlikely
Drama	unlikely
Problem driven	yes
Steps and stages	variable
Dialectical stringency	variable

Task Groups have *tasks*, which require and reward group focus and effort. Thus, they are not just discussion groups, buzz groups, or groups for other purposes. Task Groups are typically much more tightly focused: They are prompted by some specific challenge or problem that defines as well as rewards group focus and effort. They also are typically not as short term as Step-Right-Ins, but require a medium scale of engagement and a significant portion of one class session or time distributed across several sessions in a week or two of a course.

The dialectical stringency of the tasks may vary. Sometimes it can be fairly high. In the Darwinian scenario, once again, the groups need to populate their islands in a way that is thoroughly consistent with their assigned starting points, and the further implications of those starting points can and sometimes must be explored too. Other times, the challenge may be to apply a given set of standards—say, a profession's code of ethics—to an ethically problematic and unclear situation. Here again, by contrast to Step-Right-Ins, well-designed tasks for Task Groups engage the deep dialectics of the course, rather than a simpler and more defined problem that functions mostly to get students engaged and in focus or flow.

Again, too, Task Groups are essentially *groups*. Cooperation is necessary. The tasks are, by design, too big for individuals on their own, and/or require cooperative preparation or presentation. Some might be what we often call "project groups," when their chief task is to work out a specific project, such as producing a marketing plan for a community organization, or a short video on the course themes. Mutual support and joint contributions are essential to the project's success, as well as being pedagogical goals on their own, for students certainly need to learn how to work together productively in teams and groups.

Task Groups are typically not role-differentiated. There is no need. The dialectic is in the problem, not the roles. Within the group, students may sometimes take on different subtasks or make different kinds of contributions, but it is not crucial to the process that these solidify into actual roles. Likewise, rarely is there the drama of working within an unfolding story line. Here the task is the thing.

Problem-Based Learning

PBL is an exemplary Task Group–Based Pedagogy. PBL originated and is still largely used in professional schools such as schools of medicine, law, and architecture. Most centrally and obviously, it is based on *problems*. "The principal idea behind PBL is . . . that the starting-point for learning should be a problem, a query or puzzle that the learner wishes to solve" (Boud & Feletti, 1997, p. 1). This is a thoroughly Deweyan notion: True learning is driven by the learner's own wish or need to know something or resolve some pressing issue or concern.

Noting that "there is no universally agreed set of practices that must be found in PBL courses to define them as such" (p. 2), Boud and Feletti (1997) nonetheless go on to list certain expected features. Typically, PBL designs aim to simulate or invoke professional practice in some way. The problems help orient student groups, providing some guidance and urgency, but, at the same time, like real-world problems, are by design open-ended and indeterminate enough that a key initial task for the groups is to simply bring the problems themselves into better focus so as to organize their response (Boud & Feletti, 1997; Kaunert, 2009; see also Savery 2006; Wismath, Orr, & MacKay, 2015). For PBL in the humanities, see Frank (2008). Mould (2003) even links this process to Hegelian dialectic. The aim is to

> design the task and the learning environment to reflect the complexity of the environment [students] should be able to function in at the end of learning. Rather than simplifying the environment for the learner, we seek to support the learner working in the complex environment. (Savery & Duffy, 2001)

For example, teams of medical students may be

> divided into groups of five and each group is assigned a facilitator. The students are then presented a problem in the form of a patient entering with presenting symptoms. The students' task is to diagnose the patient and be able to provide a rationale for that diagnosis and recommended treatment. (Savery & Duffy, 2001)

Teams of medical students may even be tasked with running a whole simulated hospital ward. Law students may prepare a case all the way from interviewing a client to finalizing documents that can be filed and argued. My Elon colleagues' Senior Seminar students in Environmental Studies spend their term researching and preparing draft EISs for local projects (MacFall, 2012). Their EIS is not as full-scale or professionally certifiable as an official EIS, but the work is nonetheless entirely real and necessarily engaged, and often edgy as well. Students work extensively onsite and with actual stakeholders, and they present their results in sometimes contentious public forums with outside stakeholders and program faculty present.

The open-endedness of such problems is part of their challenge and their intrigue. "The benefits of PBL are not merely the production of a problem solution but also in thinking through a problem, considering alternative ideas, and justifying a decision" (Hmelo-Silver, 2000, p. 41). The aim in all of these cases is to "help students construct usable knowledge" (p. 43) through actual practice and, again, especially in unclear situations in which defining the problem is part of the intellectual and practical challenges (O'Neill & Hung, 2010).

The students begin the problem "cold"—they do not know what the problem will be until it is presented. They discuss the problem, generating hypotheses based on whatever experience or knowledge they have, identifying relevant facts in the case, and identifying learning issues . . . A session is not complete until each student has an opportunity to verbally reflect on their current beliefs about the diagnosis (i.e., commit to a temporary position), and assume responsibility for particular learning issues that were identified. (Savery & Duffy, 2001)

In PBL there is a strong temptation to picture the work of the professor on the model of Teaching as Guiding. Goodnough (2006) writes, for example, that in PBL, "learning is student-centered and occurs in small groups, teachers act as facilitators or guides, problems are the organizing themes for learning, problems are the means for the development of clinical problem-solving skills, and new understanding occurs through self-directed learning" (p. 303). I believe that this is accurate as far as it goes, but as Chapter 2 argues, I believe it does not go far enough at all. The PBL literature also strongly stresses the necessity of deft problem or scenario design. *This* role is not at all that of a mere guide, but something much more designing, co-active, and proactive. When "problems are the organizing themes for learning," as Goodnough puts it, it is precisely the impresario's role to, well, organize them for learning. Thus, Burgess and Taylor (2000) write compellingly of PBL's need to reimagine the professor's role from university teacher to "learning coordinator" and speak of that coordinator's task as, chiefly, "designing the problems," specifically the preparation of what they too call scenarios (p. 86). "The transformation in conceiving of the faculty member's role from teacher to learning coordinator is clearly needed for PBL to work well" (Burgess & Taylor, 2000, p. 93).

Some writers are keen to distinguish PBL from the Case Method (Deignan, 2009; Goodnough, 2006). Yet from a larger perspective the Case Method aligns closely with PBL. Like PBL scenarios, cases are "richly detailed, contextualized, narrative accounts of teaching and learning . . . [that] are sufficiently complex to allow for multiple levels of analysis and interpretation" (Levin, 1995, p. 63). A good case, says Barbara Gross Davis (1993), tells a story, raises a thought-provoking issue, has elements of conflict, promotes empathy with the central characters, lacks an obvious or a clear-cut answer, encourages students to think and take a position, and is relatively concise. There are case-based courses in law, applied ethics, business, and engineering, for example, and again detailed pedagogical resources for such courses may be extended in theatrical directions (e.g., Andersen & Schiano, 2014; Barnes, Christensen, & Hansen, 1994; Harvard Business School, 2015). The

PBL literature sometimes argues that the paradigmatic problems for PBL are less well defined and more open-ended than the typical case, but if that is true, this still seems to me, from the present point of view, only a fairly minor difference of degree (Merseth, 1996).

Role-Plays

Key Features

Role-Plays place students into roles, usually specific and prepatterned for engagement; hence, they tend to be moderate or large scale, and typically they are dialectically more involved and fairly stringent (Box 5.4).

BOX 5.4
Defining *Role-Plays*

In *Role-Plays*, students inhabit and enact specific roles in interaction, normally with preparation and therefore some depth, with the interaction progressively unfolding in dialectical steps and stages.

Once again, considering the 12 dimensions distinguished previously, we can give a more detailed characterization in Table 5.3.

TABLE 5.3
Role-Plays

Dimension	Role-Plays
Scale	medium to large
Urgency	variable
Readiness of entry	variable
Surprise	variable
Group	whole-group
Competitive	may be built into roles
Role differentiated	high
Role depth	high
Drama	yes
Problem driven	possible
Steps and stages	likely
Dialectical stringency	moderate to high

The Magic Circle

Dittmer (2013) speaks of a so-called *magic circle* in pedagogical simulations "in which the game's rules and player identities purportedly replace those of everyday life" (p. 495). It is a nice characterization of both the structured and the consuming nature of role-plays. Pedagogical role-plays create a *special* space in which distinctive and specific rules apply, but at the same time they are more open-ended and participant-shaped than, say, a staged play in the theater. Again, as Chapter 3 tried to show, a scenario is not a script. It is a framework, a canovaccio, although often quite demanding, within which students must, as it were, make up their own lines.

Many of the systems of roles that might be invoked to create such "magic circles" already will be familiar. A debate about some policy or activity might be reframed as a mock lawsuit, for example, and then immediately a specific set of roles and a dramatic structure emerge. Everyone understands that there will be a team for the plaintiffs and likewise for the defense, various expert witnesses, a judge, and a jury. It's just about the right number for a typical small class. The staging proper can begin by writing the indictment, perhaps with part of the class acting as grand jury, knowing that the indictment, if approved, will become the basis for the actual trial. Then comes the trial, which can also follow familiar, detailed, step-wise patterns: opening and closing statements, cross-examination of witnesses, judge's charge, jury deliberations, and delivery of verdict.

Business ethics cases might set up as board of directors hearings (board, chief officers, various advocates, lawyers, outside agitators, etc.). Appropriate classes may role-play fact-finding commissions, Truth and Reconciliation Commissions, congressional hearings, conventions, or many other adjudicative and deliberative formats. A simulation of Congress might include senators on various sides, staffers, witnesses, and sometimes more nefarious roles such as foreign agents and the like. Model UNs, of course, model global deliberations in General Assembly or Security Council formats, sometimes others. (More on Model UN in Box 5.5.) There are even models and formats for edgy encounters beyond the usual realms, such as a role-play based on Erasmus's dialogue imagining the reprobate Pope Julius II begging the angels for admission at the gates of heaven (McDaniel, 2000) and mostly nonhuman conclaves, such as the Council of All Beings (Bragg & Rosenhek, 1998).

Defined decision procedures are helpful, and in role-plays like these they are built in (Pellegrino et al., 2012). Juries, boards of directors, and the UN Security Council vote. In National Security Council simulations, the so-called faux president decides in the end (DiCicco, 2014). There are clear outcomes in conclusion, but it should also be clear that the outcomes are open. Students are not simply replaying decisions already made, as they would be

BOX 5.5
More on Model UN

Model UN simulations began almost as soon as the actual UN was established, preceded by similar simulations of the League of Nations (Obendorf & Randerson, 2013). Today, more than 400,000 students worldwide take part every year (Crossley-Frolick, 2010), in single classes or combined sections; over whole schools; and at state, national, and even international conferences. Students role-play national delegations to the UN, including main spokespeople and a variety of area specialists and advisers, all requiring extensive preparation as well as quick thinking and effective coordination during the event. Whenever possible, students are assigned to countries other than their home countries (Dittmer, 2013; McIntosh, 2001).

Concurrent committee sessions run just like real UN committees. Delegations produce and try to advance resolutions addressing the issues before the committees and the Security Council or General Assembly. Formal parliamentary debate may alternate with a variety of kinds of caucuses. Student members of Model UN clubs often run the sessions, role-playing UN administrators and staff, as well as advisers to the delegations. One or more world crises will erupt during the days of the simulation, courtesy of the student organizers, too. Some border skirmish, maybe, is quickly spiralling into war. Everyone has to respond, visibly and immediately, as his or her country, and the world, lurches toward conflict or learns to manage something better.

First-year seminars at Elon jointly stage Model UN sessions, and representatives from the student Model UN club train individual classes in advance in resolution-writing and UN protocol. This kind of procedural training can be essential for students not already disposed to role-play or drama and make the built-in dramatic structure readily inhabitable. Besides, the student trainers' enthusiasm is infectious. At the same time, a variety of other formats are also available, including some procedurally simpler ones, such as those developed by the ICONS project (Asal & Blake, 2006). Jo Ann Digeorgio Lutz (2010) reports on an especially successful Arab League simulation.

Initially introduced to Model UN in a class, many students find it so engaging that they continue after that class, getting other students involved; coaching upcoming classes; and traveling, sometimes extensively, to take part in regional or national conferences. All of this may well prove much more engaging than their regular classes. I know as much from my own early college experience. My years on the debate team were

(*Continues*)

Box 5.5 (*Continued*)

likewise intensely active, heedless of time and even food and sleep, and certainly academic in the best sense, constantly calling on argument, research, careful thinking and verbal formulation, strategic planning, and all the rest—but had little to do with my classes, which were almost all traditional. The annual debate topics, much like UN agenda items, took us far more deeply into research than any of our classes. Indeed, they called us to ransack the library (remember libraries?), and we were ceaselessly tested by subjecting our cases to each other's scrutiny in practice rounds and tournaments. We'd argue about the issues for hours in restaurants and on long van trips. And we did all this primarily for the thrill of it. Why should this kind of energy and activity be shrugged off as merely "extra"curricular?

Understanding and empathy can arise as well. Digeorgio Lutz (2010) writes of Christian women students who took to wearing headscarves out of a newly felt solidarity that surprised even themselves after taking part in her Model Arab League simulation. The challenge to thoroughly inhabit another different world perspective can be transformative.

Studies consistently report very positive student and instructor responses to Model UNs (Engel, Pallas, & Lambert, 2017; Obendorf & Randerson, 2013). As cited in Chapter 1, McIntosh (2001) concludes in a thorough and influential article that "the excitement generated . . . can be a key for opening the world to students who might otherwise have drifted through the mandatory introduction to international relations" (p. 269). Pedagogically, Model UN simulations, with one foot in the classroom and the other well beyond, culminating in intense role-playing sessions, also mandate high levels of attendance and participation, even for students who may not start out highly engaged. Engaging a diversity of learning styles also regularly "increase[s] student sense of belonging within a particular course, discipline, and even institution" (Fox & Ronkowski, 1997, p. 732).

if they were dramatically reading a play. They make decisions themselves, staying true to their roles.

Of course, there are limits to this (Box 5.6). Exxon's board of directors could conceivably vote to double hull its oil tankers or limit oil drilling in certain ecologically fragile areas, but it is not going to vote to disband the company or spike all fossil-fuel exploitation. In contrast, the national convention of the Green Party might. Best, I find, are scenarios and simulations where the question is genuinely open as well as broad: where the decision could possibly and plausibly go either way—where there is genuine drama,

BOX 5.6
Reality and/or Fiction

Must the situation being role-played be real? Not necessarily. Asal and Blake (2006) observe that "fictional cases can help avoid preexisting bias or perceptions, as well as heated emotions, but this option requires more preparation in creating a backstory" (p. 7). Because most pedagogical role-plays will have to be simplified and rearranged to some extent to work in a classroom, it may be best to imagine that most role-plays are *partially* real. Writing of the University of Maryland's ICONS project, which creates a wide range of scenarios and simulations relating to global and other issues, Asal and Blake (2006) elaborate:

> Of course, it is possible to use real-world actors in fictionalized situations. ICONS's globalization simulation is centered on the parties involved in the political economy of the Niger River delta region of Nigeria—among others, the Nigerian government, Greenpeace, Shell Oil, and the representatives of the Ogoni people—and their negotiations about the future shape of the petroleum industry in the region. Although a real-world meeting of this group is unlikely, the issues raised by the negotiations shed a great deal of light on the problems posed by globalization. Conversely, you can choose to use fictionalized actors in real-world situations. ICONS's U.S. Senate simulation uses fictional senators, but the issues that are negotiated are ones that the real Senate might consider. (p. 7)

Many—I might even say most—classroom simulations will need to be simplified to be workable in the time and with the role-players available. This tends to make even "real" scenarios somewhat fictional, such as Bernstein and Meizlish's (2003) simulation of the congressional budget process, with only the House of Representatives voting and a short checklist of budget items and options. Simulations such as ICONS and the Global Problems Summit (Krain & Lantis, 2006) work from the other direction, as it were. They are inventions from the start—there are no such conferences in the real world—but complexified in the direction of the real world.

On roles that mix idealized types and reality, I want to call again on the experience of my colleague Tony Crider:

> In many scenarios, it is both easy and commonplace to assign generic roles. The Conservative Congressman. The Skeptical Scientist. The

(Continues)

Box 5.6 (*Continued*)

Roving Reporter. In the mid-2000s, the first Reacting to the Past game set in ancient Athens had roles such as the Middling Farmer, the Fishmonger, and the Rich Athlete. Most students didn't even have a role but were just part of a political faction such as the Oligarchs or the Socratics.

In playing the Trial of Galileo game, I found that while most roles were similarly generic (e.g., Conservative Cardinal #3, Moderate Cardinal #2) there were a few "real" roles. One student plays Cardinal Roberto Bellarmine. Another plays Prince Frederico Cesi. There is much written (and even much available to students online) about these two "characters." While neither an instructor nor a game author have the time to fully populate in detail a completely fictional word, the real world we live in has a wealth of information for students to dig into. And the best students often do.

One student in my class became dejected when her character, Robert Owen, seemed destined to lose it all in a Reacting to the Past game set in Manchester during the Industrial Revolution. When we dug into Robert Owen's history, though, we found he had in reality left Manchester behind and moved to Indiana to start up a commune. While this wasn't meant to be part of the game, it ended up being a perfect conclusion for both her character and some Luddite characters who joined her.

in short, and the role-players, or at least enough of them to potentially sway the decision, will be genuinely conflicted.

As Chapter 1 reported, student and teacher responses strongly support the pedagogical effectiveness of role-plays (Loui, 2009; Pellegrino et al., 2012; Takahashi & Saito, 2011). Tobin Grant (2004) says the same in his book appropriately titled *Playing Politics,* and other political science instructors laud simulations for enhancing students' ability to view international politics from non-American and non-Western perspectives (Weir & Barankowski, 2008). Obendorf and Randerson (2013) cite a broad consensus in the pedagogical literature about the value of role-play simulations to "scaffold student awareness of global affairs and the politics of international organization" (p. 354) and about the key skills that students develop from participation, such as negotiation, public speaking, debating, parliamentary procedure, and the like.

Note that the outcomes of successful role-plays themselves are not necessarily satisfying. As Asal and Blake (2006) said,

A simulation does not necessarily have to lead to a satisfying conclusion, nor does each participant need to feel that the simulation is "fair." Indeed sometimes, the purpose of the simulation is best served if the simulation is patently unfair. For example, in the simulation of the International Whaling Commission that ICONS uses to teach multilateral negotiations, the resources of the teams are wildly unequal. This makes clear to the participants the impact of power on negotiations and allows the instructor to make points about creating procedural power when material power is lacking. (p. 4)

Because the typical role-play involves role differentiation and specificity and requires student preparation to take on roles, it tends to be moderate or large scale and mostly takes place over multiple class periods of time, with preparation phases (researching, planning, anticipating other sides' moves, etc.) a significant part of the experience as well. In this sense, the work is urgent, but not because of time pressure. Small-scale role-plays can still be run in single class periods—they are just simplified. Some role-plays can also be online, and Internet support may be crucial for in-class role-plays as well, not only for research but also for quick and secure communication, teacher management, and even foreign language translation when needed. A dedicated website can easily archive all student productions and communications as well.

Reacting to the Past

I have already had a number of occasions to call on the Reacting to the Past pedagogy pioneered by Barnard College history professor Mark Carnes. It is a pleasure to consolidate and extend some of these references now as we briefly consider Reacting to the Past as another exemplary role-play pedagogy.

Reacting, as it is called for short, places students into specific "roles informed by classic texts in the history of ideas," which they learn to inhabit in preparation for open-ended reenactments of classic confrontations or decision points, such as the trial of Galileo, the trial of Ann Hutchinson (the demands of Puritan theology collide with religious freedom in the New World), the U.S. Constitutional Convention, and the multiparty negotiations in South Africa in 1993 over that country's post-apartheid future (Carnes, 2014; Reacting, 2013). The Reacting to the Past consortium now offers a wide variety of games—about 20 fully developed and published, another 30 or so downloadable, and about 50 more in a prototype stage— and annual gatherings to test developing games and sharpen the pedagogy (Big List of Reacting Games, 2017).

The aim is not to simply reenact these debates and decisions, like (again) merely play-reading a script in which the outcome is already given. Reacting to the Past deals in historical events, with known outcomes, but in this model, the decision is once again open. Many of the games center on confrontations that could have gone other ways. Galileo could have been shut down more thoroughly. The civil rights movement might not have so insistently embraced nonviolence. There were good arguments both ways. The game's point is to understand and deploy them as effectively as possible. As the Reacting to the Past website explains:

> Students learn by taking on roles . . . in elaborate games set in the past; they learn skills—speaking, writing, critical thinking, problem solving, leadership, and teamwork—in order to prevail in difficult and complicated situations. That is because Reacting roles, unlike those in a play, do not have a fixed script and outcome. While students will be obliged to adhere to the philosophical and intellectual beliefs of the historical figures they have been assigned to play, they must devise their own means of expressing those ideas persuasively, in papers, speeches or other public presentations; and students must also pursue a course of action they think will help them win the game. (Reacting to the Past, 2017)

Preparatory materials are typically massive. Reacting to the Past games involve elaborate documentation, running into the hundreds of pages, from original sources, commentaries, historical narratives to fill in characters and their motivations and knowledge, and so on—the more varied the better. Readings in a game on evolution and creationism, for example, include extensive selections from Darwin's (1859/2001) *On the Origin of Species*, Hume's (1779/1983) *Dialogues Concerning Natural Religion* (sharply critical and indeed satirical about the creationism of both his day and, it turns out, ours), and a variety of not only contemporary creationist and noncreationist but also non- or semi-Darwinian theories of the development of new species. Extensive web resources can also be used. These may even become the main readings for a whole course, especially if the course involves more than one game. Carnes's standard lower-level history course at Barnard is built around three.

Students need to *master* the readings and look beyond them in turn. Just as in mock legal proceedings or a senatorial hearing, students carry all of the action. Unpreparedness will be obvious. Last-minute crams will not work. Again, as Carnes (2014) puts it, "no one can 'fake' a sermon in defense of Ann Hutchinson's theology" (p. 142). Thorough preparation is essential, and there will be many and often unexpected points at which students will be called on. There is no substitute for learning to think in a well-grounded game persona.

The games usually have extensive substructures, multiple stages, and many decision points. The game on evolution and creationism is framed by the 1999 Kansas Board of Education struggle over the presentation of the theory of evolution in the public school science curriculum, beginning with the election of a new Kansas State Board of Education with a slate of candidates who hold a wide range of stances on the issues, along with candidates with indeterminate commitments. After a series of debates, the rest of the class votes. The newly constituted board of education then takes on the question of standards for biology textbooks in Kansas. How should they treat the theory of evolution and its supposed creationist competitors? Members draft their own resolutions and draw their own conclusions.

Reacting to the Past scenarios can easily extend to contemporary and scientific issues as well. My astronomer colleague Tony Crider has developed a Reacting to the Past game on the demotion of Pluto from planet to dwarf planet (or, amusingly, Plutoid) by the International Astronomical Union in 2006. This move is still controversial among astronomers and obviously requires a great deal of knowledge of the solar system, rationales for various systems of classification of astronomical bodies, and even the recognition, surprising to some, that scientists actually disagree about fundamental underlying issues.

Carnes (2014) calls Reacting to the Past scenarios *games* and attributes some of their captivating power to the competitive aspect. The drama is captivating, too, I am sure, as well as the game's open-endedness and its sheer immersion and flow (Csikszentmihalyi, 1996; Heiland, 2011). In any case, captivating they are. Barnard's resident assistants regularly plead with Carnes to soft-pedal his games because they cannot get students in their dorms to go to parties or hang out instead of spending whole nights arguing about philosophy and strategizing for their upcoming reenactments of ancient confrontations (see also Sasley, 2010, on this effect for a range of simulations). Would that most of us had such complaints!

The encounters or events being modeled have winners and losers. Definitive votes and decisions are usually taken, often with huge stakes. In the class, one factor in a student's grade (although rarely a large one) might well be how successful the team is in the game. In the game, the impresario–teacher may function as gamemaster, among other things, by rolling dice to determine the outcome of a confrontation or other uncertain event. In the evolution game, the gamemaster is even invited to give school board candidates a quiz on the basics of the evolution–creation controversy (such as it is) and change candidates' vote totals accordingly. As the game manual acerbically comments, sometimes the electorate really does pay attention to how well prepared a candidate is.

Overview

Table 5.4 correlates the 12 dimensions with the 3 families of scenarios just introduced.

TABLE 5.4
Three Types of Scenarios Compared

Dimension	Step-Right-Ins	Task Groups	Role-Plays
Scale	small	medium	medium to large
Time pressure	high	fairly high	variable
Readiness of entry	high	high	variable
Surprise	yes	maybe	variable
Group	any	small-group	whole-group
Competitive	possible	likely	may be built into roles
Role differentiated	unlikely	unlikely	high
Role depth	unlikely	unlikely	high
Drama	possible	unlikely	yes
Problem driven	yes	yes	possible
Steps and stages	unlikely	variable	likely
Dialectical stringency	low to moderate	variable	moderate to high

I reemphasize in closing that Step-Right-Ins, Task Groups, and Role-Plays are by no means the only possible types of scenarios. The chapters to come offer many examples of all of these but also of other types of pedagogical scenarios. The families elaborated here, however, seem to me to be the main types found in the teaching literature today and are central to my practice as well. This is in part because they represent especially logical and synergistic ensembles of features or choices along the described dimensions. For example, Task Groups are inherently problem-driven and of course involve groups, but they need not be highly role-differentiated. There can be exceptions, of course, but there do seem to be natural kinds of pedagogical scenarios, and these are I have tried to highlight here.

Still, from a generative point of view, one could take this list of 12 main dimensions of pedagogical scenarios as variables and vary them, in imagination, to explore new possible combinations. Try inventing new possibilities. For example, a highly role-differentiated but small-scale and urgent scenario might be quite practical in a class in which specific roles were already well established—say from some larger ongoing role-play or some context outside of the class proper. Sometimes I even have my students role-play each other. Or maybe . . . competitive dialectical dramas?

6

DAILY SCENARIOS
FROM MY CLASSES

Stepping Right In to Critical Thinking

My What Can We Know? course is an introductory philosophy class that surveys basic rules for analytical inference and the appropriate use of evidence while at the same time grounding those rules in basic epistemology. It is a practical course, in my vision, even as we read Socrates, Plato, Descartes, and Hume along with a critical thinking textbook. And so we "step right in" and, as Chapter 5 suggests, right away on the very first day.

Playing Sherlock

The first theme is careful observation, and what Sherlock Holmes would call *deduction* from it. Accordingly, the first readings for the course are selected Sherlock Holmes stories, assigned online in advance of the first class meeting. Thus we start even before the first class, so to say. When we first gather, moreover, we do not start with a class list or syllabus—the syllabus is online too, and my set-up e-mails will have asked students to read it and respond with questions—but instead we start with, yes, a whodunit.

Epitomizing the theme of observation and deduction, in short, my strategy is to immediately make the students themselves into detectives. We do not just *study* Sherlock Holmes—we *become* Sherlock Holmes. Again—this is how impresario–teachers operate!

Students walk into the room to be handed a picture mystery—a several-page case summary, mostly photos, of a suspicious death (Black, 1983). Maybe it is suicide, maybe it is murder, and if it is murder, there are multiple suspects. The students' job is to figure out the clues, mostly visual and requiring careful observations, and then figure out from the clues what actually happened. Pick a partner or two, I say—most of the students don't yet know each other, so this is also a way to meet—and get to it.

Thus the first moments of the first class meeting are already, in effect, a workshop. We segue into a whole-class discussion at various points. Still no plenary opening, though—we're simply on task. I ask for clues that students have found, noting that this is exactly what Holmes would do: observe as carefully as possible. Even the smallest details—the slight unraveling of a rope (or not), or a medically implausible alibi—turn out to be revealing. In this case, two or three clues lead us fairly readily to conclude that this death was not a suicide. Then, who did it? Back the students go to work with their partners again. I circulate and drop hints, and eventually we come back to share more clues and deduce the answer.

This is focused and difficult work. It is not simply a make-work or socialization activity to get class going. The scenario "progressively unfolds," in the language Chapter 3 adopted from Ruth Clark (2013). As the first clues are uncovered and deduction proceeds, students realize that more is yet to be uncovered—and again more still. Time is tight, too. Other teams are also on the case.

Among other things, the intended message is: This is a class in which you will be expected to *think,* hard, and take an active part, right out of the gate—because that is what we just did. Do not wait to be told how to do it, and do not worry about the details (Wismath et al., 2015), but come in here every day alert and ready. This class will meet your readiness. In fact, it will *demand* your readiness, and be thoroughly enjoyable to boot.

Twenty minutes in, we may finally gather to talk as a whole group. We discuss the mystery, examine our process, and go on to adumbrate Holmes's methods generally (maybe on an individual check-in sheet, a sort of quiz on the first day—better have done the readings, eh?). We do talk about the course, at least a little, if there are questions. At the end, I give the students another mystery in the same format. Many take it back to their dining hall or apartments and immediately tackle it with friends or suitemates. And so we have stepped right in indeed.

Mysterious Objects

Another kind of Step-Right-In is what I call *Mysterious Objects.* Near the door will be a box of little things that students can pick up when they come in, but few will recognize. What are they? "I have no clue," somebody usually says. Oh, yes you do, is the reply. Many clues. Find them and deduce, Sherlock-style—this is the day's warm-up. What is the object made of? Are there any markings? Why would something be made just like this? Can you infer what it is from these clues?

One of my standard mysterious objects is the twist-on wire connector familiar to electricians. Few students know what it is (although I once had a student who claimed that his uncle invented them). Cheap little plastic casing (so cheap everyone can get one—a big advantage), some grip or wings on the sides, a metal spiral inside—that is it.

Why these features? Are there clues here? Remember, I say, none of this is accidental. People have designed and produced this object, indeed apparently en masse, for some purpose, and that purpose drives the design. Therefore, we should be able to deduce the purpose from the design, even if at first we do not know what it is, if we look and think carefully enough. The metal spiral, for instance, can function to screw on . . . to what? The plastic can insulate . . . what? Looking really closely, we see a little "UL" logo on the side. Google it. Underwriters Laboratory—an independent lab certifying electrical equipment for insurance companies. Are we making progress?

Web Sleuthing

Next meeting, the mysterious item may be a website. I send students a link, and again they're off. Here, for instance, is a site that for a mere $10 offers you a chance to be whisked off into the future before you die and to be resurrected when medical technology exists to greatly prolong your life, all to be paid for by the tens of billions of dollars that even a single dollar earns if invested at compound interest for a millennium or so. For real, some elaborate scam, a lighthearted joke—what is this?

Someone will raise their hand and start guessing. No, I say, don't guess. Play the sleuth and look for actual clues. Observe and explore first! Who is behind this site? What is in the fine print? Does the site display an organization with the longevity and legal acumen required to make a credible promise of this sort? Does the PayPal link actually work? (It does. Hmm . . .) What do other online sources say? It turns out, for example, that this site is included on certain lists of online scams. But how reliable are *they*?

The offer presupposes the possibility of time travel, someone points out. Yes, but the website is explicit about this. Whoever is behind it does not take time travel as a given, although they do offer extensive citations from scientists and others to suggest that it may well be possible. Might this caution be a clue? If it were an obvious scam, would they be so hedged? It's only $10 for, in effect, a bet on a kind of immortality. Why couldn't that be a serious, if rather offbeat, offer? Isn't it at least worth $10?

Another way to find out what would happen if you send in $10 is to actually send in $10—which, I eventually reveal, I have done. The class is amused and intrigued. "What happened then?" they eagerly ask. I got back a certificate and an instruction sheet. I bring in copies. Everyone examines them closely. They don't look too convincing—but in fact I did get *something*.

Among other things, the instruction sheet requests members to arrange for someone to report their death back to the time travelers so that someone can come back and rescue them just before. In one class, some students therefore suggested that one of them specify my death moment as right then, right there in the class, so that we can test whether anyone actually shows up at the last minute to save me. I demurred, on the grounds that I did not want to take even the slightest chance of having to leave everyone and everything I love (let alone them!) just to take up a long life many centuries later—or of seriously annoying an envoy from the future who turns up to discover I am actually not dead but just testing them. But you see the point—and those students certainly got some serious credit for the day.

In any case, you can see that the question is real and intriguing. Nobody made up this site merely for a class exercise—though there are websites like that; in fact, I have whole lists of them and put them out to students as well. They all bear more careful sleuthing. As Holmes would say, often the tiniest and most unintentional clues reveal the most. Deeper habits of mind are key: looking carefully; not taking any website for granted; and not taking one's own, off-the-top-of-the-head reactions for granted either. And, in case this is not already obvious, this work is utterly engaging for everyone. As class proceeds, many students may be online, usually the bane of allowing laptops in class, but they are following up links or cross-checking this site on others—not off-task at all. Class is too interesting!

Task Groups for Whole Sessions

Teachers who want to try out scenario-based teaching might start with Step-Right-Ins like these, even if what follows is a more standard class. Gradually, perhaps they will get longer and morph into Task Groups that occupy whole classes. They can become not just lead-ins to the students' main work together but a significant or even complete part of a class session.

Chapter 5 cited one classic exercise for a class on problem-solving or critical thinking: NASA's challenge to build a lander to protect an egg from breaking when dropped onto a hard surface. One of my follow-up Task Group exercises ups the ante with a challenge to construct a working wind-up clock from a big box of mixed parts. Originally, I found these clock kits in a kids' science shop. They have about 30 plastic parts and include step-by-step instructions. With instructions, this activity is at about a sixth-grade level. Without instructions, it's a challenge even for teams of college students, especially because they have no experience with wind-up clocks in regular life anymore (or building things generally, for that matter).

Again I will narrate a bit of the story to help give the feeling of how an impresario–teacher might unfold and manage such a scenario. Teams need to start by looking carefully at the parts they have available. Then they need to consider how such a clock actually works, and therefore what parts it needs. A spring, obviously. Then what? Some way of gearing down the spring's unwinding, yes? So maybe in 20 minutes they manage to reconstruct the gear train.

If they let the spring go with this, though, it runs down to nothing in five seconds or so, spinning some gears off their shafts to boot. Clearly there must be some way of regulating and greatly slowing down the unwinding. What could that be? Back to the parts box—what kinds of parts are left? They see a pendulum. Could this regulate the unwinding rate? They may picture a grandfather clock. Think about this. What is the pendulum doing? Once again, the teacher might point out that in a designed device such as this, every part is exactly fitted to the function. You can infer the functions from the parts and vice versa. So what kind of linkage is needed to make the pendulum a regulator? And what sort of linkage is suggested by the available parts?

The challenge has certain milestones, such as completing the gear train, so students can mark their accomplishments along the way, as well as clearly and functionally defining the next challenge. Hints can be strategic and clearly represented in the problem before them on their workbench, such as how to run the two separate hands of the clock at different speeds on the same shaft. Once they see their way to that, they can finish the face. Still, it is usually a race with the timer—we only have the class period—but hints can be varied depending on how far each group has gotten and how much time is left, so that most of the clocks end up mostly complete, and usually with a great sense of accomplishment to boot. In how many other classes have they experienced such intense concentration for so long? "My brain hurts," someone will usually say at the end. Ah yes, I answer. This is *college!*

Box 6.1 offers a few more thoughts on work of this sort.

BOX 6.1
More Notes on Staging

As Chapter 5 also emphasizes, Step-Right-Ins can be used across the curriculum. Analyze a poem or newspaper story. Identify a flower or a crustacean (better, just carefully note its defining characteristics; actually finding the taxonomic name isn't the key skill and can be done in plenary session).

(Continues)

Box 6.1 (*Continued*)

Design the smallest possible self-sustaining physical system with life in it—a challenge I use in my environmental studies classes when we take up the subject of sustainability.

Once again, a certain urgency and focus can be indicated in the very staging of the room—setting the scene, indeed. Worktables can already be set up with some intriguing project, and students can begin on them the minute they enter the room, so that others then enter to find ongoing work already. Maybe there is some sort of challenge on the board or a handout. Students gather and begin to work while the teacher circulates, explains, challenges, and teases.

I always ask for my classes to be scheduled in rooms with tables and chairs rather than desks, which allows more flexible set-ups in general but also has the particular advantage that workgroups can be automatically created simply by setting up the tables separately with a few chairs around each one. Students sit down in workgroups from the start. Supplies can be laid out in advance if needed, or readily distributed table by table when the time comes. I bring large poster-paper pads, large sticky pads, and cases of colored markers. Sometimes, in the Darwin scenario for example, the working product may be a poster that can then be displayed on the wall or whiteboard and explained by the student group. We'll put up all the posters before beginning the explanations/presentations. Just that, on the usual bare walls, already transforms the room into a much more lively and exciting space.

Use timing deliberately as well. In a workshop where the work begins as soon as students enter the room, no one necessarily takes much notice of the official beginning of the class period, and the activity goes on until it comes to its own completion in the fullness of time. Only then might the teacher and/or student leader call the group together and into the next phase of the day's work. Again the symbolic aspect is also important. The message is that this class is always active, inviting, running over the boundaries of the period—like life, eh?—and with engaging challenges.

Stepping right in means, well, stepping right in. Thus, for better or worse, I forgo almost all of the usual introductory scaffolding. Otherwise, in my view, by the time we get to the actual work, it has often been overly worried and predigested. The life has started to go out of it. Students in traditional classes quickly get used to ponderous windups, moreover, and therefore learn to tune out the first two or three repetitions. I first noticed the contrast when I started singing with advanced enough musical ensembles that the director would give us instructions in rehearsal exactly *once* (if that), and everyone accordingly listened and was ready to go after that one instruction. What a contrast, I realized, to the usual scene in school. But our students are entirely capable of listening the first time, too.

In general, I would rather have my students learn to confront (and welcome) new challenges and figure them out for themselves. It's even better when the Step-Right-In manifestly depends on the readings, so that students are again emphatically signaled that they had better show up fully prepared. They can hit the ground running, alert and prepared, if we not only manifestly expect them to do so but also structure that expectation into the setup itself.

On that note, did you notice that this chapter itself just stepped right in? No introduction, no explanation, no justifications. Confusing? Or energizing?

One last point. A useful design feature of the clock-building and egg-drop challenges is that the criteria for success or failure are crystal clear. The egg survives or it doesn't. The clock runs properly or explosively unwinds, jams, or just sits there doing nothing. The criteria are totally given by the specific task itself. This also relieves a major potential source of time delays and burden on the teacher. Students do not need their instructor to come around to evaluate their products. They can test them themselves. Definitive feedback is built into the activity itself.

Talk Shows and Panels

There are other kinds of scenarios into which a class may be invited, or more or less required, to step, and not just at the beginning of a class. They can start (and stop) anytime. Indeed, the recognition that such scene shifts are possible and even likely—once they've seen them a few times—is intriguing to students. It keeps them always a bit on edge. Students quickly learn that something unexpected can be expected nearly every day in my classes. Here already, for better or worse, things can get far more dramatic than students typically expect from their school experience.

Bring Your Microphone

A talk show, remember, was the very first example of an alternative teaching scenario in this book. Some days a teacher might just pull a microphone out of his or her pocket and begin prowling the aisles—of course, set up in advance— asking questions of students, but talk-show style. This may be planned, or even unplanned, at the beginning of class or anytime along the way.

For most students who watch television, the talk show is a readily recognizable format and one that is easy to join both because of its familiarity and the genial insistence of the emcee. Yet, a surprise! Suddenly their teacher, a moment ago so safely professorial and distant, is now in their face, requiring that they have something to say. Apparently they're on the air, and immediately they have to venture some thought. Then there is something to work with, ideas for others to react to. No time to remember that this is after all *school*. With just an attitude and the barest of props, then, you can almost instantaneously evoke an entirely different set of responses, switching from what may seem like a stilted class discussion to something on the spot and thoroughly unexpected and enjoyable.

Social psychologists speak of *scripts*, meaning known patterns, usually quite specific, that may be invoked socially and familiarly and into which people can step almost automatically. Again, not *script* in the sense that it dictates specific words, but specific styles of interaction are still given. Broadly speaking, students know what to do. Of course, school has its scripts, too, in this sense, but the dynamics of a talk show are different and typically far more engaging than the usual class discussion. It is a much freer pattern of interaction, for one thing, and also more insistent. The host is expected to be provocative. Rarely is there waiting for the raising of hands. Instead, there is an expectation of a certain eagerness to join the exchanges, and usually there is the possibility and even expectation that what is said can be a bit edgy or at least unusually forthright, all of which serves the energy of the scene as well as the learning.

Don't Look Back

Here the impresario–teacher deliberately and theatrically creates an alternative space—the scene and, more broadly, the scenario—and walks right into it without looking back, expecting students to follow immediately and enthusiastically. She brings this whole pattern forth, in this case by resolutely, insistently, and even a little recklessly embodying it herself.

My students know I am play-acting an emcee. My questions, too, may not be ones I would or could ask of them if I were playing the teacher role. That is part of the talk show scenario, and of course the students accordingly also know that they can dodge many of those questions in a variety of ways. Which they often do, skilfully and deftly. A lot of laughter may be part of the scene, but it can stay serious, as well. The humor often enables the seriousness.

Maybe I put on a tasteless or dated bowtie while students are still trying to figure out what is happening, make a joke about plugging in the mic when really I am just stuffing the other end of the cord into my pocket (they laugh . . . and then forget . . . because they know I'll be after them in a minute), hit the music, and start up the show with a canned spiel, a few jokes, and the like. But then there we are. I begin asking questions of students in a somewhat louder voice, maybe motioning to an imaginary TV camera or dropping hints about a worldwide radio audience along the way. No explanations—who needs them? No waiting for students to raise their hands. Everyone's fair game, but it doesn't seem like an intrusion to call on them uninvited. It's just part of the scenario. Immediately, though, we can get into the real themes of the course.

Both my voice and my persona will vary. I'll be more insistent, less polite, more wheedling, or provocative. I've just made room for this by wholly jumping into the talk show scenario in the first place. Among other things, I consider this an offering of a certain kind of space to my students. It is only fair to ask them to take the risk of play-acting in the scenario by manifestly play-acting myself, even more risky as it may be, out in front. Students follow, and usually happily too, even when they are on the spot, at the other end of the mic, or know they soon could be. Without even having time to recognize it, they are actually in the thick of real thinking and fast interchange. Still in a deep way, they know they are nonetheless personally safe—that is a key responsibility of the teacher too, of course. They can play, but on the scenario's terms, which underneath the banter is still focused and pressing. We are after all exploring a theme, working out or critiquing an argument, exploring different points of view, or solving a problem. It *is* school, actually, but in a dramatically different key.

Planning and Scaffolding . . . or Not

Talk shows might also be announced and worked out in advance, so students have time to prepare. With preparation they obviously can go deeper and with more background, backup, and organization. The tradeoff is that the event can also be more stilted and nervous. Precisely the surprise character of the impromptu talk show can overcome nervousness. There's no time to get nervous, for one thing, and the manifest surprise for everyone (sometimes even me, if it's impromptu) also signals lower stakes. Obviously students cannot be expected to be fully organized, with data at their fingertips, if the whole event has just happened at the drop of a hat. They are less on the spot and can actually speak more freely. However, they still can be expected to have decent command of what they were asked to have read in advance. Students will be far more likely to do the readings after some command of the readings has been called upon in a few extemporaneous talk shows or similar formats. Like the Boy Scouts, their motto has to become "Be Prepared!"

Once again you'll note that I offer no scaffolding for such an event. In my view, a long windup (explanation, self-justification, etc.) would suck the air out of it and tune the class out. There is nothing like the electricity of just shape-shifting into it. There may be some confusion the first time, along with delight. After that, I have found, there isn't. Often students will plead for more.

Panels

Panels are a closely related kind of scenario: Think of them as talk shows to which limited but more formal roles are added.

Students might enter the classroom one day to find a few chairs set up in the front of the room, the rest of the room with half-circled chairs like a studio. A few of them volunteer—or are "volunteered"—to occupy the chairs and take up assigned roles—yes, on the spot—based on the readings (again, better be prepared, eh?), recent class themes, or current events. On some kinds of panels, it can be useful to have some panelists be themselves—twenty-first-century college students—which also makes for an easy way to persuade/conscript students who might otherwise be reluctant. Sometimes the panelists may be recruited or alerted in advance. Other times, not—in some ways, they are freer when everyone knows the entire event is extemporaneous. The teacher then can become the interviewer or panel host—again a microphone can be useful—and jumps right in.

Panels can also build on course work. In my upper level Marx/Darwin/Freud course, students prepare graded research briefs on each of the three figures. Students' briefs in that class must be only one single-spaced page long, but accordingly research-packed, concise, and punchy—every word must count—and must include at least two detailed, reliable, and supportive references or links on the subject, from which the brief demonstrably draws. These briefs are then uploaded and become the assigned readings for the final week of class on each figure, as well as potential outlines for students' term papers for the class. They pick one theme to expand on, bringing in the other figures, as well as resources from other students' term papers (the authors get credit when other students cite them).

One feature I like about this design is that the range of applications we consider is mostly shaped by students' own research choices—not by me, although I also write a sample research brief myself on each figure as a model and as a way to discuss another theme that we might not have had time for in class. Another thing I like about this design is that students are thereby primed to take part in a panel. Instead of the stilted script of "reports," we have something much more engaging and efficient. On the days when we consider the research briefs together in class, we have 25 briefs and 100 minutes. My strategy is to set up about panels of 5 to 6 students at a time, centered on a shared theme or topic, not announced in advance, but there will be a schedule, with names, on the board when they walk in. The students on each panel in turn are called to the front of the room, sit in the guests' chairs, get interviewed by the emcee (me, at least the first time), and take quick questions from the rest of the group as well. Strict time-keeping (by a designated student) ensures that everyone gets their turn in the limelight. Vigorous moderating ensures that discussion remains fast-paced and on topic.

The first time, this is all new. After that, students come with expectations. Often a student in the class volunteers to take over the emcee role. Once I actually had an aspiring professional emcee, good at it already, with a thoroughly winning personality. Then I either just sit and watch ("on the side" for once) or jump on the panel myself, probably in some role (say a modern-day critic of the figure in question) to help out—or make trouble.

Visitors and Impersonations

Guests

Teachers and sometimes students may invite experts or advocates on some key class theme to visit the class and make a guest presentation. Usually, especially if the visitor is another professor, the expectation is that the visitor will essentially lecture: that is, present some material from an authoritative point of view. It can become a standard class, just with a different teacher for the day. This has advantages. It regularly brings in others, it keeps the class manifestly permeable to the outside world (Sandy, 1998), and the sheer novelty of different voices helpfully mixes things up. Besides, because guest speakers are not the regular teacher, they are also not grading the class and probably have no personal relation to the students in the way a regular teacher does. This can free students up to be a little more challenging than they might be with their regular teacher.

There are ready ways to sharpen this dialectic and heighten the drama. Rather than the guest simply taking over the Sage role and the Stage for the day, for starters, one might at the very least make the visit an energetic dialogue between the regular teacher and the guest. Of course, the first key to scene staging in this case is to be sure the guests are ready (ideally eager) for this. Establish enough respect and clarity of expectation in advance that the teacher and visitor can demonstrate a genuinely respectful and well-informed disagreement for the students—who can then be invited to join in the same spirit. With guests who are game, you can use more deliberate staging to advantage, too. Argue from opposite sides of the room, maybe, with the students between you. I and my guests have sometimes dressed up a little, or barged in on each other apparently without warning. Again the symbolic aspects are key. Here the students are literally put into the middle of a debate, rather than just hearing about it or analyzing it from the outside.

Sometimes I invite a guest who challenges everything we've been studying in the course, such as the PhD microbiologist who is also a Biblical literalist/Young Earth Creationist who visits my Darwin classes and defends a 6,000-year time table for the whole history of the planet. He's serious. Most of the students will have none of it—and I make sure my guest knows this in advance, too, out of respect for both him and the class—but of course they have to *argue*, to dig deeper, to make Darwinian moves on their own.

I am not necessarily after fireworks here, although they may happen. It would be easy for such a visit to reduce to just a staged clash of views, but it is also not hard to make it much more productive. As usual, the essential thing is to set up a scene whose own thoroughly engaging dynamic pushes the action, the thinking, the learning. In this case, the visitor presents for maybe half an hour; then we have a round of quick clarifying questions, then more systematic arguments. In his last appearance we were joined by one of Elon's evolutionary biologists, who had a fair amount to say, too, and not all of it in disagreement. I or a capable student moderate to ensure that a range of views is heard, and our guest or guests are heard out. Typically after a 100-minute class of this, a fair group wants to continue, and we stay on in the classroom if we can or find a table in a nearby coffee shop.

Remember again, then, that scenarios needn't involve role-playing. Just having a visitor can be a dynamically structured situation, even if it doesn't have the equivalent of plot development. A thorough exploration of an issue or a topic has its own dynamic and dialectic.

Visitors used to be limited to the immediate locality. Potentially fine guests anywhere outside your area would be unlikely to be able to come. This has changed completely, however, with the advent of online video-conference options. Now people can visit your classroom literally from anywhere. Thus, my colleagues and I regularly bring authors of class readings as guests into our classes from all around the country. My classes have conferenced with authors as far away as Australia, where one generous soul even got up in the dead of the night to talk with us. Some authors of widely used academic readings actually offer this as a service. Even the sky's not the limit. Courtesy of NASA, elementary and secondary school classes have even Skyped with astronauts on the International Space Station.

Impersonations

In literature and philosophy, if you read original sources, most of your authors are long dead. How we might wish, per impossibile, to be able to talk with Socrates in person, Dickinson, Gandhi, or Marx! Or to join in an exchange among several of these luminaries who never could have met in real life either.

Who would you really love to have visit your class? Who would students be most surprised and thrilled to see walk in the door? So what if they are dead—bring them in anyway. It just takes a visit a costume shop, some work on accents, and more or less the same sort of planning you'd do anyway. Scene-setting can be simple too. On some days when the students are expecting me as usual, the person who walks in the door is . . . me, but not in my usual self. Or maybe someone else, like a colleague, can be induced to impersonate a historical figure they know well, and thus can walk in on a regular class and "surprise" me as well. (Do not assume your colleagues wouldn't do this for you, by the way, just because they might not go so far in their own classes. You can always ask.)

Costume is critical to mark the shift, but it need not be much. Sometimes just a suit jacket can be enough—at least for me, since "normally" I do not dress up. My Descartes may be merely a period hat and a fencing foil (visibly blunted point—just to be clear). In some ways, a full costume would be more distracting. It is more effective to leave most of it to the imagination, offering just enough to clearly mark the role. With light props, you can also flip in and out of the role more easily, which I find useful both pedagogically and dramatically. Just put the hat on or off as needed. Accordingly, my costume drawer (yes, I do have a costume drawer) includes a lot of small props for this purpose: wigs, canes, a toga, Benjamin Franklin-style spectacles, pipes, top hats, pocketwatches, along with wilder props such as alien ray guns, Mardi Gras masks, capes, magician wands, and so on.

I will admit to even dressing up as Daniel Quinn's (1992) *Ishmael*—a gorilla—which takes a bit more costume. But what better way to take up Quinn's series of Socratic dialogues with a gorilla than to bring Ishmael himself into the discussion? (Again: we don't just *study* Ishmael's dialogues—we *join* them.) Students become more able to see the world—and human presumption within it—from a more-than-human point of view, which of course is exactly the goal. Here is a gorilla right in front of them, and indeed in their faces. Sometimes if Ishmael visits another class, students do not know who is *really* in the costume, which is usefully unsettling as well.

Not Just Performance

Some colleagues have imagined that impersonation is just lecturing in costume. One could certainly do that, but much more is possible. After all, by the time the class is ready for whatever appearance you are making, students presumably have already read and maybe discussed "your" works or the positions for which you want to speak or that you want to challenge. There is no reason to simply *tell* students anything. You want to answer their questions, engage them, and even provoke them. You want to give them at least a glimpse of what it is like inside "your" thought, and the best way to do so is to think *with* them, or perhaps to some extent *against* them, but in any case in a thoroughly interactive way that makes good use of the dramatic possibilities as well.

Again, then, as the coda to Chapter 4 points out, this is not a performance—not if that is supposed to mean that the "audience" remains passive and merely spectatorial. Interaction is key. Imagine a class visit as Socrates, for example. In person, he would work entirely in questions. So do the same. Ishmael does, too, by the way. He is in effect an other-than-human Socrates. Or suppose you barge into a Darwin class as a bombastic critic of Darwinism—perhaps a nineteenth-century clergyman much like the notorious Bishop Wilberforce. Get outrageous enough—parody "yourself" just enough—that some student will interrupt to object. They can see the game that is afoot. Then you are off and running. Here, from the start, students realize that they are also *inside* the scene, on the stage, so to speak, part of the event, just as much as the visitor/teacher is.

Jean-Jacques Rousseau recently visited my Philosophy of Education class. They'd begun the class with me in my regular person, quickly moving into groups with the challenge of extending Rousseau's (1762/1979) model of ideal education in *Emile* (the week's reading) to three specified modern settings: to early twentieth-century public schools with large classes and immigrant populations; to today's multicultural classes, including ready Internet access; and to a twenty-second-century class setting whose conditions that group could specify (they ended up on Mars, with "Emillennia's" tutor being an artificial intelligence). As the groups readied their answers to present to each other, I exited the room (no one noticed), returning in character 10 minutes or so later—as usual, with no warning and no explanation—for the event.

"Rousseau" made himself in effect the moderator and questioner of the student panels' presentations. His sometimes exaggerated reactions and bad French accent (I practice accents—not well but enough) were entertaining, but the laughter eased the way for serious and probing exchanges about his philosophy of education in modern practice. His reactions of both horror and intrigue at the modern or future worlds the student panels presented both personified Rousseau's philosophy of education concretely but also symbolized for students—and in the end for me, too—how much a radically changed world asks of any such historical philosophy of education in modern application. Plus, we all had a blast. Why not?

Behind the Mask

From the teacher's side, the experience can be powerful as well, for different reasons. Typically, I find myself becoming more insistent, less professorial even than usual, and somewhat carried away, as I imagine real actors must feel (Wyman, 2008). It takes emotional and intellectual preparation. I have to close the door of my office or find some private space and consciously shift identities, talk to myself in the new voice, close my eyes and picture the world, physical as well as intellectual, from which I am coming. Ishmael, not surprisingly, is the most challenging to take on (you do not want to hear me talking or growling to myself as I get ready, but I find it immensely helpful to do so), but I try to give the same investment to whatever the role may be.

Of course it also takes serious, down-to-earth, academic preparation, too, like a thematic outline to hold in your head and even, for me at least, some in-character jokes. Every time, I reread the texts in question and try to hear the person behind it, even read some of it out loud so I feel the writer's distinctive cadences in my own voice. I want to act and respond as the visitors would, marshal reasons as they would, but also *feel* what they would feel. Behind the mask, wearing the hat, manifestly play-acting someone else not the teacher, I am freer to be that person, to provoke or even insult, within limits of course. The students, meanwhile, know I am playing a role—that they are safe even so. As long as they know they can trust me in my regular appearance, they know they can trust me even when I am being outrageous in costume. But at the same time, I can use the outrageousness to engage and provoke in ways I normally could not.

Finally, one note about endings. Given what I have said, it will not surprise you that my practice is to stay completely in character. In fact, this is something of an emotional necessity for me. At the end of such a class I am simply incapable of turning right back into my usual self. My head is still in the Forum in Athens, Ishmael's cage, or some generation starship. I don't even try to take off the costume and resume my usual role. I leave in character, and that is it for the day. Students can visit my office a bit later if they need to see me. I am always apologetic for missing class: "What happened? *Really?* How come I always seem to miss these visitors?"

Showdowns: Or, My Willing Colleagues

There is a further step that I have sometimes been able to take with impersonation scenarios: events with more than one impersonator in the scene,
interacting with each other as well as students. Naturally, these call on my
colleagues, who I would like to credit with creditable and generous respon-
siveness. Here are two vignettes by way of illustration.

Epistemological Survivor

Students in my What Can We Know? class debate Descartes's and Plato's
epistemologies. They defend Cartesian or Platonic views and critique the
other in panels. They have a few days to prepare for this. The format is a formal debate style embedded within a "show," sometimes with a student emcee
or myself as emcee with an invited (in advance) student sidekick.

The ultimate panel comes at the end. After several of these debate panel
days, the course ends with a visit by a panel of all of the course's key figures. Descartes shows up, as well as Socrates, Hume, and the Radical Skeptic
as represented by Descartes' "Evil Demon" (I call him the "Omnipotent
Trickster"). Who are these eminences under the assumed identifies and costumes? My philosopher colleagues!

The event runs like TV's survivor-type shows. Student panels, again with
preparation and coordination, are responsible for each stage of the questioning, after which the rest of the class votes the contestants one by one off the
epistemological island, so to speak. The drama heightens down to a final
showdown between the last two left standing. (One time Descartes and
Hume actually tied—the perfect ending.) My colleagues deftly role-play the
contestants; student panels even more deftly rise to their challenge. I produce
the show with show-style lighting, studio-style seating, and prizes (chocolate
bars! Philosophical glory!). It's provocative, dynamic, memorable, informa-
tive, and thoroughly fun. Students bring their friends, and sometimes other
faculty members come too. It is an *event*, a memorable ending, but also and
crucially a sharp and sustained philosophical interchange taken on and run
by the students, for which the whole class has urgently prepared.

When Marx Met Darwin Met Freud

For the final regular meeting of my last Marx/Darwin/Freud class, I set up a
poster session for the students to present their final projects, a paper building
on their and some classmates' research briefs, as described previously, integrating the thought of all three figures around some issue of interest to them. This
work was underway as we met for the last regular session. They needed feedback, among other things, and I also wanted the whole class to see just how

wide a range of topics and approaches was being considered. As usual, I mean this literally: I want them to *see* it, visually, in front of them.

So they made posters, and a third or so of the class at a time put up their projects, on the wall or on easels, and the rest of us circulated to view and discuss them. It was an energetic scenario, basically a poster session. Some of my departmental colleagues came and even some other students passing by joined us to look at posters as well.

This was all that anyone expected. It was certainly a good way to see everyone's work in progress, on the walls. I helped with the setup and briefly launched the scene. It hardly needed more, since most students were already familiar with poster sessions. They launched right in. Unnoticed then, I slipped out after 10 minutes.

A bit later, all of a sudden, in barged Marx himself. Loud, intrusive, dogmatic, outrageous. He cast his eyes over student posters, sometimes reading them out loud, often outraged or outrageous, lauding but also challenging the authors, with knots of students gathered around. More of a costume than usual—the iconic beard, for example—my last shot at dressing up for them.

This much perhaps still did not surprise students. By then they expected such things of me. Still, challenging. He gave no quarter. But then, suddenly, what? Someone else appears, too. Apparently a determined naturalist decorated with flowers, a stuffed bird or two, and a taxonomy book. Darwin?! But ah, he says, what have we here? A poster, with a student author next to it and dealing with Darwinism's application to modern education? Or some modern form of creationism. And soon another knot of students is joining another critical discussion about another topic.

Presently, Marx, upstaged and annoyed, stomps over, and he and Darwin go at it, again with the student's theme and project visibly front and center. But then again, on the edge of *this* crowd, students gradually become aware of yet another stranger, this one a more unobtrusive observer, looking a bit . . . Viennese? Freud??!

Yes, now the whole complement is here. Darwin is insistent, firm, and acerbic. Freud tries to get inside everyone's head, makes various insinuations. Marx and Darwin both had major issues with their fathers, didn't they? Perhaps their iconoclasm has some roots in their childhood? And do they in turn take kindly to being pop-psychoanalyzed?

The cast of this little encounter/drama, along with me, is two of my colleagues. Some of the students know them, but most of the students don't. For all they know, they almost *could* be Darwin or Freud. Picture being a student, then, with a poster on professional sports, contemporary politics, or the healthcare debate, trying out Marxist, evolutionary and psychoanalytical views on your topic, and now right in front of your innocent academic venture, and in sight of half the class, Marx is berating Darwin for his views on your topic while both are being psychoanalyzed by Freud. The students, willy-nilly, are once again right in the middle of it.

Then after a final explosive three-way encounter, we all stomp out. As usual, I don't come back. And that is the end of the course as well as the day. How else would Marx/Darwin/Freud have it?

CODA
Own the High Wire

Chapter 4 points out that one task of the impresario–professor is to set the pace. You'll have noticed, I am sure, that many of my scenarios tend to be *fast*. Typically I want the work to be and feel urgent, even if there is not quite enough time. There is certainly no time for distraction or off-task discussion or indirection. Thus full attention can be structured in. Presupposed is a certain level of urgency and risk to which I now want to briefly speak.

The Uses of Urgency

Urgency tends to arrive, as I have tried to illustrate, with the first minutes of the first day of my classes. In this I am deliberately confounding student expectations of the first day. Usually they expect just to be given a syllabus and maybe a brief course description or an introductory lecture. In my classes, they already are likely to have had a reading assignment, nowadays easily sent out in advance via e-mail and the class Moodle page. The syllabus will also be online weeks before the term starts, and they are expected to have read it, too. Then, the very moment they walk into the room, there is work to do, and challenging collaborative work with definite answers to boot.

By design, in short, from our first moments together, we are together in a *live* space in which things are happening. Fellow students are active, the teacher is fully present and already engaged with them, often some interesting or energizing music is playing, and there is some project to sit down and undertake.

Traditional schooling may literally teach slowness and inattention. Students get used to a certain ponderousness and habitually come to fill the extra time with texting, daydreaming, or off-topic talk. At first they bring the same habits to my classes. Soon, though, they will be caught short when they are suddenly expected to be finished with a project that they have barely gotten around to starting. Next time, they jump on it. There's excitement in this, as well as a new kind of self-respect (Sasley, 2010). This is serious work, and here they are in it already.

I would rather have a Task Group not fully finish a deliberation than have them finish before the allotted time and peter out into off-task talk or checking their cellphones waiting for a plenary session. My Step-Right-Ins and Task Groups are generally specific and demanding and probably focused by a worksheet or a target object, with a filled-out worksheet expected both as a reference for on-the-spot reporting out to the class, if requested, and to be handed in for attendance and check-in credit at the end. Students also quickly learn that I am looking more for process than product—the worksheets are a way for them to record both. All of this, under time pressure, keeps them resolutely on task. Again, I am much more interested in their experience of working flat-out on a task than on their actually completing it.

Two other features intensify the urgency. First, the challenges are *real*. They visibly and energetically engage the world, typically beyond but including the classroom, and consequently also have real criteria for success or failure, such as sleuthing a website or working out a developmental hypothesis with a dozen other students on the classroom wall. Second, the challenge may be *extreme*. Quite likely it is at least unfamiliar, and it may be beyond what students ever expect to be asked to do in classrooms or school. Find space aliens? Try to answer an armed Descartes who is skewering arguments right and left? *What!?*

I do plan occasional slower days in my classes—for discussion, maybe, "like a normal class" (as my students often put it). Just by virtue of contrast to our class's norm, however, such days can also call forth a high level of engagement. I also teach one *extremely* slow course: a January-term course in Zen Philosophy and Practice, co-led with a Zen master and friend. Even here, however, tempo is still key—indeed, it is featured and accentuated. We ritualize a slow tempo, in fact, always beginning and ending with half an hour of meditation, timed by a student leader with bells and clappers, who simply starts with the bell at the appointed time, nothing necessarily spoken at all, so that no one else has to think about time—or words—at all. Then, about mid-month, the class goes on a four-day silent retreat, which is the same pattern writ large: up at 5:30 in the morning for long bouts of meditation throughout the day.

Co-Opting the Multitaskers

The bane of the modern professor is supposed to be student multitasking: taking notes in a lecture or even half-participating in discussion while texting with friends or surfing the web for news or shopping. Researchers debate whether multitasking is now developmentally wired into young people's brains. Regardless, I don't propose to fight it. I propose instead to *co-opt* it—in fact, to turn it from a problem to (yes) a resource.

My classes are themselves often exercises in multitasking. Regularly two or three things may be happening in the room at the same time. Debriefing a scenario in my Philosophy of Education class, for example, we might have a discussion going on in class at the same time that two or three other intersecting exchanges are unfolding in the day's Google Doc for analysis, which is projected in real time onto a screen at the front of the room as well as on individual students' laptops. It can be almost too much for any of us, but the sheer amount of processing that is enabled in a short time can be prodigious—and it can be revisited later at a slower pace as needed. I usually assign a student or two to organize and tighten up each day's Google Doc, after which the collected Google Docs become a class resource, visited by all of us repeatedly over the term. Still, the unparalleled generativity comes from the urgency and focus of the class right in the day's classroom. This is the key: *by design, everyone has to multitask just to keep up.*

Also, sometimes the use of such technologies can become an issue within a simulation. DiCicco (2014), for example, offers an illuminating and sometimes amusing discussion of the use of technology, from PowerPoints to cellphones to up-to-the-minute news reports, in National Security Council simulations. Real councilmembers might multitask just as our students do, and for the same mix of good and not-so-good reasons. So how would the real National Security Council deal with it?

The Uses of Risk

Of course staging scenarios can be risky. A scenario may simply fail, it may unfold unhappily or half-heartedly, or students may prove unable to take up the roles it offers them, if not prepared, for whatever reason, with enough information or conceptual basics. The action can slow, stop, or go wildly off track. Maybe the teacher has misjudged the tempo or students' level of engagement. And some days a group may just be "off" for any number of other reasons.

The trade-off is that risk creates a high-wire effect that gives everything an edge. Indeed, it can give a whole course a constant edge, even when we are doing more "normal" things, because students never quite know when the high wire will reappear. In short, I argue, the potential of failure also can energize. Risk is actually part of my method.

I have never walked an actual high wire at any serious height above the ground. But I—and I am sure you, too—have certainly been in enough risky physical situations to know that they call forth complete presence to the task and utter alertness in the moment. No one goes through such an event list-lessly or half-heartedly. No one even *watches* listlessly or half-heartedly. Every witness as well as every participant is pulled into the heart-stopping intensity. Just watching a wire walker, you find your own body involuntarily moving back and forth to correct and keep balance. At the level of instinctual engage-ment, you're up there too.

I have spoken of Improv comedy as a theatrical analogue. Improv actors operate without script or preplanning, essentially making up the show as they go along, in full view of everyone, often in response to completely ran-dom audience suggestions. Every moment of every sketch is essentially hang-ing over the abyss. But the result once again is that everyone is pulled into the intensity and improvisation. Again, it is worth considering that Improv largely attracts the same demographic as our students: 20-somethings look-ing for something live and edgy. So let's give it to them, I say—or rather, let's invite them to co-create it with us.

It does take adjustment. Students are not used to being responsible in this way, and at first they may not recognize what my colleague John Sullivan used to call their response-*ability*. School tends to inculcate passivity and caution. Still, our students remain spirited beings. (So do we, right?) Give them half a chance, and more than enough of them will step up that most scenarios will fly.

Leading With Risk

In speaking of this issue in Chapter 1, I have already mentioned colleagues who lament students' self-protectiveness and unwillingness to take risks. Why don't they step out more creatively, we wonder? Why aren't they more ven-turesome? Many answers have to do with students' individual background and situations, and to these of course we need to be sensitive. However, from the present point of view, there is another general and obvious, if disconcert-ing, answer. To put it baldly, it is that we rarely take such risks ourselves. Students' apparent risk aversion reflects our own. We do not offer good mod-els, and consequently safe spaces, for serious intellectual risk taking.

Of course, again, the impresario–teacher designs the work, scene, and tempo of the class so that the sought-after intellectual stakes and complexi-ties emerge out of the student work that ensues. This is the prime work, and for many teachers, it may be the only work. But we ourselves can also model the kind of playfulness and edginess that most fully energize many scenarios. When we put on a costume or wig, or role-play a new persona deliberately and theatrically, we create an alternative space for interaction. Even the rela-tively sober Chapter 4 of this book still pictures impresario–teachers walking right into new scenarios without looking back, expecting students to follow. Such a teacher is already "all in," having manifestly set in motion a situation that she cannot resolve alone. The upshot is that, unexpectedly and inescapably, students are invited to go all in, too.

I argue that it is only when we professors ourselves manifestly cast ourselves into this kind of uncertainty and exposure, as an act of trust and a visible condition of greater mastery, that we can justly ask students to do the same: to step out of their studied unobtrusiveness or the air of self-possession that the typical passivity protects, and put themselves whole-heartedly and unreservedly at the same adventurous edge. We know that teachers' attitudes are a central part of the *hidden curriculum* (Barbour & Barbour, 1997)—or as Sandy (1998) defines it, "the unconscious and unintentional aspect of the classroom whereby what we do comes through much louder than what we say" (p. 49). Thus, I argue, not just the first but also the most visible and venturesome high-wire walkers in our classrooms need to be *us*.

And for our own sakes as well. Writing of a nursing professor who systematically adopted acting games in her "Nursing and Management" courses, for example, Diamond and Christensen (2005) tell us:

> Using this technique affected the faculty member teaching the course as well. She found herself considering a broader range of perspectives when looking at the material in preparation for class. She took more risks and relinquished some control of the session in exchange for becoming more open to spontaneous student contributions. Overall, the process rejuvenated her view of and approach to the curriculum. The payoff was a higher energy level and a greater level of insight on the part of everyone involved. (p. 63)

I would only add that the risks that we teachers take sometimes need to be less intellectual and literally more theatrical. This is because our students are not generally in a position to appreciate intellectual risks in the way that our professional colleagues can. Our own risk-taking, by means of leading the way, needs a more visible modality: that is, as I have been urging, dramatic ventures or challenges. We already relinquish our aura of authority and control by launching into a role-play or simulation while manifestly not knowing what is going to happen or posing creative-thinking challenges to which we clearly do not know the best or all the answers. Top it off with a costume and a bad accent—at least that is one way—and, I have found, most students have all the invitation they need to join in the same spirit.

7

ADVENTURES IN
ROLE-PLAYING

I n Role-Plays, students inhabit and enact specific roles in interaction, normally with preparation and therefore some depth, with the interaction
progressively unfolding in a number of steps and stages. Chapter 5 lays
out a general framework for Role-Plays and briefly explores some existing
paradigms. This chapter offers detailed accounts of some of my own more
adventurous designs.

These can make for long stories. Role-Plays' designs and enactments can
be complex and dynamic, and like any good drama need some care in the
retelling. Their pedagogical effectiveness is also clearest when illustrated in
detail. It is one thing to simply report that a class negotiated some international crisis at the UN or simulated alien contact. It is another thing to
describe how it actually unfolded, blow by blow, with some of the backstory
too. The electric moment in Carnes's first Reacting to the Past game when
the Confucian chief minister threatened to behead (throw out of the game)
anyone who disrespected the emperor, and even the opposing faction grudgingly complied; or alien-contact teams racing across campus to mysterious
landing sites, missing hidden warnings inside messages that appear to beckon
them, not knowing what awaits them—moments like these of "heart pound-
ing intensity" (Carnes, 2014, p. 5) only appear in the finer-grained stories.

Some such stories are also necessary to demonstrate the depth and
creativity of student engagement and uptake. These scenarios enable
moments when "everything comes together" in sudden and "all-consuming"
moments of "insight and magic," in Heiland's words (2011, pp. 122, 125).
In this spirit, I offer the detailed narratives, especially of the more adventurous methods, as a kind of proof of concept, if you like, for certain especially
edgy methods where the pedagogical research cannot go, or has not gone.
Narrative is sometimes the only way (Eagen, 2002; Whitehead, 1967).

A Congressional Hearing

We have considered the court case or formal hearing as a prime example of a ready-made setting for Role-Plays. The format already exists in a well-developed form, and students are usually familiar with it or at least its general feel. Add a few specifications, and you can be off and running.

For contentious issues that have public or potentially legislative dimensions, even if not a criminal or civil suit, the format of a congressional hearing is likewise quite suitable. The following is an extended example from my Environmental Ethics class.

The Question

My Environmental Ethics classes do not debate oil pipelines or factory farming—those debates too readily become familiar set-pieces. Instead, we debate questions that call on the themes of the class in what I intend to be freshly revealing and provocative ways, and ones that cast the values at stake into an especially revealing silhouette. In my last class, it was test-tube or in vitro meat (IVM): animal flesh produced without actual animals.

IVM can be produced by stimulating the right kinds of cells in nutrient solution in laboratories and thus, potentially, on an industrial scale. Although much remains uncertain, it seems at least possible that we could entirely end the monumental animal suffering presupposed as a matter of course by the production of meat today. Not by everyone becoming vegetarian, though, but by producing animal flesh in a radically different way that causes no pain or other harm to actual animals. Still, although one of the chief objections to eating meat would thereby be removed, eating IVM would remain the consumption of animal flesh—a form of barbarism, or so it still seems to some—and new reservations arise, such as the questionable morality of "playing God" by massively rearranging the reproduction of animal cells. The effects of industrializing such an entirely new food-production process are also wildly uncertain.

In short, the issue is genuinely unclear. Card-carrying environmentalists can differ about it quite dramatically. Much depends on exactly what kind of environmentalism one embraces and for what reasons—which is why the whole question is so useful for a course like mine, for the fundamental aim is precisely to bring out underlying value frameworks and bring them into contact and dialogue.

Preparation

The course design took us through a variety of frameworks for environmental ethics, each with a range of practical questions, IVM among them, as constant touchstones. But a certain pressure was also on. Students knew from the outset that the course would end with a mock congressional hearing on a bill to ban IVM. Eventually they would have to take—at least try on—a position using course resources.

Through discussions and exercises periodically in the first half of the semester, the students gradually sorted themselves into advocacy groups. Some chose mainline environmentalism, which tends to enthusiastically favor IVM because it is predicted to be vastly more efficient than meat production. Animal rights groups favor it, obviously, because it could vastly reduce animal suffering. Other interest groups formed, such as cattle growers (against IVM, in unexpected alliance with a nascent Native People's caucus), the World Council of Churches (ecotheologians and others concerned for the integrity of the natural world in its own right), and various other groups organized by enterprising groups of students, such as Citizens Against Test-Tube Meat, a front group for ranchers and chicken-growers.

Not knowing the other sides' arguments, teams prepared for every eventuality, anticipating a wide variety of possibilities and developing their responses accordingly. With me and each other, they explored implications of our environmental–ethical frameworks with detail, persistence, and inventiveness. They brought in outside research, sometimes even outside experts. Some switched positions (I finally set a deadline after which they had to stay with their current stances for purposes of the hearing), and all refined them. Anti-IVM groups prepared a draft bill to ban IVM to use as the basis for discussion and negotiated with each other to refine and complete it.

Hearing Days

Hearing days finally arrived. We remade the classroom into a genuine hearing room, with table mics (as props), lights, a raised dais, published speaker lists, and proceedings. Having caught wind of it all, a university reporter arrived to take pictures for university publicity, but the students just saw an energetic photographer and took him to be another of my stage props—I didn't correct that impression until later. One of the pro-IVM groups set up a table in the hallway outside the classroom, unannounced, and cooked up tantalizing samples of what they said was IVM—actually soy gluten chicken substitute. Confronted with the thing itself, who would eat it? Most everyone, it turned out. What did this presage?

For senators, I recruited other environmental studies faculty members and student veterans of my previous courses. Dressed the part, they mounted their dais, sat down, and began to call testimony and cross-examine the witnesses. I served as committee counsel. The witnesses sat and sweated under the lights. Individual senators had their own agendas (I encouraged this for realism and unpredictability), not necessarily sympathetic to the witnesses or even giving them the time of day or conversely hyping them all out of proportion. Hidden agendas and weaknesses in arguments were ruthlessly exposed.

After the first session, everyone scrambled to reconfigure and prepare for the second session two days later. The scenario allowed for any interest group to be recalled for more questioning, especially on the basis of subsequent testimony, after the prescheduled testimony was completed—and some were—so everyone had to listen to everything intently. Questioning could be intense. Front groups were openly accused of being just that. Factual allegations were systematically challenged and backed up or fell away.

Eventually, like a real congressional committee, the senators took their own stands and argued among themselves, in public; the rest of the group listened and sometimes needed to be gaveled into order. Then they voted. The draft bill badly failed in this instance: It was not that senators had no reservations about IVM, but the general view was that a ban at this early stage was an overreaction. (In my latest iteration of this scenario, though, the ban passed.)

After the vote, "reporters" asked for statements and reactions from the interest groups—their last act in character. A small group of communications majors wrote a draft news report on the proceedings and outcome. Then we broke and debriefed the event in our own persons. This took another class session, followed by a reflection paper on the process and also the issue itself (Auman, 2011). Students had been thoroughly inside their positions and therefore taking a more partial view of the issue as a whole. This was their chance to step back out of those roles and discuss and even debate the issue one last time—but now from a far more informed and engaged place.

Expanding the Circle

Some single-session events in my Ethics and Environmental Ethics classes illustrate other kinds of role-play as well as various sorts of structural analogues.

Tables Turned

My Ethics classes stage debates about the human use of other animals for food, product testing, and the like. However, as by now you'd expect, I do not stage simple yes-or-no debates among students in their everyday selves. The scenarios within which we find ourselves are just a little different.

I ask students to start with a thought experiment—an imaginative leap. Let's suppose that aliens have taken over the Earth. Their power compares to ours in about the same way that ours compares to the other animals'. Alas, the aliens are quite like us in another way, too: They see "lower beings" mainly as resources for their food (Foer, 2010; McGinn, 1993). Their attitude toward humans mirrors the attitude you sometimes see on bumper stickers today: "I love animals—they taste good." Sure, a few of them are sentimentally attached to us and refuse to eat human flesh or use human-tested products, but the majority are dismissive and treasure the familiar and long-taken-for-granted pleasures of their palate—genuine pleasures, to be sure—too much to look closely or care about what happens to us as the darker side of their culinary preferences.

Nonetheless, for whatever reason, the aliens have agreed to set up a tribunal to hear one last plea from humans against their proposed exploitation of us. Our job is to prepare for that hearing. The alien team is always the most popular. Just dressing up and acting the part can be delightful, but it is also a chance for vegetarians to be heard for once, and many of the other students can already begin to glimpse what is coming. Still, the bulk of the class ends up in the role of humans. Three or four teams start to prepare. What will their case be?

Preparation time is typically short—maybe just a day. Normally I design this exercise to open and frame a deeper discussion, rather than develop it fully—that's what later sessions are for. But here too there is a twist. Anticipated by the others or not (I have done it both ways), another party will also show up for the actual hearings: other animals. Yes: The humans end up trying to make the case against the aliens eating us in the presence of other animals that we eat. The animals have a voice and representation too, or they simply disrupt the proceedings until they are heard.

Both aliens and animals have a field day accusing humans of hypocrisy. The animals don't hold their fire. The aliens are bemused by humans' discomfiture. Meanwhile, of course, the stakes are enormous, and personal for anyone who understands the underlying logic—modeled, as is my method, by the structure of the scenario and gradually sinking in for all. Again, it is not necessarily that humans cannot make a sustainable argument in this setting, but it is difficult, and again the caught-in-the-middle position of the humans, literally before us here in the very stage-setting, itself builds in most of the necessary feedback. Especially, it exemplifies one essential feature of moral arguments: they must not be self-serving or depend on special pleading for oneself (or one's species). The same rule for one applies to all. Under that simple and basic constraint, made visible right in front of us, what can humans say? If it's wrong to eat sentient "lower" creatures, surely it's, well, wrong to eat sentient "lower" creatures, isn't it?

This scenario can be staged with various degrees of structure, levels of risk, and tempos. I have done it with almost no warning at all, early on in a class, sometimes even on the very first day. I bring a few animal masks, some alien-looking bric-a-brac, a gavel for the moderator (sometimes me, sometimes a student or colleague), and off we go. Other times, students have a few days of warning, which roots the problem deeper in their thinking. They scour the vast literature for the best arguments they can find, agonizing and puzzling their ways through it. Sometimes they invite friends and roommates to come and watch the proceedings. It naturally becomes a touchstone for the rest of the course.

Expanding the Circle in Plain View

One can think of the history of ethics in general as a dialectical expansion of who counts, or what the ethicist Peter Singer (2011) calls *the expanding circle*. At a certain point in the moral evolution of the West, moral consideration was only applied to the free citizens of one's city-state: at the iconic moment in Athens, for example, only to adult land-owning male citizens. Slavery was widespread in the ancient world, as well as reaching into near-modern times, and slaves were usually considered mere property, to be disposed of as owners saw fit. The European conquerors of the Americas saw the native people as animals, sexual objects, circus attractions, slaves, and finally just impediments—certainly not as fellow human beings.

Under relentless moral criticism, though, the small and self-congratulatory moral circles presupposed by all of this eventually came to seem utterly and indefensibly circumscribed. Slaves, non-Greeks, and Native Americans have the same self-awareness, rationality, vulnerability, and so on that were the reason that the in-group supposed itself to have moral standing in the first place. Logically, they could not be excluded from morality. The "in" circle had to expand—radically, in fact, and even unimaginably to some in the previously privileged group. Egalitarian ethical recognition eventually—although in some cases only after a very long time—followed suit.

We may hope that we have reached a point at which all human beings, whatever age, gender, and state of ability or disability, have moral standing. In principle, at least, we know that we all count, though on the practical side, don't we know, there is work yet to be done. Yet conceptually and morally too it turns out that the struggle is far from over. The exclusion of the rest of the world beyond the species boundary is now coming into question. Might that exclusion be arbitrary in much the same way? Certain other animals, at least, arguably have the same type (not necessarily degree) of self-awareness, rationality, vulnerability, and so on that are supposed to ground the current human in-group's moral standing. Maybe such nonhumans must therefore be included in excluded in morality too. Why should moral standing stop at species boundaries any more than stopping at one gender, race, or city-state?

This kind of expanding circle is a thoroughly enjoyable topic for a lecture in ethics classes. A Sage can lay out the progressive expansion step-by-step, attending to the driving force of the argument's logic each time. Because students are typically provoked by the arguments, but in different directions, traditional engaged teaching methods are also readily invited. On this topic I acted the Guide myself for years. Students would present the ideas rather than me, or we staged a simple class debate between different points of view.

Impresario–professors, though, will notice right away that the expanding circle is close to a visualizable scene. It's a visual metaphor already. Thus the possibility of a much more dramatic pedagogy emerges. A circle that expands—why not literally stage it? As usual, the aim would be to design a scenario so that students are led by the set-up itself to work out and apply the argument's key ideas or movements. The dynamic of the scenario should propel students into the key recognitions and expansive steps, with minimal nudging if necessary, so that they essentially reinvent the moves of the expanding-circle argument. Concretely, then, in the classroom, why not represent this by an *actual* expanding circle?

The Line

Here is how it works in my current design. On the appointed day, students walk into our room to see a line taped straight down the middle. All the chairs are crowded onto one side, and nowhere near enough for all the students either, so that late-comers end up sitting uncomfortably on the floor. On the other side of the room, spacious and lovely, there are some comfortable armchairs, a potted plant or two, along with a table already set with festive drinks. Three students, one male and two females (handpicked in advance by me, but they don't know this), get to sit on the far side. Everyone else, crammed into the other side, gets a three-inch-by-five-inch card when they come in, assigning them some other-than-human identity, ranging from chickens and cows to apes and whales, redwoods, rivers, mountains, and the Earth itself. They also get a handout listing all the species and Earth beings present in the room.

Everyone is curious about what is happening. A few have already gotten it. I ask them to explain. They say: It looks as if we are, right now, physically enacting the usual humans-only ethical situation. Indeed, I say. Look around. Humans stand on one side of a supposed a hard-and-fast ethical line between them and the rest of the natural world. And the stakes are huge. In our model, the out-group merely mostly sits on the floor, and the humans just have nicer seating and some drinks. In the real world, the humans would be eating you, shooting you to mount on the wall, poisoning you to be less "bugged," destroying your habitat to build more suburban swimming pools, skinning your offspring for shoes, or digging you up to burn to run air conditioners and accelerate global climate change. And why not? *You don't count.*

So there is the line—currently between humans and everyone else. Our room is divided in half by the tape. The question is: Can anyone else argue themselves across it? The rules are: Everyone in the in-group, at any stage, gets a vote, whereas any out-group that wants to try gets a chance, collectively, to make their case. The "outs" have to figure out how to do so, in what order and groupings, and what to say.

Once again, they'll note that their readings can help. Singer (2011) and others map expanding-circle arguments in a general philosophical way. Now the students, transformed into other-than-humans of all sorts, actually have to use such arguments to get themselves over the line—arguing to the in-group, whomever it happens to be at the time.

Planning first. I send the humans out for a walk—they don't get to overhear the strategizing. The rest of the natural world starts planning, hurried but excited. Often some argue for an all-or-nothing strategy: Everyone tries to get over the line at once. But this tactic is usually rejected—most vociferously by the otherwise top-of-the-queue candidates—as too risky. We can't risk trying to bring all you riff-raff over with us all at once. Already re-enacting Singer's approach, the cannier participants usually win out with a sequential strategy, beginning with the other-than-humans most similar to humans and gradually expanding the in-group before the farther-out beings come up for a vote.

The humans return, and we are ready to begin. But wait! Just as the formal arguments are about to start, I feign instructions from above and throw the two women out of the in-group. Mirroring the earlier evolution of ethics, it turns out that they, too, have to justify their ethical standing. One single male is left alone on the in-group side of the line, then, occupying the well-appointed half of the room in splendid . . . isolation. Oh, and what does this allegorize, exactly?

In the meantime, I appoint or introduce an Ethical Argument Referee, usually a colleague, sometimes a student veteran of the course or an outside philosophy major who is good at arguments. The referee sits right on the line, like a soccer or tennis line judge, ready to blow the whistle—he or she literally does have a whistle—if anyone makes an illegitimate argument. In particular, no one is allowed to argue on the basis of their *usefulness* to the in-group. They have to give *ethical* and not merely instrumental grounds.

Another key distinction they need to mind, again structured into the situation—in this case personified.

The Action

Now the arguments begin in earnest. The women try to get (back) in first, and everyone else queues up depending on their affinities to the most recently admitted in-group. Overall, the argument works by a series of small and individually compelling expansions of ethical consideration, based in each case on specific morally relevant similarities between the in-group beings at that stage and the next larger set or circle of beings trying to get in. Students now see this clearly: It is their necessary argument strategy. Usually they all get in in the end—this is environmental ethics, after all—but they need to come up with decent arguments, mandated by the scenario setup: again, morally relevant similarities with the current ingroup. Apes and whales argue that they are virtually the same as humans on the basis of similar mental capacities. Cows, bears, and other animals argue on the basis of shared sentience (Regan, 1983). Meanwhile, even plants have goods of their own, which they strive to achieve, and arguably having that much in common even with an enlarged all-animal in-group might entitle (certain) plants to moral consideration—of course in their own ways. It would not mean having human rights but such moral respect as befits plants. The circle could expand very broadly in the end (Rolston, 1999).

The referee also has a lot of work, despite the seeming obviousness of the distinction between ethical and instrumental reasons. There is nothing like being whistled out of order a few times to drive student groups (now, certain animals, forests and trees, etc.) to heed the distinction.

All sorts of intriguing things happen along the way. Whenever a new group gets in, many joyfully cross the line to the in-group side. Others stay back, wishing to remain in solidarity with their erstwhile excluded companions until they too can move. Some reject the whole set-up. Last time, Moon and Asteroids (I expanded the other-than-human roster beyond Earth) refused to even play the game. We don't want your consideration, they said. Pig and Mountain, alarmed, warned them that this is a real question. Already there are serious proposals underway for asteroid capture and moon mining. But we are not like you, they said. You need to learn to value what is *different* from you as much as you value your selves. Octopus and Sycamore are nodding too. Thank you, Moon!

By the end, then, the class has enacted the essential logic of the extensionist argument, as well as experienced its potential limits and defects. They've lived it—they've had to argue themselves across the line, at each step trying to widen the circle of moral consideration by expanding the criteria or commonalities appealed to. Each group is virtually forced by the structure of the situation to make arguments of commonality with the in-group, not resisting the idea of a moral line as such, but in fact embracing it—for the other side of insisting on commonality on the in-side is to insist on difference or distinction on the out-side. Pleas for generosity for ones' own group do not necessarily extend to the next in line.

Of course, the in-group *could* say no at any stage—and the votes are seldom unanimous—but the momentum is toward inclusiveness, and the key thing is that participants have to figure out the reasons. Once we are back together, out of role, though, we can stand back and look at the whole model and ask about it in turn. Is arguing on the basis of similarity to the in-group actually the best, wisest, and most necessary strategy? Some have questioned this, including me, in some writing that the class eventually considers (Weston, 2004). Other models of far wider moral consideration are possible, including starting the other way around, with an initial presumption in favor of the inclusion of everything (Birch, 1993). In short, then, students can also critique Singer's extensionist model, and again, they are in the best possible position to do once they have lived it themselves.

Cultures of the Imagination

The coda to Chapter 3 introduced the Life in the Universe course that Tony Crider and I co-teach as an honors class—an exploration of the search for life, especially intelligent life, beyond Earth, and its means, assumptions, and implications. Part of our class design involves an extended Role-Play modeled after an activity created by Professor Jim Funaro (1994) of Cabrillo College, called "Cultures of the Imagination" (COTI).

COTI is a multiday, nonstop workshop in which two teams independently construct whole civilizations, originally one alien civilization and one future human civilization, and then bring them together to role-play a first-contact situation.

> One team constructs a solar system, a world and its ecology, an alien life form and its culture, basing each step on the previous one and utilizing the principles of science as a guide to imagination. The other team designs a future human colony, planetary or spacefaring, "creating and evolving" its culture as an exercise in cultural structure, dynamics and adaptation. Through a structured system of progressive revelation, the teams then simulate—and experience—contact between the two cultures in real time, exploring the problems and possibilities involved in inter-cultural encounters. (Funaro, 1994)

The final stages of that "real-time contact" are staged as the closing plenary of a larger conference also called "Contact," a regular gathering of people interested in SETI, including NASA scientists, social scientists, philosophers, ethologists, and science fiction and science writers. I took part in the 2012 iteration—an utterly absorbing experience. Imagine a team of diverse but imaginative and high-octane professionals, from evolutionary biologists to cultural anthropologists to science fiction writers, together conceiving a whole alien civilization, rethinking evolution (as it happened in our case), conceptualizing an entirely different kind of life-form, its development and eventually form of shape-shifting star-sailing (Weston & Sibelman, 2012), and responding to a crescendo of contact events as the ultimate moment neared—first of all in the isolation of our little room (spaceship), then landed on an alien planet, in front of the whole conference.

Bringing COTI Home

Our classes' COTIs are built into the course over half of the term, at the same time as students are learning the basics of astrobiology and the epistemology and technology of SETI, as well as a range of related topics—a good bit of it driven by their COTI work itself.

Students begin by forming into the two teams. One year we worked up a Hogwart's-style sorting hat to assign them teams, massaging their entries behind the scenes; another time we staged a ceremony in which they were invited to align themselves. Enjoined then to keep the work secret from the other group (although members of the other group may be their close friends and even roommates), they jump into in- and out-of-class meetings to begin to envision, in detail, an alien or a future human civilization. Tony and I offer extensive guidance on a handout (Handout 7.1).

Our students have pulled off three spectacular—and spectacularly different—COTIs, on the edge all the way. The first group's eagerness for the scenario was immediate, and the effect only intensified for subsequent cohorts who heard the stories through Elon's fairly tight honors program. It helps that our honors sophomores mostly live together: Apparently the COTI work becomes one of the main topics of conversation almost immediately, from shared meals to late-night dorm rooms. It adds to the intrigue that they have to keep it secret from half their friends. It is all part of the game. Tony and I don't talk about it with each other either, but for weeks, we get late-night or weekend Skype calls, while some of our scientist colleagues are inundated by the *weirdest* needs to consult.

HANDOUT 7.1

Sample Instruction Sheet for "Cultures of the Imagination"

Our experiment begins with a great deal of brainstorming, inventing, and planning. Here are some parameters.

Earth-originating civilization:
- Start by projecting an Earth-originating civilization roughly 100 to 200 years in the future.
- Your civilization will launch a mission to the stars. Thus, you must be space-faring in some way, although it needn't be anything like the current way. This enables the contact part of the game.

Aliens:
Your civilization should include these elements:

- Some type of intelligent being or locus of intelligence—that's you!—plausibly grounded in an evolutionary backstory (biological and/or other)
- A highly developed mode of community or organization of these beings (coordinating and integrating the lives and actions of many such beings over space and time)
- Developed institutions and practices, such as arts and communicative methods and means, something like science, art, philosophy, and religion (or if you lack some of these things, you should have some plausible account of why and what you have instead)

Ground rules:
- *Secrecy!* Teams do not talk at all with each other about your team's work for this project! Don't give anything away! The intrigue of this experience lies partly in the encounter with another intelligence that is as unknown and unpredictable to you as possible when the contact begins. One professor will work with each group, and we do not talk to each other about this work either—an independent (and tight-lipped!) gamemaster will be our only means of coordination about this until the event itself.
- *Physical possibility.* Your civilization's mode of life, transport, and so on shouldn't violate known laws of nature. No traveling faster than light, no ESP, nothing that some kind of natural and cultural evolution couldn't somehow produce.
- *Thick backstory.* First, there must *be* a backstory. How did your civilization get here? Why is your being the way it is? Second: the backstory must, at the very least, *hang together.* Ideally its elements should virtually necessitate each other (e.g., if your planet first called forth intelligence in packs of omnivorous, roving, dexterous apes—just saying—then the eventual civilization's art and religion and even behavior in space should be ape-like too). But, of course, there are other possibilities.

We're looking for you to write up the backstory or in general some kind of detailed account of yourselves. It's ideal for some sort of wiki, for example, with an interlinked set of entries that team members can work on semi-independently. However, it might suit some civilizations better to write yourselves up with epic poetry or mythology. But a presentable and detailed model is essential. Among other reasons, it will be necessary once the contact experience begins. We can almost guarantee that contact will call on some quite unexpected aspects of your civilization, so you need to have thought about as many basic aspects as you can beforehand. In the event, you'll need your backstory as a ready-to-hand reference.

- *Push the boundaries.* Earthlings: 200 years is a very long time! Two hundred years back, remember, was 1816. Who could have even imagined the contemporary world then? Aliens: remember, in a galaxy with 40 billion or so potentially habitable planets, some of which have been so for maybe 10 billion years, just about anything physically possible is, well, possible. Think of your job as making one such story *plausible*.

Aliens: Here are two different kinds of methods you might use to evolve yourselves.

- *Natural evolution.* You might develop your civilization in the way it might unfold through evolutionary time. We will assign you a solar system with a variety of possible origin places (e.g., at least one planet in a habitable zone around the stars, along with potentially habitable moons of a massive planet, etc.). Then consider how life might begin in such a place and what kind of life it would be. What characteristic forms would it develop into? Then consider how some of these might become intelligent (while still, surely, reflecting their unique biology in their modes of intelligence). Then consider how this creature might develop culture and civilization (as previously defined).

  This should guarantee that you have a thick and connected backstory. At the same time, remember that evolution, both biological and social, is not unilinear. Just look at what evolved on Earth, in basically the same natural environment: everything from whales to mosquitoes to mushrooms to us. Accidents play a role, too. If a meteor impact hadn't wiped out the dinosaurs, mammals might never have taken over the world. The same goes for technological evolution. So your story does need to hang together, but it can still be a sort of random walk.

  Be careful here not to slide back into basically human types of biology and intelligence. You could do so, but even if you use Earth-based models, there are multitudes of other-than-human possibilities: forms of intelligence or proto-intelligence, such as bees and ants (hive minds), cetaceans who live in the deep and communicate by sound/music, and even (arguably) artificial intelligence.

- *Hyperextension/specialization.* This way, you develop your civilization by starting with certain key traits or features that you might imagine a being to exemplify or a civilization to embrace and even deliberately hyperdevelop over a long period of time (e.g., millions of years). This works best for civilizations well past the biological evolutionary stage, if that is your inclination. The natural evolution method has the great advantage of automatically generating a thick connected backstory, but the possible disadvantage that by focusing so much on the early stages (totally fascinating, for sure) it tends to stop a few stages beyond where we are—hungry new spacefarers—with little time left to go into later and (arguably) postevolutionary developments that might carry a civilization/being far beyond its biological roots. Already we can imagine this even for ourselves— and our species has barely popped into existence. What would a million-year-old civilization be like? You still probably will have some biology, or at least were created initially by some biological beings whose evolution needs to be part of your backstory, but by now can imagine that your beings have had the chance to thoroughly re-engineer themselves, maybe multiple times, or create new forms of intelligence and organization, which in time have taken over, generated new forms in turn, been subject to further accidents, and so on. Meanwhile, biology may go in all kinds of alternative directions, too.

If you take this approach, begin with some feature(s) or practice(s) that you want to imagine hyperdeveloping. This should be a quite specific idea (e.g., music, martial arts, symbiosis, cosmic healing, etc.). Then give yourself a few million years to play with, work through some stages without necessarily thinking you have to know where it is going to end up (it's evolution again, but now technological and cultural—enjoy this!), and see what might result in the end. Work out the end result in detail. Be creative about how it might be represented. (And consult your professor! We're going to be looking for coolness; careful development, in which your whole team collaborates extensively; and usability, in the sense that your model enables you to respond quickly to a range of possibly quite unexpected challenges and opportunities. You don't want to be making it up on the fly!)

COTI #1: *The Invasion of Aurora*

Our first COTI's alien group invented a form of intelligence synergized with the trees of their planet (Aurora), themselves highly interlinked through root and tendril networks, an adaptation to Aurora's weather extremes (high and volatile tides and storms due to gravitational swings from Aurora's double-sun system and multiple moons—the lifeforms need to respond). The Aurorans spent long meetings working out the species' biology (partly photosynthetic, so we learned all about carbon cycling, photoheterotrophs, and plain heterotrophs—a great way to learn basic biology for me, too), and in the end there were elaborate illustrations and models of cat-like, canopy-dwelling creatures. All the science as well as extensive mythology and culture went into our private wiki, Aurorapedia, which grew by leaps and bounds.

The human team, meanwhile—the KICK Astronauts as they immediately decided to call themselves—worked out in detail a vision of a plausible human future. Decidedly cockier, they devolved into a mission of scientists whose strings were pulled behind the scenes by billionaire philanthropists looking for resources and spectacular new museum specimens. They wrote elaborate scientific autobiographies, posting these proudly on a crew website likewise secret for the time being. They worked out protocols for evaluating candidate planets' physical and chemical properties—again thoroughly working from the scientific aspects of the course and well beyond—as well as search and contact strategies in the event that life and potential intelligence are discovered. All this was filtered through their adopted personae that they designed as (mostly) anthropocentric caricatures.

We allotted 2 class periods (100 minutes each) with an optional third for the contact experience proper. Almost all of the other work was outside of class, although we had occasional (separate) group meetings at the end of some class periods.

Day 1 was the approach. The KICK Astronauts attempted contact from a distance, but naturally they came up blank—the Aurorans had no radio. (This was done by our gamemaster, a role adapted from the Reacting to the Past design—in the event, a third colleague—running up and down stairs between the command area of the starship and the Auroran island, aka our classroom.) They also did a long-distance surface probe, coming up with just ocean and forest (in fact, Amazon rainforest as viewed through Google Earth).

Landings

On Day 2, there were a series of landings: that is, appearances in our classroom, which had been thoroughly transformed into a blazing hot, windy, vine-thick rainforest planet, projections on the walls and windows covered with yellow and red cellophane to simulate Aurora's two suns, Blaze and Bashful. The Aurorans' report described the first landing:

> [There is] a commotion on one of the adjacent islands. Fire, noise, movement. For us this creates mostly confusion. We've not had volcanoes in historical memory; fire is tightly controlled (and honored), and other land creatures are unknown on Aurora. . . . The result is twofold: to drive us to clump with each other . . . . and to entwine, as is our wont, with the fronds of the great trees in order to find out through the network of tree awareness what is happening on the next island. But Tree Mind gives no clear message

either, since whatever's happening is nothing that fits any known pattern for them either. So we remain in confusion at the point when totally unfamiliar beings suddenly appear near our circle.

To the human party, of course, all of this looked quite different. Their first landing party simply failed to discover intelligent life, as defined by their standards, of course. They had more or less operationally defined "intelligent" simply as "humanoid." A second group was therefore instructed to land on an adjacent island, with the rest of the KICK team observing the landing via a FaceTime video call from the command ship (downstairs seminar room):

> Shuttle Two has landed. They appear to be in a lush, green forest. The Commander describes the island as extremely windy and hot [*the Aurorans had turned the thermostat up to 95 and were running multiple big fans*]. After some observation, debate, and attempts at contact command determined that Shuttle Two has discovered what we would classify as "pets." They are the size of a cat with hard shells and many legs [*here they were looking at Auroran self-depictions posted on the walls*]. They are very loud creatures and seem to be whistling, making sounds that are musical in nature. [The KICK Foundation President] is satisfied with the discovery. . . . All [of] the [crew] members on [Aurora] are directed to capture a pet to bring to the ship for experiments.

The KICK team did indeed "capture a pet," and the Shuttle One crew brought this Auroran team member back to the command ship room for observation. Meanwhile, some of the human crew went rogue, trying to make contact with the Auroran "specimens" before they were frozen en route back to Earth, and murmuring mutiny before the return shuttle mission to the surface—although eventually, despite misgivings, they went along.

Meanwhile, the Aurorans were in confusion.

> We trade half-thoughts and fear through our panpipe-voices as well. The invaders observe for a short time and then begin vocalizing with each other. They don't have any coherent language that we can tell, and certainly nothing beautifully expressive like our voices. They are moving around, beginning to encircle us. They pay no attention to the trees, confirming their utter lack of intelligence. This continues for some time. Suddenly they grab several of us. This produces mostly confusion also. We don't have predators: nothing in our natural world comes along and grabs us.

In the melee that followed, one of the humans ended up getting swarmed by Aurorans, not necessarily with any hostile intent, but this resulted in her death (called by the gamemaster). This shook the humans—although it turned out they'd half expected the whole landing party to die—and led them to withdraw to their ship.

But not for long.

> Not long later there is commotion on the island on the other side of us, and invaders appear yet again. They are using panpipes again and a few of them seem to make a certain connection—it's still not possible to tell what they are saying, but it does resemble our voices somewhat . . . . They bring small fires as well. It appears that they are using all this to get us to follow the music or fires as a lure toward their metal containers—as if we hadn't see what happened when our former companion was carried off in one.
>
> In response they get only clumping, pan-piping, and a few mildly defensive displays from us. After a very short time, the invaders tire of this and become aggressive again, grabbing and hauling off two more of us. Others begin tearing down tree fronds, something inconceivable to us. We are piping and whistling furiously at them and moving around as fast as we can. The trees are waving. Soon they back away, take our companions, and leave.
>
> Shortly there is fire and a strange object moving into the sky—and then, somewhat later, a bright star is seen, slowly fading away. We are left to come to terms with our losses—three of our companions, one badly burned island, deep confusion over what happened and who the invaders were, and a nascent sense that the world and even our own potentialities are different than we ever imagined.

Aurora Was Shaken!

The KICK Astronauts left in elation. Only one crew member was lost, and a nice cargo of "pets" was collected for their sponsors. The Aurorans were devastated. Some Aurorans even refused to talk to their friends in the KICK group after the experience closed. The Auroran group met again, a long, hard meeting, and finally came to terms with what happened partly by rewriting Auroran mythology, essentially on the theme of "the gods must be angry." All of this then was worked out with many backs and forths on Aurorapedia. Aurora had become a real world in which they needed to make sense of what happened.

> Yet there is also an intuition that this time the invaders really are gone, and that Aurora will come to terms with these events its own way. We conclude, back in our diminished circle, sadly but determinedly, with our mantra: "On Blaze! On Bashful! On Aurorans all!"

At the same time, of course, we took up the whole experience in class, unveiling all the secrets at last, and tried to come to terms with what happened. In whole-group discussion, face to face with their colleagues back in their roles as fellow students and friends, it took long and impassioned discussion to understand the denouement together. The former KICK Astronauts, now abashed, ended by offering a formal apology and calling for a moment of mourning. What happened, we realized, was exactly the sort of miscommunication and unwitting disaster that the contact literature warns of. Tony and I wrote later:

> It is all very well to imagine that of course *we* would pick up on alien intelligence if there as any to be found, and that we would avoid, through sheer good will, the kinds of misadventures and cascading-to-lethal mis-understandings that so often emerged in previous human-to-human or human-to-other-than-human "contact" situations right here on Earth. In the event, however, this very class went quickly and enthusiastically down the very same road. (Crider & Weston, 2012)

That was the basis on which this class finally, slowly, reconciled them-selves to what happened: it is actually, alas, a very old story (see Box 7.1).

Box 7.1
Our Epic Finale

For this course, we construct what Tony Crider (2015) calls *epic finales* in place of the usual final exam. These are, as by now you'd only expect, more scenarios.

In this first iteration of the course, the finale was actually two sce-narios (Crider & Weston, 2012). The first part followed on our class dis-cussion, on the last day of regular class, of Kubrick's (1968) classic film, *2001: A Space Odyssey*. We'd emphasized the sheer alienness of the alien in the film, along with Kubrick's 1960s vision of alien contact and the film's suggestion that the development of human intelligence was sparked by alien intervention. Then, for the final, the students entered the classroom to find it completely empty except for an eight-foot black monolith akin to the one in the film. There was no warning and neither instructor any-where to be found. What were they going to do with that?

In the event, they did a variety of things, including attempting to decode a few other potential signals we might have left in the room, and eventually moving the 200-pound monolith down 2 flights of stairs to set it up in the sun, remembering that in the film the sun's rays triggered it to send a message. For them, what this ended up triggering was an intense discussion (we recorded everything: the room's cameras and mics were on) about how the class had changed them. One student summed it up beautifully:

> If we were to find aliens sometime in the future, that is the unknown. That's what this [exam] is for us. It is the unknown. We don't know how to respond. There's no rules. There's no correct way to handle this. If we go out there and find aliens, that is exactly what it is going to be. It is going to be, "What do we do now? What are they expecting of us?"

When we first heard this comment (on the tape), my reaction was, "That's an 'A' moment right there!" Because we (the instructors) are the *they* of the last question, we note, too, that the question essentially puts us into the problem—as the metaphorical aliens.

The second part of this finale spoke directly to the denouement of the first COTI, and I'll let Tony take the story from here.

> During our first COTI scenario, the KICK Astronauts ended up capturing and enslaving several of the Aurorans as pets, all as part of their futuristic mission plan to explore and discover sentient life. In our COTI postmortem discussion, students compared this abuse to that done by humans to humans in the past (e.g., Spanish conquistadors) and claimed that they had learned their lesson. Do not mistreat others. The second part of our finale was intended to test just how deeply they learned this lesson.
>
> After concluding their engagement with the Monolith, students were vanned to a house off-campus (still no instructors had appeared), and in the backyard they were greeted by three chickens. The yard also had a dinner table with five cheese pizzas, one barbeque chicken pizza, and a bowl of sunflower seeds. One student cautiously examined the table and said, "I think we are supposed to do something with the chickens." However, another student quickly chimed in, "I think we're just supposed to eat," and within minutes all of the pizzas were gone.
>
> Ideally, the students would have seen this as a test. After all, we left a very obvious camera, also running, on a tripod pointing at the pizzas. Unbeknownst to the students, these chickens would eat sunflower seeds from the palms of human hands. However, the thoughtless action of the group trumped thoughtful inaction of the individual. They ate the alien/chicken pizza right in front of the aliens/chickens. It turned out that they had more learning to do.

(Continues)

Box 7.1 (*Continued*)

> Crider also noted that, in the following years, we encouraged and later required students to record and submit videos of themselves responding to similar scenarios. In each, we crafted a new epic finale to get students to demonstrate, rather than describe, their mastery of topics from the class.
>
> Given that today's students nearly all have phones capable of video recording, it is easy for them to document themselves working through these scenarios. These memorable endings for each class helped both the students and us to fully see what they had (or had not) learned and how they had (or had not) changed.

COTI #2: Look Out, Universe!

We varied one aspect of Funaro's (1994) original COTI model for the second iteration of the class (he has varied it too, and in the same direction). This time both teams developed alien civilizations, between which contact was then simulated. The instructions varied somewhat but still set up the same basic encounter scenario.

This time one team evolved the *Lorem Animae* (LA), a kind of bio-engineered, bioluminescent air-balloon jellyfish with an embedded and transferable virtual intelligence, supposedly confined by design to the desert-like wreckage of their creators' planet, but in fact contriving to send messages—somewhat disingenuous pleas for help—and even probe messengers (digitized versions of their own intelligences, effectively on suicide missions) into deep space.

Theirs was a dark and ambiguous story. The LA were inspired, in part, by a TED Talk by science writer Ed Yong (2014) describing a number of ways in which parasites can take over the brains of much larger creatures, even sometimes mammals. The emerald wasp, for example, uses a stinger/probe that's also a sense organ to find the cockroach's brain and inject the mind-controlling venom that changes its operating system. The LA team began with the conception that we might have such powers, except of course (of course!) only to be used for the good, like expanding our knowledge of the universe.

Or—really? We (I was adviser to this group) also began, seemingly independently, with the idea that our creators somehow were destroyed, or destroyed themselves, because they'd created a doomsday weapon of some unknown sort. The confinement of the LA was part of their creators' penance. Only slowly did it dawn on us that we LA ourselves, unwittingly endowed with an immense and extraordinarily dangerous mind-capturing power, might be that doomsday weapon. The two strands of our imagining met and fused—a spooky moment. Actually, I am not sure that all of us ever fully recognized it.

We began sending pleas for help into space across the radio spectrum, followed up by an elaborate self-documentation largely in the mythic mode, including a sort of cultural last will and testament from the LAs' creators to guide their creations and inheritors. This had a false bottom, however, because it turned out that another faction of the creators buried their own, much darker account of the LAs' genesis beneath the official plea. It was not settled, even within our group, which one was true, if either was. We didn't see the need, and indeed the whole scene was much more interesting if that question were left unsettled. (Let the aliens figure it out.) This second account was all there in the revision history of the "Last Testament" Google Doc, quite accessible to anyone with but a single click . . . if anyone thought to look. Would they?

The other group fashioned themselves into a robotic intelligence calling themselves the SAVI, an acronym derived from the name *scienti appetenari vita intellig* in the bad Latin of their creators, the Flebians: It was meant to roughly translate as "new life knowledge-seeking intelligence." Originally the Flebians—or, more likely, rogue scientists among them, very much like certain leaders in the SAVI group—created the Disassemblers, intelligent robots programmed to seek the secret of life by disassembling any and all living things they encountered. Alas, the defects of this programming were not obvious to the creators until too late, when the Disassemblers were reproducing wildly and taking down the Flebians right and left.

All the Flebians could do before wholly succumbing was to create another species of SAVI to try to counteract the Disassemblers. These are the Preservers, programmed to track Disassembler activity and stop them forthwith, by violence if necessary (but, oddly, only when they are actively disassembling or about to do so—ah, robots!). Otherwise, the two species of SAVI coexist more or less peaceably and have various interesting and harmless peculiarities, such as a tendency toward electronic self-stimulation and a penchant for bad Flebian movies. But the whole civilization, if you could call it that, is trigger-happy. At a moment's notice, the Disassemblers could be off on another search-and-destroy mission, with the Preservers in hot pursuit . . . as was about to happen.

Crash Landing
Contact began unexpectedly early when one of the scattershot LA suicide missions arrived at the SAVI home planet (in reality, a student from the LA group crashing the other group's meeting room) and encountered

their species. Immediately, it (he) was surrounded and disassembled by Disassembler SAVI. Before going completely inert, however, it managed to touch one of the SAVI, whose neural network it was able to briefly commandeer, unbeknownst to either her or the rest of the SAVI, and from whom it was therefore able to download her language, radioing this back to its compatriots literally with its last gasp.

As it happened (and, to be honest, by design), the SAVI thus touched was a native Georgian speaker. So naturally the LA took Georgian as the SAVI language and composed solicitations in Georgian (courtesy of Google Translator). This utterly befuddled the SAVI in turn, of course, except for the one student who knew the language, but neither she nor any other SAVI understood why the LA would be communicating only to her or how they could know Georgian or any SAVI language in the first place.

Now both teams act precipitously. The arrival of the LA probe triggers the immediate launch of Disassembler missions back to the LA planet, now locatable, along with Preserver ships in hot pursuit. The Preserver faction also sends ahead a radio message, meant as a warning, which predictably the LA only partially decode, presuming far more than they should about the intent of the message (never imagining that it could be a warning, they interpret it as an invitation) and about the universality of symbols (an arrow is necessarily a pointer, eh?), and therefore totally misunderstand, ending by returning a lovely but wildly misconceived welcoming note . . . in a Georgian music video. Of course, the SAVI in turn can make less than nothing of this. And all the while the destroyers draw near.

Encounter

This lead-up took place over several days, including one class day. The following class day was the day of actual contact. The first Disassembler ship finally arrives, picking up ever more elaborate messages en route from the LA, including the music video and the false-bottomed Last Testament, but only partially read—students in the first Disassembler-SAVI landing group frantically trying to digest it from their smartphones as they sprint across campus to the mysterious LA-specified location. The GPS coordinates, they discover, lead them to the campus Black Box theater—the LA planet? They completely miss the hidden layer in the revision history.

The Black Box, true to its name, is pitch black inside. Only a few dim multicolored light sticks wave on the far side of the cavernous space. Eventually their sensors adjust (the lights come up a bit). There's someone there! Recovered, the Disassemblers methodically decimate the LA welcoming committee. In the nick of time, the LA rally when they discover the SAVIs' brains' vulnerability through their eyes, the one spot to which, weirdly, the LA are already predisposed to attach themselves to capture others' neural networks.

In the midst of this carnage a first contingent of Preservers arrives and immediately takes on the Disassemblers. Now we have the bizarre spectacle of two factions of an alien race fighting it out on the surface of the LA planet—with physical weapons. They called them "ice picks," no less, since the SAVI do not have the peculiarly insidious mind-capture capacities of the LA. The gamemaster has the students fight rock-paper-scissor style. Soon more corpses litter the floor. The advantage see-saws, but eventually the LA and the Preservers create a kind of common front when the LA discover, via the reappearance of SAVI thought killed, that the SAVI have spare bodies in their ship. Weirdly also, the SAVI are downloadable intelligences much like the LA, but their bodies are much more durable and readily manufactured. And there are extras. Cautiously, a deal is struck with the Preservers to share some of those spare bodies. Hastily and portentously, the first LA-Preserver/SAVI hybrids appear on the scene.

Fight to the Death?
But the Disassembler-Preserver ice-pick battles still rage. The LA-Preserver hybrids join, desperately trying to fight off the remaining Disassemblers. Finally, more or less by chance, only two fighters remain: one Disassembler and one LA-Preserver hybrid. The fate of the universe is now down to one ice-pick battle. Utterly improbably—we could not possibly have orchestrated this—these two last combatants now make a series of identical moves. Rock-rock, paper-paper. . . . They stalemate literally 10 times. Equally improbably, in reality, these combatants are close friends, philosophy majors, and among the best students in the class. Finally, they just stop, refusing even the gamemaster's demand that they fight to the bitter end. A new kind of recognition dawns, even for the programming-bound SAVI: that the Other, having repeatedly and consciously risked death to realize its destiny, is a fellow, like being, with whom somehow the universe can be shared. Philosophers will recognize that these students have just reenacted a version of Hegel's (1977) famous master–slave dialectic—without either of them (yet!) knowing Hegel.

Reinforcements arrive from both sides until everyone is in the theater, but they find a wary but peaceful exchange taking place that leads in the end to a general détente. Unhybridized SAVI Disassemblers are persuaded that they have gotten what they came for. Shields are set up to protect the LA from detection by further unenlightened Disassemblers. Meanwhile, the LA have acquired their jellyfish-ish hearts' desires: durable bodies and the means to manufacture more, with spaceships to boot. Warily, they part, and everyone can breathe again.

Denouement
Again the two groups debrief separately first. What happens next? For the LA especially, it turns out to be unclear, for in the process the LA have uncovered their own hidden history and powers. Once again, the ramifications extended well past the contact encounter proper.

> We have begun decoding a data-set deep in the Lorem Animae consciousness that has lain dormant and unseen since the beginning of our existence. The further we delve into this information, the more evident it becomes that the Creators' message is *not what it once seemed!* Our true history has made clear that we are more powerful than we ever imagined. . . . There are immense implications of our ability to control the minds of creatures we make contact with. Paired with a newfound ability to travel through space and our insatiable curiosity, it is hard to imagine a force that can prevent us from going and doing wherever we please.

Thus, precisely at the long-awaited moment of their liberation, the LA also lose their innocence.

> Some LA are ecstatic with the potential we now see in ourselves, and are eager to commence immediately in using our power to seek out whatever mysteries of the universe we can discover. Others have become nervous, fearful even, as this new knowledge has been revealed. . . . They refuse to accept their ability to conquer. . . . The divisions deepen.

Finally, they know who they really are—or are forced to recognize it, and the veneer of benign intentions, its falsity sensed by a few all along, is pierced for all. Some LA quickly launch expeditions to other planets, whereas back home the conservative faction becomes increasingly restive. It is even possible that the civil war (over them!) that destroyed their creators will be reenacted, despite all best intentions, by their creations. Unregenerate Disassembler-SAVI, meanwhile, newly energized by the discovery of unsuspected forms of life and intelligence elsewhere, launch missions to search for the planet that actually speaks Georgian (that's us, fellow Earthlings). Tony takes the precaution of repossessing the ice picks (it's his team), but the fate of the universe remains unsettled.

COTI #3: "All Mother!"

For our 2016 iteration we returned to one future-Earth scenario (my team) and one alien (Tony's).

The first thing that year's alien team noticed was that they were all women. Accordingly, they created an all-female species, the Deryajin, reproducing by cloning, or so it seemed (they took on a mythic and metaphorical style that made their explanations and proclamations at once genuinely poetic and hard to decipher), and tracing lineage back to a primal mother, "All-Mother," who'd become an all-seeing and all-providing God figure who also appeared as their moon's planet, hanging close in the skies, although even this basic astronomical fact had only recently been discovered.

The basic Deryajin form was a sort of gelatinous blob, although highly differentiated within. Different adaptations could be grown or grafted onto their bodies, as either trophies or out of necessity, for the Deryajin were also in trouble. In the fairly inhospitable solar system in which they found themselves, their home environment was under the ice crust of a moon whose liquidity was maintained by the heat of the moon's iron core. This core was slowly cooling. Providentially, All-Mother then created a path—"All-Mother's Crater"—to (what they then discovered was) the surface of their moon, where thin deposits of certain metals from space included Helium-3, a helium isotope they use as a new heat source. Although natural Deryajin cannot live at the surface, with bioengineered modifications they can. Thus, a race of miners was created, not coincidentally providing a way to exile Deryajin misfits, who are mostly but not entirely successfully brainwashed into viewing themselves as sacrificial heroes. The rest remain below in a medieval sort of caste society whose ruler reincarnates the timeless All-Mother.

We Earthlings, meanwhile, began our move toward 2216 by imagining cultural and scientific transformations in 50-year intervals, each subsequent stage reacting to the last, to give us more of a systematically imaginative and unpredictable process rather than taking just a single step out 200 years. Finally arriving at the twenty-third century, we found ourselves in a sort of cultural funk. The whole planet is thoroughly humanized—even many domesticated species are in some degree of communication and league with us—and artificial intelligence manages everything, except that it remains utterly uncreative. It turns out that you can't program true creativity—it is the last remaining human superiority. But it is attenuating quickly.

What needs reenergizing in 2216, then, is—who would have thought? — Earth's *art*. A renegade zillionaire outfits a kind of nomadic art colony to seek new inspiration in far-flung space. A gaggly outfit of latter-day Gauguins, without (let's hope) the syphilis, is about to set forth. "EARTH without ART is EH," they intone, a slogan borrowed from an ancient (i.e., early twenty-first century) bumper sticker. Their starship—christened *Amanuti*—is itself a work of art and a living being at the same time (bioengineering, at least, has greatly progressed on Earth) and is rather like a massive tree, in that it is designed to take root in alien soils and shelter tree-housey dwellings. In space, *Amanuti* can also assemble and disassemble itself, the befitting outward form of the bohemian collective it shelters inside.

In the same ragtag spirit, only the loosest protocols are set up to deal with unexpected contingencies like, say, running into aliens. The artists are much more interested in alien landscapes. And again, why mightn't this be exactly the case?

Encounter

By way of preparation, the week before the full-scale enactment, *Amanuti* goes for a trial run, taking our treeship (van) to an inviting nearby planet (the college farm) and trying out our art supplies. Already then there is art on our walls and paint under our fingernails. Then *Amanuti* sets off to the stars.

Fast forward to contact week. Coming into the assigned star system, the artists naturally head for the most aesthetically appealing body, which is definitely not the Deryajin's ice moon. *Amanuti*, landed and taking root, is a huge and welcoming old magnolia tree on campus, large-canopied and readily climbed. From this base, our bee scouts go out (not robotic bees but real bees, in partnership and communicating through, of course, the famous bee dancing; in the actual event, we used a small drone with a camera piloted by a colleague.) Art proceeds apace, but no aliens show up, a matter of no great concern to us, officially, but since it will not make for contact, our gamemaster fairly quickly deposes us from our little alien Tahiti, announcing that the planet's biota is turning incompatible with *Amanuti*, and pushes us back into space.

Back in our *Star Trek*-like computer-room-turned-ship's-bridge, the next moon comes into view—in fact, the flat, pebbled, sun-baked roof of the university gym across the quad. Desolate. But wait! Onboard sensors (binoculars) show something moving on the surface—the first time the Earth team catches sight of aliens. Quickly they go into action: Out go our allies/scouts (the drone again, this time buzzing and thoroughly spooking the students representing surface-mining, semi-slave aliens), which show also, after all, an aesthetically suggestive landscape—not Tahiti, but maybe Antarctica. Let's explore this.

Paused there, action resumes on the second day of enactment. Dispatched from our control room, our intrepid but phlegmatic pilot, not too fond of the artists but doing his job, takes a landing team down to explore the ice moon and its strange fauna. Unexpected events then quickly cascade. Uplink (FaceTime) is lost almost immediately, first of all—an unplanned feature but utterly realistic in the event. ("This is just like it would be, isn't it?" said a student to me as we were in the midst of it. Yes, indeed.) In the tree-ship, the Earth crew panics and readies a rescue probe. Meanwhile, the initial pod lands, and the first encounter takes place on the surface of the moon. Neither side has any idea what is going on. The miners are programmed to simply mine. Only one less brainwashed miner shows much interest. The Earthlings' lovely drawing and dancing has no effect—for the Deryajin, who evolved in utter darkness, have no eyes!

Meanwhile, back on the treeship, frantic research turns up a bizarre coincidence—and true story. This solar system was actually beamed some music from Earth, all the way back in 2001, as a so-called "Russian Teen-Aged Message" on, of all things, the theremin (Zaitsev, 2002). Maybe the aliens would respond to theremin music? A flash drive containing the original transmission is dispatched to the landing party via yet another pod. At first it agitates the aliens, but then they settle into it. All-Mother, it turns out, remembers. But the fragile peace is soon shattered when one of the artists—and, alas, our mission photographer—approaches too closely, as photographers will do, and then is physically restrained and "assimilated" by the Deryajin miners. This looks like murder to the Earthlings, who naturally panic, abandon their easels, and flee to their landing pod, in turn assailed by other miners. Soon thereafter, though, the now zombie photographer's body approaches the pod. Through her now-commandeered voice, the Deryajin manage to communicate an invitation/demand for an audience below the ice (in a circular multistoried chamber of the gym, in fact) with All-Mother/Queen herself.

Denouement

Two humans finally go, more or less picked on the spot: one is the hapless pilot, the other is an artist. In the audience, neither side understands what is happening very well, but the encounter nonetheless seems to end satisfactorily, with the Earthlings' acceptance of an offer/demand, which the Deryajin will henceforth call a consortium, obliging them/us to assist the Deryajin in finding more Helium-3 elsewhere in what some of the Deryajin are beginning to understand is a vastly larger universe than they ever imagined. Or possibly to move the entire race to some other planet or moon not afflicted by their current global cooling.

Of course the artists are actually in no position to deliver any such thing, but they are certainly not going to confess as much. They only want to escape with a little art for their trouble—or just plain escape. Meanwhile, for All-Mother and her minions, the event takes shape in their fairytale universe, in which the Earthlings are known as the Rigid or Rigidlings, on account of lacking the gelatinous, water-adapted bodies of the Deryajin, and their appearance is credited to All-Mother herself, while opening up for her bio-engineers a whole new set of possibilities through study of the unfortunate photographer's assimilated body. Their later final report admits, "We have yet to reach the outcome of our formation of the consortium between the almighty Deryajin and the selfless Rigid," another way of saying that the Earthlings have just fled, no doubt finding better artistic inspiration in alien-free places. But they maintain a forlorn hope.

Earth, for its part, does get some art out of it. One feature of the art colony that all of us Earthlings liked from the beginning was that our reports and results were not just verbal. Students actually began imagining and producing new kinds of art—at least attempts at it—which became part of their final product. Aliens remained incidental. Unprepared for premodern or other-than-modern thinking and unassisted by any anthropologist or specialist in radically cross-cultural communication—oops—the artists never understood All-Mother either, nor did they even try very hard. A real ancestress? God? The Deryajin world is permeated by mother-being and mothering, but it all seems to the Earthlings as so much talk. We just want to paint!

In turn, their own loose talk and incomprehension are misunderstood by the Deryajin, one of the priestesses even writing that, "From the few words I understood, I have come to learn that their queen, Earth, also knows of All-Mother, and they have come to unite with us." That was my favorite line of their final report, so exactly does it capture how an alien might misinterpret contact. At the same time, it is heart-breaking in its innocence and wishfulness. What poignancy awaits us in the stars?

Notes and Overview

Our COTIs have indeed created "magic circles" (Dittmer, 2013): special spaces in which special rules apply, at the same time far more open-ended and participant-shaped than, say, a staged play in a theater, and the effect can indeed be magical, in that possibilities normally unsuspected in regular interactions, classroom or otherwise, are welcomed and indeed almost required.

Role-Plays are in part *play* (Huizinga, 1950), but at the same time, the roles will likely be highly differentiated and demanding—something to rise to.

In the context of our class, the COTIs succeed both dramatically and dialectically for the same reasons. They produce encounters that really do manage to model the profound uncertainty and unknowability of encounter with the genuinely alien—of course in an extremely partial but still recognizable way (Crider & Weston, 2012). Right in front of them and in their own actions under pressure, students can see incomprehension and radical nonrecognition play out, even down to truly ludicrous encounters like that between a ragtag nomadic painters' colony and a desperate but eyeless underwater race on a dying moon. Really it *is* likely to be that strange. Likewise, no amount of conceptualizing in class discussion about the underlying ideas and pitfalls in extraterrestrial contact can take the place of sprinting across campus, like the first SAVI landing groups in COTI #2, on their way to an unknown destination, hotly pursued by their own fellows, bombarded by unintelligible or confusing messages, with unsuspected hidden layers only discovered later, heading perhaps to their deaths or to . . . what? Students experiencing themselves in the roles was crucial. *Then* they knew something about "contact."

After these adventures, our students say that they had never dreamed that contact could (and plausibly would) be so complex, contingent, and fraught—and this even with two groups of similar contemporary U.S. college students knowingly doing the simulating. It happened repeatedly, in different ways, across all three COTIs. The groups consistently misunderstood each other, even more or less in their real selves (i.e., they weren't just pretending) even with slowed-down action and teacher and gamemaster processing, and thus vividly came to realize how *total* such misunderstanding would be if such an encounter were actual. (The same kinds of reports turn up in the literature, by the way, in student reactions to some thoroughly terrestrial simulations, for example about opposing positions in international climate change mitigation negotiations [Pettenger et al., 2014].)

Tony and I have also been struck by how deeply many participants came to inhabit their invented species or world. It was not just the team spirit and the T-shirts. As I have said, we require a variety of kinds of feedback and concluding thinking, but the most welcomed and intriguing part is how the teams carry on in their roles after contact. In COTI #1, the Aurorans methodically rewrote their mythology on their own private wiki, while the KICK team celebrated their successful return with specimens. In COTI #2, an LA faction enthusiastically began plotting to, well, take over the universe, still unable or unwilling to come to terms with the lessons of their own origins, while others were genuinely troubled, again in their own persons as well as in their roles. Echoes of their creators' doomsdays began to sound. In COTI #3, the Deryajin ruling class, finally beginning to glimpse what art is—not easy even for the humans, who mostly just traipsed off to paint while their patron fumed about obliterating the ice moon in retaliation for the taking of the photographer—decided to suppress art as they understood it completely, weirdly echoing Plato's banishment of the poets from his ideal city-state, and to reeducate those drawn to it, exiling them to the miner class on the surface, all the while awaiting (but deep down, do they wonder?) salvation from the skies.

In the end, of course, we step all the way out of the roles and come into whole-class reflection. Here I do not dispute the value of debrief—it's our chance to stand at more of a distance, beginning to leave the magic circle, but it is certainly not forced from the instructor side. The students are thoroughly provoked and deeply curious, and they carry it themselves. They are the ones who spoke the profound and poignant all-too-human analogues of the invasion of Aurora. In COTI #2, both teams marveled at their frankly spooky convergences. Both teams independently imagined themselves as derivative/created beings who destroyed their own creators; both backstories had hidden layers; and both teams even named themselves in bad Latin. Was it something Tony or I said? The SAVIs' one point of weakness—their eyes—was the one point to which the LA were predisposed to target for brain capture. Why? What if it had been even slightly different?

As we resurface we also turn to other details. We track the other group's world-creation as narrative. How did you get there? We relive key moments from the perspectives of the key actors. Maybe there is even art to view. And how about that drone? Teams go on to produce their own final reports—graded, finally, by the other team's professor, along with all the supporting material generated in advance: chiefly backstories in a variety of formats, like wikis, team bios, letters of application for Earth missions, histories of the future, newspaper editorials from 2205, or whatever it may be.

Many of the COTIs at the Contact conferences have ended with one or the other side getting wiped out. In our own, COTI #2 had that distinct possibility as well, but some advance tweaking by our gamemaster—the only one who could see how things were shaping up several weeks in advance—plus the resistance of two key players at a key moment prevented it. One could certainly argue against this kind of intervention. Funaro (1994) insists in his account that death to one side is not at all a failure on the metalevel, but Tony's and my view is that we are running a one-time event for each group of students, and from that perspective a somewhat less bleak outcome is significantly more encouraging and suggestive, although in each of our COTIs, too, the long-term prospects are unsettling or at least unclear. It is actually saying a lot that most everyone survived. May it be so when the moment comes for real. Maybe some of these students will even be in a position to help.

8

WHOLE-COURSE SCENARIOS

This chapter explores a type of scenario that essentially constitutes an entire course. Here the scenario does not merely co-extend with the class, like some of the Role-Plays described in Chapter 7, but essentially *is* the class. Whole-course scenarios, therefore, go beyond the typology of scenarios outlined in Chapter 5. Sometimes they can encompass smaller-scale Step-Right-Ins, Role-Plays, or other more specific scenarios, but the setting is a meta-scenario that frames the entire course. The largest dynamically structured situation in this case is the project of the course as a whole.

A Self-Constituting Ethics Class

Early in my career I found myself teaching an upper-level ethics course centrally considering the moral and political philosopher John Rawls's (1970) theory of justice. Rawls's fundamental idea is that a just social arrangement is one to whose principles the involved parties would have agreed if they were unaware of what their particular place would be in the eventual arrangement—that is, as if they might end up occupying any of the roles within it. To arrive at moral rules, Rawls argues that we must abstract out of both particular situations and particular persons to some extent to the moral essence behind them. It turns out, moreover, that this abstract social contract situation, or what Rawls calls the *Original Position*, can be modeled quite precisely using game theory, thus allowing determinate solutions, specifically Rawls's famous principles of justice, specifying that all "primary goods"—liberty and opportunity, income and wealth, and so on—are to be distributed equally except where an unequal distribution is to the advantage of the least well off.

Designing this class, I realized that it too would have primary goods: grades, naturally; learning, for sure; support by the teacher; and ample time to do the required work. Here was the occasion of one of my first serious ventures in scenario-setting, although I did not yet have any terms for it. As an experiment in thinking about justice ourselves, why couldn't the class decide how some of its own primary goods might be justly distributed? I was not ready, at that point, to imagine setting up a class to reinvent the Original Position itself. I was ready, though, to challenge the class to devise just procedures for part of the design of the class, and to see how close to Rawls's principles their own would come.

For part of their graded work for the class, each student was expected to pick a major theme in the theory of justice and lead a 30-minute class discussion on it. The available presentation slots were listed in the syllabus and distributed evenly through the term, running from about the fourth week of class through the fourteenth. Students needed to distribute themselves likewise. But this choice was not neutral from the student point of view. Some strongly preferred to go early and have met the requirement, or might have other reasons to go at some particular time, but in general the preference was to go as late as possible, for the sake of having the most time to prepare and also to hear other students' presentations and pick up hints from them and their reception.

Obviously, not everyone could do so. One primary good of the class, then, was the chance to get a desirable spot on the presentation schedule. We needed some fair way of signing students up to the available slots (taking the distribution of slots as a given, which could be rethought too, of course, but I held firm there). So I put the challenge to the class: You figure out a fair way to do so.

I did not specifically say that everyone must agree to whatever system they decided on. They could have decided by majority vote, by appointing a class dictator, or by dumping it back in my lap as the local benevolent despot. However, during the event the students recapitulated a key Rawlsian requirement right away: essentially, universal consent. Whatever plan is adopted must be agreeable to all. No one was willing to put themselves in a situation where a majority or a despot could disadvantage them against their will to serve others' (even most others') interests.

Some kind of lottery naturally had a strong appeal: that way everyone obviously had the same chances at advantageous spots. Presumably a lottery would be at least a baseline arrangement that would be agreeable to all. But a lottery is not necessarily the *best* agreeable arrangement. For one thing, students who prefer early spots, or other spots that most students did not want, surely should be able to take them. That is better for everyone.

For another, although some inequality seems inevitable, perhaps there could be some systematic way of alleviating the burdens of early slots, again out of fairness. Just as Rawls suggests, everyone wanted to make the least well-off as well-off as they could be, including perhaps special advantages by way of (some) compensation—because they could turn out to be one of them.

The system that the class eventually devised and agreed upon was complex but took account of both of these points, drawing on a lottery with a variety of adjustments both before and after the results were known. The beautiful thing was to watch students' energy come alive with the challenge. Everyone in the room had something serious at stake. Everyone knew that everyone else had to be brought along. Students had hints and directions from the general theme of the class, but they had to apply them and in so doing test the theories, knowingly recapitulating them now with a deeper understanding. By the time they got back to Rawls, they read him—usually a notoriously difficult figure for undergraduates to understand—with recognition, appreciation, and even amazement at how closely they had approximated him . . . or, more accurately in the event, vice versa.

Co-Constituting an Ethic

Now, twenty years or so later, I am teaching Elon's Ethical Practice course, which aims to develop students' understanding of the nature of ethics, provide some basic familiarity with landmark ethical perspectives and principles, and improve students' ability to make a constructive ethical difference in their lives and in the world. The text I use is my own third edition of *A 21st Century Ethical Toolbox* (Weston, 2013), which brings a wide set of practical skills into play: being more alert to the moral dimensions of everyday life; articulating moral values, both in their own terms and against the background of moral tradition; critical thinking; dialogue skills; integrating values rather than perpetuating or exacerbating conflicts; creative problem-solving and moral vision; and practical and persuasive skills to inspire larger ethical changes and organize groups to make a real difference.

Pedagogically, by this time, I am most of the way to a conception of Teaching as Staging. My previous ethics courses had indeed been practice-based and included major service components—in fact, the *Toolbox* textbook arose out of them—but now I have learned to go still farther. Befitting an impresario, my bent is immediately to ask how I could set up scenarios that put students into dynamically structured situations that would lead them to unfold the key ethical dialectics largely on their own. So it was time to truly go all the way. Let the very work of this class be to constitute itself as an ethical community. Let everything be on the table: how the class is going to operate and make decisions; what our daily expectations of each other will be; how we will decide our major outside engagement or service project and our approach to it; and how the classwork will be organized and, yes, graded.

The typical ethics course, even if taught actively, still invites students to debate or analyze someone else's behavior, often in abstract or hypothetical situations. The aim of my new and all-out design would be to build *our own* ethic together, in dialogue with the tradition as represented in our practice-oriented textbook, and put it into our own practice in some creative and effective way outside the classroom. The aim would be to actually *enact* ethics as an ongoing, compelling, semi-negotiated set of agreements with others, and as a co-responsibility, not arbitrary or distant, and not something that we can just opt out of if it proves inconvenient.

Strikingly, these presuppositions mirror the broadly constructivist conception of knowledge that underlies PBL and other scenario-like pedagogies described in this book. For example, one key task of forming PBL groups is often for the group to set its own ground rules (Burgess & Taylor, 2000). In my class, I now proposed to frame this work as a microcosm of ethics itself.

First Steps

Imagine, then, an Ethical Practice class settling in on its first day. Here we are, I said: A group of people who have chosen to come together with certain educational aims—to learn something about ethics. The stakes are significant: ethical learning itself, obviously; the productive use of each other's time, in general; appropriate care for each other as fellow learners in this class and fellow members of our university community; and, yes, individual grades in the end. These already invoke broad ethical ideals. Our first project will be to spell out those ideals, and then begin to extend them into determinate and specific enough agreements to apply to our actual interactions. Our project will be to construct and consolidate our own class ethic and then put it to use between ourselves and in the larger world.

Student scribes went to the board and we began making lists—this is, again, five minutes into our first meeting. We want to learn productively, of course. What sorts of responsibilities does this set up for each of us? Fairness is crucial, but how shall we understand fairness in this context? What is a fair way to decide on a major class project, for example, when not everyone may be equally committed to or capable at the work? Grades are on the table, too. What is a fair way to grade such a project? And how specifically shall we balance productive learning against, say, fidelity to our personal and academic relationships, or fairness, should they conflict?

Students brought forward various possible class agreements addressing such questions. The readings from *A 21st Century Ethical Toolbox* scaffolded this work, helping us identify and explore the families of moral values that each proposed agreement invoked—making the point, among other things, that ethics in fact starts "in the middle of things." That is, we brought to our nascent class community a wide range of preexisting needs, expectations, commitments, and habits, such as social and ethical norms from our family life or earlier schooling, as well as those that we are called on to adopt as members of a university learning community in general and of this university in particular. Our task was not somehow to start from scratch but to co-construct a workable modus operandi out of this complex and rich inheritance. *That's ethics,* I argue, or at least a big part of it—and, naturally, it was manifestly the task before us.

Setting the Rules

My classes have pulled back from formally requiring unanimous consent for specific agreements, worrying that one or a few recalcitrant members could block agreements that everyone else favors and that might be necessary to make further progress. One class adopted a basic rule requiring a three-fourths supermajority to establish any other agreement. Notably, however, we unanimously consented to this basic rule. How else, the students asked, could we ethically start?

In fact, strikingly, in the event, almost all of the specific agreements adopted by that class were by consensus. Moreover, class members consistently and emphatically committed to hearing out anyone with reservations (i.e., rather than just pushing proposals through with a three-fourths vote), even gently prompting and prodding class members who showed hesitation to express their reservations and typically adjusting the proposed agreements accordingly—because, they recognized, next time the would-be holdouts could be themselves. Halfway through we even added a formal proviso for appeals, reassuring dissenters that they could appeal if they wanted to, but also suggesting a distinction between an issue about which they did not care *that* much and an issue about which they really needed us to think more.

A later class did something similar: In that case, a two-thirds vote was required to make rules, but elaborate procedures were again added to ensure that the minority was heard and responded to in an ongoing way. This group also specified that the project vote in particular had to be unanimous at first, but the backup was that if no agreement was reached in the first meeting, on our next meeting only a two-thirds vote would be required, allowing if necessary for a "loyal opposition" group who would agree to go along but also stand apart to constructively critique the project as it proceeded. So the question to prospective opponents was not exactly whether they could grudgingly go along with a supermajority, but whether they could join such a loyal opposition. In that class, 4 (out of 24) did at first, but they quickly joined the project as it morphed partly due to their stance.

In both classes, the students' care for each other was exemplary. I also made a point of highlighting how radically different even these fairly sensible moves are from what is usually done in group decision-making. We are too used to accepting tyrannical majorities. To the students' credit, each of these moves was their invention, with only the lightest prompting.

Most discussions were conducted in talking circles or with a talking stick rather than the usual mode of hand-raising or free-for-all. Student facilitators ran most of the discussions, both to ride herd and sometimes to prompt more engagement. This was not my idea, either: Students voluntarily decided to require themselves all to talk. Both classes also took it upon themselves to forbid texting in class and closely limit their cellphone and laptop use, to take care not to begin packing up until the day's student moderator declared class over, and many other things that we normally leave to professorial imposition, if we address them at all. Again, I did not bring up any of these things, although my opinion was solicited and considered.

By design, my role in group agreements was also up to the group. I ended up with one vote on most matters, like everyone else. Subsequently, I was on the losing side of some votes. Students were solicitous and careful with my views, as they were with each other's, while not afraid to disagree with me either. Of course a preset ground rule was that I did have the right, indeed the responsibility, to override certain class decisions if basic academic standards or personal rights were being infringed. This too is a provision the group arguably should accept on Rawlsian grounds, but regardless, it was not open for their agreement. In fact, not surprisingly, we never got anywhere close to needing such an override.

These classes spent many sessions working out the rules. We took our time to explore and invoke varied moral values from the frameworks we were studying—our way of reviewing, exploring, and testing them. This is not mere prelude, I insisted: It is deep and real work. At long last, it produced agreements governing our general procedure as well as many specific specifics: everything from our basic ethical attitudes to sourcing information, how we listened to each other, and establishing student moderators and tone monitors. Students even proposed and committed to learning everyone's name, immediately set up a procedure for name drill, and learned them all within two sessions. The final agreements were posted on the class website, along with most of the preliminary versions; each student got an individual printed copy and also signed a large public copy that was posted on our class-room wall for every subsequent session.

The Projects

Now came the project question. *A 21st Century Ethical Toolbox* (Weston, 2013) ends with a challenge to undertake a major ethical change project: a project that manifestly works from a moral vision (the theme of the book's last chapter); a project that aims, at least partly, at *structural* change—crea-tively addressing causes and not just symptoms—while engaging stakehold-ers as partners (not just a form of unilateral do-good-ism); and a project that sets in motion processes of change that can sustain themselves beyond one class's engagement.

This is a tall order, of course—on purpose. I wanted to challenge stu-dents to think beyond the usual service projects, indeed to think bigger in general. The very act of canvassing potential projects and creatively amplify-ing and extending them was already, once again, a major and striking part of the learning. Student groups worked out and presented various possible projects, often with outside advice, eventually with detailed information, posters, and open-ended brainstorming sessions. Again, I said, do not think that the only point is to arrive at a project as quickly as possible. Although we can only pick one (or perhaps combine several), just look at how much we are learning along the way about how much we can do and how creatively we can push the usual limits. By the time student groups come back to the class with worked-out proposals, there are typically half a dozen thoroughly engaging and genuinely change-making possibilities before us.

One of my classes ended up producing and distributing an ethical cook-book for their fellow students: a guide to sustainability, social justice, and per-sonal responsibility in eating and cooking choices, written with a special edge because they took themselves to be writing for themselves, in effect, unlike any other cookbook available. In addition, it was written with special flair, with illustration and narrative too. Students ended by cooking their recipes for an all-campus café/banquet at which we also distributed the cookbook.

Another class decided to partner with a local homeless shelter, making a point of working *with* the shelter's guests rather than *for* them. We began to meet in the shelter for regular class sessions, as well as to help out at meals and in the evenings. Our partnership culminated in daylong workshops to build about 50 bunk bed frames to replace and expand the shelter's mea-ger and battered supply, while facilitating the university's donation of used mattresses—still in excellent shape—that otherwise would just have been discarded. The students got firsthand instruction from some of the guests not only in life's hard knocks but also in how to handle power drills and screwdrivers—an entirely different relationship with "The Homeless" than they had dreamed of before. This led to uncomfortable questions. Here are people who are completely capable of building their own homes—some even had trucks full of tools—so what stops them? How could capable home builders be left homeless? The answers might be quite different than we thought: certainly complex, and less readily politicized.

Yet another class eventually elected a project of working with elderly people, trying as far as possible to approach them without the stereotypes of aging that surround us today. The impetus was from our reading of a selection from William Thomas's (2004) book, *What Are Old People For?*, arguing that we profoundly misconceive the aged by conceiving them as failing adults. Thomas argues for a category of "post-adulthood" instead. It is possible, he holds, to relate to the aged in their own different terms so as to create and affirm a new kind of elderhood he calls *Eldertopia*.

This one came close to home. We approached it cautiously but with good heart. Many students spoke of their own relation to grandparents, past or present, both pains and joys. Some admitted confusion about how to deal with older relatives who are (as they put it) "losing it." Many also spoke of missing older people in their lives. In fact, they proceeded to assign themselves Thomas's entire book—again, their initiative—and the project became an effort to try out Thomas's vision in practice.

We established a liaison with a local retirement community where, for the remainder of the term, we visited, volunteered, and partnered with residents in all of the sections: some in independent living, some in acute medical need, some with serious dementia. Here I was most strongly impressed with the students' sheer generosity and openness of spirit. We ended up walking into many difficult and trying situations, aiming just to be fully present to them and help as best we could. Back at school, we processed the ongoing experience together. Poignant but soulful and penetrating talks.

Students were also intrigued by the liberatory possibilities in Thomas's conception, with its potential to transform their relations to their own older relatives. Gradually something else also dawned on them: that their own aging is also at stake. It is way down the road for them at present (a lot closer for me, as I kept reminding them), but we will all age. They found themselves considering how they themselves might take on aging differently. We brought all of this back to share with each other in ongoing class meetings as well.

One goal, remember, was to make our service reach beyond this one class and term. Therefore, structural change was a question we also pursued with our various visitors and advisers. We considered trying to make our campus more welcoming and accessible to aged people (e.g., imagine regular groups of seriously senior citizens in the dining hall—how transformative that might be both for them and for students!), building more student involvement into classes that the university already runs for older local residents, or bringing older neighbors into college classes, as well as building stronger connections not just to one retirement community but to communities of older people all around our campus.

Moved by their own experiences working with elders, and contrasting them with their own fears and expectations beginning this work, this class made a strategic final decision: to make a class video about our experiences at the retirement community to be used by Elon's Volunteer and Service Learning offices, as well as the staff at the retirement community, to help orient and inspire future volunteers and address the kinds of uneasiness students often feel about working with aged people. This video project was inspired by various advisers in the volunteer office and our main liaison in the retirement community, as well as some remarkable student interest and capabilities in documentation and publicity. Class members did all the organizing and filming for the video—I was even out of town the day they did it. They took the most striking care to ensure that every class member appeared in it and had a voice, and they drew on Thomas's book in eloquent and heartfelt ways. I am happy to say that, four years later, our film is still in just the sort of use we hoped for it.

Philosophy of Education: Or, The One Course That Rules Them All

A Philosophy of Education course examines the assumptions underlying teaching and learning while, of course, actually engaging in teaching and learning. Could this potentially dizzying degree of self-reference be part of the reason that today the subject is not often taught? Contrariwise, mightn't an impresario–professor take precisely this self-referentiality as an unparalleled pedagogical opportunity? Logically, one can lecture about the limits of lecturing, or discuss discussion, but to do so in practice may feel paradoxical, edgy, or maybe prone to getting impossibly tangled. This very kind of paradox and edge, however, would attract an impresario's inventiveness. Why not do such things precisely *as* paradoxical, visibly and even enthusiastically on the edge?

Suppose that a lecture or discussion—and, soon enough, wilder pedagogies—were enthusiastically and visibly *staged*. That is, each pedagogy might be enacted precisely and explicitly as a scenario that students and teacher together could vividly and immediately inhabit and, at the same time and by the same means, could put before themselves in a highlighted and focused enough way that students and teacher can readily examine and question those pedagogies for their philosophical underpinnings. Actually enacting a pedagogy could be made a means of exploring that pedagogy's philosophy. The pedagogy of each individual scenario would simply be each day's philosophy in action.

Thus we can envision not only a thoroughly engaging course that mines the seeming paradox for all it is worth but also a kind of laboratory course in philosophy, where the daily enactment of pedagogies is the ongoing experiment and meta-scenario that constitutes the class itself. The class in its normal activity becomes the laboratory—both subjects and experimenters at once—and the continuously varying scenarios are the experiments.

This is my Philosophy of Education course. I have led it at least a dozen times, in varying forms (e.g., Weston, 1991a, 1998), but the basic design has remained the same. Readings introduce each pedagogical scenario in the context of the larger philosophical system within which it arises, which proposes answers to basic questions about human nature and about the nature of knowledge and of the world such that, or insofar as, it can be known. In class, we explore how each system's answers determine and undergird a pedagogy—using that very pedagogy to do so. Eventually we step back from our pedagogical enactment in turn to analyze and critique the pedagogy and its underlying philosophy. For critical analysis and response, multiple enactments deriving from a particular type of philosophy of education can be addressed in a regular paper due every several weeks, when a session can be dedicated to working them through. In other iterations I have distilled each day's enactment to an hour or so, leaving about 40 minutes (in 100-minute classes) for analysis. Either way, the aim is to enact and experience the pedagogy *and* to explore and challenge it critically and against the background of a range of alternatives, and all more or less at the same time.

Beginnings

As by now you would expect, the first day of this course is already a full-on activity: an introduction to the main idea and method of the course. Immediately we take up the idea that every pedagogy is a philosophy in action. We consider it first in microcosm, on the level of specific pedagogical items: the classroom itself, for one, and specifically the ubiquitous classroom desk, which for this purpose has the virtue of being able to be set up on top of a table or something as a display and thus framed in an unfamiliar way.

The desk, then. Let's not sit in it—*look* at it for once. What is it like? Why is it like that? Its surfaces are all metal and hard plastic, for example. It's not comfortable. Why not? Students have to be kept awake? But why is that? Movie theaters don't have seats like this, but people don't fall asleep in them. Our typical classroom desk is also not made for interaction—the irregular-shaped, sloped tops manifestly do not fit together into larger shared work surfaces—but they do seem to be intended to lead each student to self-confine into a smallish volume, presumably so that the maximum number can be crammed into a given-sized room. At the least, the typical desk markedly confines physical movement in ways that other seating does not.

We discover, in short, that even so simple a thing as the all-too-familiar desk actually embodies certain very specific and possibly troubling assumptions about the nature of learning, such as that students need to sit still for it, apparently against their natural tendencies. Likewise, the desk embodies assumptions about the nature of teaching, such as that it is a form of one-way mass communication. Standard school desks are made for listening, and as individuals rather than as contributors to an active and interactive group.

The logical next question—still on the first day, still by way of getting started—is how *else* could classroom seating be designed? Drawing pads and markers come out, students work in groups, maybe on the floor (goodbye, desks!), and in 15 minutes we reconvene to survey a range of alternative classroom seating possibilities that also embody, now manifestly and intriguingly, alternative philosophies of education. If at all possible we try to mock up a few of them, right then and there. Sit in them. How does the room feel now? Who are you, as a student, now?

The aim of this course, I can now say, is to look at pedagogies in the same light: again as applied philosophies of education, to which there are also, yes, alternatives.

What's next? From both a thematic and a dramatic point of view, it seems sensible to survey pedagogies historically: that is, broadly and roughly speaking, to start with tradition- and authority-based philosophies of education, moving through progressive and liberal philosophies and pedagogies in modern times, to liberatory models that are quite contemporary. But the question of tradition is not neutral. Whose tradition? How far back do we look? It took me some time to realize that arguably the oldest of all pedagogical traditions actually is *initiation*, in the ceremonial and ritualistic sense of indigenous peoples. Native peoples have specific ways to bring young people into capable and conscious possession of their heritage: through personal modeling and mentoring, typically by tribal elders, manifested and completed by certain rituals, often physically and spiritually risky, through which the initiates embrace and visibly take on the larger human identities that make them who they are (Annerino, 1999).

The challenge for classroom enactment is to capture the spirit of this kind of learning in a single session, and without appropriating or romanticizing native ways. My solution is to concentrate on the ceremonial aspect, highlighting and mobilizing the special energy of transition or passage for the class, because we stand at a special moment of transition ourselves (Box 8.1). Here at the beginning of our course, students can ritually invoke their own changing identities as beginning students of the philosophy of education.

BOX 8.1
Initiation

First enactment, the second day of class. Students have been asked to dress up and be on time. Now they are solemnly greeted, one by one, outside the classroom door by the college chaplain and the college president—both surprise guests—along with myself and sometimes another colleague, all of us in full academic regalia. We walk together into the darkened room and take seats in a circle.

Silence, and the dark. Then the chaplain begins, speaking of the widest circle of all: the 14-billion-year-old spree of the galaxies, the very first arisal out of darkness. She paints a picture of an evolving universe, every atom in our bodies first fused in other suns; planets coalesced out of the whirling gas and dust; water coming by the trillions of tons from comets; the 100-million-year-long dance of the dinosaurs; and still later, barely a millisecond in cosmic time, 100,000 years of little bands of humans learning to talk. The whole cosmos stands at our backs. *And thus*, she declaims, *the light of the cosmos burns in us!* She lights a candle, the first spot of light in the room.

The president follows, invoking the 1,000-year history of universities. The fire that so benignly burns today in the middle of our ceremony reminds us also, he says, of early scholars who dared to challenge their days' orthodoxies and paid the ultimate price—some actually dying by fire. Even today, there are more than a few places where serious and independent-minded study can endanger your life. In short, the freedom and heritage we presume here today were won at a fantastic cost. Generations have struggled and died to make this possible, and the struggle goes on. Suddenly the class no longer feels like a random and passing study group. Instead, we inherit all of this struggle and hope. It's not just the cosmos that stands at our backs but also this whole long struggle. What will we make of it?

Now the president lights the second candle from the first. The university from the universe! *And thus*, he concludes, *the light of learning and inquiry burns in us.* Let it be so!

A colleague may speak next for the discipline of philosophy within the university, and then, finally, me, for the inheritance of philosophy of education within philosophy proper. Accordingly we light two more candles, each from the previous one. Opening the shades then, it becomes the students' turn. One by one, solemnly, each student is invited to rise, give their name, and light their own candle from the candle of philosophy of education. The light, the fire, and the passion are now theirs—lit ultimately, and today visibly, from the very fires of creation. We chant some words to this effect together. And thus we conclude our beginning. We're initiated—literally.

One common student reaction to this enactment is that this sort of self-location is really a sort of prologue to education, not exactly education itself. Already this leads to some interesting recognitions. In the modern West, we are much more apt to think of learning in terms of acquiring discrete bits of information. On an indigenous view, though, knowing who and where we are—acquiring a world picture within which all that information makes sense—not only *is* learning but also is the most fundamental learning of all. "Remember who you are!" is the most basic imperative of many tribal cultures. It does not merely mean being an Inuit or a Lakota or a twenty-first-century American but knowing your place in the *cosmos.* Being at *home* in the cosmos.

There are some echoes of such rites of passage in a few modern practices, such as the bar or bat mitzvah preparation and ceremony that brings a young person into the adult Jewish community. But normally we don't think of ourselves as inheritors of supernovae and Socrates. And yet we are. Everything we do is framed by larger meanings, and we are quite literally made of stardust. Being thoroughly grounded in this world is knowing *that.* It might even be argued that this is what the modern West has forgotten, which is partly why so many people feel so rootless and out of place. What is more important to know than our place in cosmos and in (long) history?

In the debrief some students also worry that the ritual was predetermined and simply given to them. True, this initiation session looks nothing at all like a modern classroom give-and-take. Yet already we can make the point that the modern classroom give-and-take should not be presumed to be the only desirable pedagogy either. It too has specific and

(Continues)

Box 8.1 (*Continued*)

arguably limiting assumptions behind it. Moreover, even in this ceremony students arguably remained active, in at least the sense that the ritual also asks for a commitment. True, most of the time they only listened, but the whole dynamic of the ritual headed toward the end, when they committed themselves to this class against the nested deep background the celebrants gave to it. Bride and groom don't talk much at wedding ceremonies, either—but "I do" says everything. Likewise, in their own words of commitment, our students also *do* something—something enormously important, and the condition for all that is to follow.

Traditional Western Pedagogies

Initiation may be followed by a drill-and-practice session: memorizing, by rote, a list of basic terms in the field and names of key figures and schools. The goal is not only to jump-start the course conceptually—the terms are necessary and useful points of reference in the field—but also to inhabit another and also unfamiliar pedagogy, this time a fairly unpleasant one, too, in an insistent and artfully exaggerated way. We address the same questions in the analysis that follows: What philosophies of the self and knowledge does a memorization-based pedagogy presuppose?

Drill can be staged in a variety of ways. Professor Frances Bottenberg, my co-teacher for one lucky recent iteration, deftly played it as a stereotypical schoolmarm. I have combined it with frequent quick quizzes so that memorization gets quick feedback, reinforced by student-student coaching—all of this loosely inspired by the Keller Plan or "Personalized System of Instruction" (Buskist, Cush, & DeGrandpre, 1991). Well-designed multiple-choice quiz questions can themselves teach—they call for careful distinctions to which the teacher can return as the quiz is debriefed—and then can be repeated so that the correct distinctions can be made and secured in the next quiz. By design, most students end up acing the third or fourth quiz. Correspondingly, though, lost in all the activity and time pressure may be the critical recognition that the entire list of key concepts is predetermined by the teacher, and none of them is acquired at any depth, at least not yet. This point certainly comes up in debrief.

Then comes a lecture—an overview of the field from Plato through Rousseau to the present. Students are expected to treat it as they would any other lecture. The content is entirely serious and essential to the class. At the same time, to clearly mark the lecture as a scenario meant for critical analysis, I stage it with a vengeance. I set up the room as a lecture hall: all seats in rows facing forward, a nice solid lectern, and ideally a stage, so that I in my academic gown can not only shield my body from the students but also literally stand above them. I go long, on purpose, taking questions only at the end—just a few, preplanted, and as mundane as possible. "What were Plato's dates, again, please?" No other contributions from the class. I even solemnly interpolate some nonsense about two-thirds of the way through, some lines from Edward Lear maybe, into my declamation, to see whether anyone is actually listening. (We return to this in debrief [Box 8.2]. It turns out that by then, most students have long since tuned out, just as the data suggest.) I may even bring in amplification and turn up the volume, sonically as well as symbolically dominating the space. Saging staged, indeed.

BOX 8.2
Troubling the Lecture

Students will have read Freire's (1970) critique of lecturing, as well as Burgan's (2006) defense of it, so we can come quickly to the philosophical and other criticisms of lecturing raised in Chapter 2. Still, to actually say such things in a classroom—the bastion of lecturing, after all—and moreover for this class's teacher himself to treat it so unsympathetically, is provocative and unexpected to many students. Even a few weeks into this unusual course, it can still come as a shock when we subject lecturing to analysis and criticism.

Students relax a bit when it becomes amusing. I talk openly about what it is like to be the lecturer: to so thoroughly dominate the space that I can even talk utter nonsense—as, in fact, I'd done—and have students solemnly write it all down or take no notice at all. This self-mockery opens up a space, ironically, for taking the critique seriously. Analyzing and criticizing my own role while at the same time *in* the role quite literally epitomizes the course theme and activates the dialectic—key roles of impresario–teachers, remember, according to Chapter 4—and helps us move more fully into the critical and imaginative space it asks of all of its participants.

For this debrief we may reenact the same room formation in which the lecture took place. We can look, then, at how the teacher's authority is reflected in and buttressed by the structure of the classroom. Borrowing a leaf from Theater of the Oppressed, we may even switch places with each other to get different perspectives on the room. Do you see how the usual front-focused, spectatorial layout discourages communication among the students, allows easier professorial control, and conveys the message

(Continues)

Box 8.2 (*Continued*)

that—by literally creating the reality that—the teacher stands apart from the students and relates to them only en masse? Do you see how amplification gives lecturers the space of the classroom free to themselves, filling the room with their voices alone, free of challenge, ratifying and, yes, amplifying their sense of authority and power?

This may be the first time in their entire school careers that students are invited to systematically analyze and critique—not just complain about—some key aspect of school; the first time that they recognize that the all-too-familiar academic forms embody a definite philosophy of education that is also not the only possibility. Some start complaining that they can no longer take their other classes sitting down, literally. I did warn you, I reply. Now let's see what else is possible.

After the lecture, I usually set up a law school–style session. Once again the room is set up in a (literally) teacher-centered way, again featuring me as an authoritative figure. This time, though, *they* talk at my command. I cross-examine students on the day's reading, calling them by name randomly from a deck of cards visibly in hand, making each stand up and answer, sometimes a long set of rapid-fire questions with no quarter given, sometimes switching rapidly among students.

Few students have experienced such teaching firsthand. At most, maybe, they have seen caricatures of it in films like *The Paper Chase* (Paul & Thompson, 1973). Almost all seriously dislike the level of tension it creates. At the same time, they also acknowledge that it keeps them attentive and sharp in ways they rarely experience with other pedagogies. The effect is actually electrifying. No one is looking at their laptop or out the window. The key feature, as argued in the law school literature, is that every student knows that at any moment he or she may be on the spot to answer the next question. Indeed, they have to think as though they have actually been asked it—for (the argument goes) they'll be on the spot in this way in their eventual practice of law (Garrett, 1998; Mintz, 2009).

In point of fact, many lawyers never see the inside of a courtroom. Pedagogically, however, the method does have some strong points. Student participation is required, not merely invited, but at the same time the format automatically precludes a few students from dominating the class. The instructor gets a good sense of how prepared the students are in general. Besides the high level of tension, the chief disadvantage is the method's almost necessary concentration on specific facts, contentions, and analysis, to the neglect of other dimensions of a subject or a reading, such as its rhetorical and emotional dimensions, its suggestiveness, and the possibility of more charitable or imaginative but less literal readings.

The dynamics need careful attention, too. Despite the fact that the session consists largely of students rather than the instructor speaking, it remains a profoundly teacher-centered method. Once again it is striking to experience from the professorial side. You are utterly in control, and feared too, as it becomes quite clear that you know all the answers. The trick is to sustain this appearance of omniscience by the simple expedient of selecting all the questions in advance and deciding how you will pursue them, and moreover setting yourself up to judge students' answers rather than proposing any of your own. Students almost always miss this aspect of the staging entirely, and typically are outraged when I point it out. As you should be, I answer, happily back in my own person.

Progressive Pedagogies

An early scenario in the progressivist section of the course is a workshop in which students and I develop a paper-grading rubric for the rest of the term. We work out a draft and then jointly test it by grading sample anonymous student analysis papers from this very class, comparing and discussing our results. I grade them right along with all the students and explain my grades and my thinking as well. All of this out loud, together, in a full regular enactment for the class.

Part of my aim is to simply focus on the course writing rubric to help students understand the papers' intentions and improve their responses. This is one reason to stage this workshop fairly early in the term—right after the first paper, usually. Just as much, though, my aim is to demystify the grading process by discussing it explicitly, by putting students into the place of grader as well as gradee—again an unaccustomed place for most students, despite most of them having been graded since the beginning of their school careers—and by sharing my own grading practices and thinking, which is only fair considering that they are going to be subject to them for the rest of the term. Thus this enactment is meant to exemplify a Deweyan democratic approach to class work. Students now have a hand and a voice in how they are graded. After this, whenever they bring in papers for analysis days, they start by using the agreed-on rubric to both self-grade their own paper and grade another student's as well. By the time I get their paper, then, there are already two other responses to the paper using the shared rubric, all of which the writers get back along with my own response and grading using the same form.

We read major parts of Rousseau's (1762/1979) *Emile*. A second pro-gressivist enactment thus begins in student groups with the challenge of extending Rousseau's model of ideal education to three specified modern settings: early twentieth-century public schools with large classes and immi-grant populations; today's multicultural classes, including ready Internet access; and a twenty-second-century class setting whose conditions the group could specify. This is already energetic and challenging work. But a bigger surprise awaits, as Chapter 5 has already explained. As the groups ready their answers to present to each other, Rousseau himself shows up, cocky hat and bad French accent and all, making himself in effect the moderator and ques-tioner of the student panels' presentations.

The aim is a vivid, fast-paced, and consistently challenging application of Rousseau's philosophy of education to modern settings—to discern the essentials and adapt them to radically changed worlds. Pedagogically, too, there are new elements: group work, their first in this class (and what is the underlying philosophy of *that*?); the playfulness of my appearance in costume and character (and why not?); and the sudden and insistent mod-ernization of what may seem a classic philosophy—even, as it turns out, to twenty-second-century Mars, where last time an *Emile*-style tutor reappeared as an artificial intelligence. So the session ended with an eighteenth-century philosopher in conversation with a twenty-second-century robot. With a lit-tle prodding, a few suitable props providentially provided, and the inspira-tion of my own appearance in costume, the twenty-second-century student group was even moved to bring the robot onstage. Rousseau, naturally, was both utterly confused and thrilled.

Further progressivist sessions have included an on-the-spot talk show with students role-playing all the major figures we've read so far, plus our university president (this time role-played by a student: many eagerly volunteer) and a few students appearing as themselves, spokespersons for all. Another session is usually a distinctive kind of science laboratory (Box 8.3).

Regularly at this point I also take my Philosophy of Education classes to join the university chorale for a rehearsal. A few students have had some choral experience, most have not, and none of them has considered it as a pedagogy. Yet it is a strikingly Deweyan scenario, or so I argue. One key aspect is that every participant is required to venture something. They have to open their mouths and sing—everyone, constantly. The chorale scenario is also, like almost no classroom, necessarily and energetically cooperative. Everyone's success depends on everyone else succeeding. People have to listen carefully to each other, matching notes and voice tones, while carrying their

BOX 8.3
Reaching for the Moon

Students enter yet another day in a Deweyan classroom to notice a large white Styrofoam ball on a pole in the grass out the window, some distance off. Moon-ish. Today is a day for scientific inquiry, I say, and you can start right now by figuring out how far away that "moon" is.

After a moment some people head for the door. Maybe they can pace it off. Wait, I say, I forgot to mention: You can't leave the room. You're stuck here, like the ancients who figured out the distance to the real moon long before anyone could leave Earth.

Now what? Ideas go up and down. Shortly someone remembers trigonometry—though, until now, they have probably never been invited to use it to make an actual measurement. If you have a right triangle and you know the length of the baseline, measuring the angle on the other end of the baseline allows you to figure the length of the other sides with a simple equation. I give them the equation if they need it.

But how, stuck in the classroom, are they going to measure baselines and angles? Students form teams and puzzle it out. Soon, sometimes with hints, they decide to use their cellphones to take two photos of our little Styrofoam moon from two separate windows of the classroom. The two shots show it in displacement, of course—differently located against the distant background. Students can measure the distance between the two points at which they took snapshots (I bring tape measures)—that's the baseline. Then they figure the angle they need for the trigonometric calculation by overlaying printouts of the two photos and figuring the apparent displacement of the moon in moon diameters, which they can convert into degrees when I tell them the apparent diameter of the moon in degrees. Then they calculate, sometimes getting the real distance within inches.

Good. Now, I say, I want you to figure out the distance to the actual moon.

They stare at me. It seems impossible, only for some expert or someone with a big telescope maybe, just for them to look up, but here I am, asking them to figure it out, themselves, right here and now. Apparently I am quite serious.

So they talk again. Soon they realize that they can use exactly the same method on the real moon. If they take two photos of the moon from different points a known distance apart and at the same time, they can calculate the moon's displacement against the stellar background by overlaying the photos in the same way (again I will tell them the actual

(Continues)

Box 8.3 (*Continued*)

moon's apparent diameter in degrees), and then, once again, it's just a little trigonometry. For the real moon!

They wonder how separate the two photo-points have to be. Could they try triangulating just from two opposite sides of campus? Ideally I'd have them try it and find out for themselves, but in this class we haven't the time, so, no, I answer. Across campus there will be no detectable shift at all. How about if a confederate drives an hour away the next clear night? No. In fact, it's best if you try for . . . several thousand miles.

This sounds impossible again . . . for another five seconds. Then students realize that of course they can mobilize family or other students and friends elsewhere in the country or abroad. Soon they are at it, making contacts and coordinating plans. On the next clear nights, they and their contacts take simultaneous shots of the moon; their contacts e-mail their photos back; student teams equal-size the two photos and coordinate the overlay using background stars (so there need to be some stars in the photos too) and run the numbers.

Not everyone succeeds. The weather may not cooperate: They need a cloudless night sky at the same moment at two widely separated locations. But in the end many do. Some get surprisingly close. They are shocked, proud, and a bit, well, moonstruck.

Debriefing, we look at math anxiety: its causes and forms, including its effects in this scenario. Even with hints and encouragement, and the support of teamwork, more than a few students in my classes close down the minute they realize that the problem before them is trigonometric. What were their own high school math classes like, then? Some make only half-hearted efforts even when they seem to understand the logic, and consequently also go nowhere. Again, why?

Even proficient STEM students, meanwhile, often regard science as a mere collection of facts to be learned. Debriefing, I tell the class that this scenario was initially prompted by a student comment to exactly that effect. What would Dewey say? Science on his view is fundamentally a kind of *inquiry*, even out into space. And it can be *thrilling*, as well as deeply affirming of the power of the inquiring mind. Perhaps this scenario at least gave them a hint of that thrill—for some students, the only time in their entire science education that they were asked to truly *be* scientists, as opposed to simply taking in scientific facts.

Ancient Greek astronomers figured out the distance to the moon more or less in the same way—making simultaneous measurements several thousand miles apart even without precise clocks or cellphones. How did they do that? I leave that question for the class.

own lines. They also have to listen to the director's directions, and the first time, too—again, an unusual demand for many of them. Everyone needs to be on the edge of their seats—or perhaps they are standing with no seats at all.

What if all our classes were like that? Why aren't they?

Critical Pedagogies

Another major segment of the course explores a range of *critical pedagogies*: philosophies of education that consider education as inherently implicated in power relations and often complicit in various forms of social domination, the aim being emancipation instead. We'll return to Freire (1970) for the positive part of his *Pedagogy of the Oppressed*, alongside Belenky, Clinchy, Goldberger, and Tarule's (1986) *Women's Ways of Knowing* and bell hooks's (1994) classic plea, *Teaching to Transgress*.

Women's Ways of Knowing (Belenky et al., 1986) is a close developmental study of women's experiences in higher education, grounding a program for reform in turn. Thus I may make our opening day a workshop to essentially create our own developmental theories. Increasingly large groupings of students are challenged to sequence increasingly large sets of epistemological attitudes—mostly their own, some from the readings—eventually commandeering whole classroom walls to work out and display their systems. Much in line with Dewey as well as the later stages of Belenky and colleagues' (1986) developmental theory, the underlying meta-message is that knowledge is not an already given system. It is not fixed and complete and just presented to students to assimilate, but a construction, a hypothesis, a pattern that someone thought up, like students just found themselves doing on the classroom walls in this enactment. All such constructions remain open to challenge and change as well. Inevitably, students also leave asking where they themselves stand in the schema they have devised and where they might go next.

Teaching to Transgress (hooks, 1994) sets itself against the boundaries of sexism, racism, and classism, as well as against the usual distance that insulates professors' lives and hearts from students' (Box 8.4). For a first enactment, we may meet, with permission and appropriate courtesy, in the one space on campus where Black identity is affirmed and Black heritage at Elon is celebrated. How does this space feel to us, we ask, as mostly White people? Why do we never see these pictures anywhere else? Is what we take to be "normal" campus space just, more accurately, *White*? (Not to mention, as hooks [1994] also calls it, *bourgeois*; e.g., in its restrained model of classroom decorum.) Professor Prudence Layne—friend, colleague, and faculty member who can more or less channel bell hooks—joins us and does so, challenging me, too, to be personal in ways that normally I am not—as if my whole self were not engaged anyway.

BOX 8.4
Come as You Were

One follow-up to the hooks reading is often a "Come as You Were" party, based on a suggestion of sociologist Inge Bell (1999). Students recall or reclaim enough of their family histories that they can come in the garb and with some stories of a grandmother, great-grandfather, or other distant but known ancestor, and also with some food that ancestor would have offered or enjoyed. It's a party: we introduce ourselves, tell our stories, and share our food.

But the feeling is more poignant than festive. Most of us are down-and-out refugees from war, famine, or persecution. Bell (1999) writes of her students' enactments:

> Here is a Chicano student whose family lived in a Chicano neighborhood near the Mexican border for generations. They were former landowners, pushed out when the Anglos grabbed California and reduced the family to the poverty of farm laborers. . . . Here is a young woman who was, herself, born in Taiwan and whose own parents had an arranged marriage. She tells us that it seemed to work about as well as most marriages she sees around her in the United States. Here is a young man whose ancestors were queens of Hawaii. (p. 122)

For my part, this day I am my grandfather Harry Ogoroskin, refugee from Russia's prerevolutionary pogroms, bearing Czarist buckshot in his chest.

The seeming middle-class homogeneity of most of the students dissolves before our eyes, this day, into something much more varied and interesting. It isn't just other people who have an ethnic or a racial identity, hyphenated like "African-American," while the rest of us are just "American." No—all of us have a race; an ethnicity; and varied, endlessly fascinating, and sometimes tortured backgrounds. All of us could be said to have hyphenated identities, whether we embrace them or not. Some of my students will reclaim their "Irish-American" background for the day, their ancestors come here fleeing the potato famine as families starved back home, not even considered White by many of their new countrymen. Here are Black students whose ancestors somehow survived the brutality of enslavement and crossed the ocean like so many cattle in the holds of slave ships—and whose histories accordingly were lost, even deliberately destroyed, before they even arrived. Here are Native Americans, the only ones who can truly claim "American" without a hyphen.

Once a couple of students in a class came as their great-great-grand-fathers only to discover that not only immigrated to America on the same ship from Germany but also ended up in the same steel mill in Bethlehem, Pennsylvania. (Both families had very thorough records!) Almost certainly they knew each other back in 1885. Perhaps they were friends. Now they embrace each other again, scruffy, astonished, overcome, in the person of their great-great-grandchildren, 130 years later, in a university classroom in North Carolina.

We are in this room full-fleshed, for once, all voices heard and all voices equal. hooks (1994) insists that "accepting the decentering of the West globally, embracing multiculturalism, compels educators to focus attention on the issue of voice. Who speaks? Who listens? And why?" (p. 40). This too is *education*!

Liberatory Pedagogies

Finally, we turn to philosophies of education that question education as such at deeper and systematically more radical levels. Inge Bell's (1999) concern is with *wisdom*, which she argues is not at all the same thing as knowledge. In fact, she says, it may well be at odds with knowledge. How much of your education right now, she asks, brings you into the presence of joy or makes you "more, balanced, alert, effective" (Bell, 1999, p. 78)? If the answer is not much, then how come? How could we all do better in this way?

Certain enactments now address this question. We undertake a walking meditation, for one: the slowest possible walk, across the quad in front of our class building, barefoot maybe, on some beautiful spring morning. It takes an hour, maybe, to go 100 feet. Students feel self-conscious and silly for the first 10 minutes. After that, usually, they are just present to the birds or the grass beneath their feet. It's a powerful thing to do—it can carry you away. When we talk later, someone tells us that she fell in love with the beauty of our campus on her first visit—that's why she came—but today was the first time since then that she felt she'd really seen that beauty again. By now she's crying. How can we walk through all of this and miss it? Why, the students ask, was everyone else walking so *fast*? Like us too, all the rest of the time, someone adds. All this wonder, and we walk through it like overwound wind-up toys.

In other iterations of the course, we have spent a day and a night at a local Zen monastery, getting a glimpse of what truly deep silence can feel like. Or a week without TV. Or, reading Foster's (1989) *The Book of the Vision Quest*, we may undertake our own mini-quests, seeking out affinity creatures from beyond the human sphere and eventually bringing them back into a fire circle ceremony. Here we edge out beyond the human world—but more on that in the next chapter.

Most of the term we look at either traditional apologists for schools or various philosophical reformers, but at the end we come to figures who are explicitly, and shockingly, against anything like schools as we know them. In *Instead of Education*, John Holt (1976/2004) derides the idea of "getting learning" as if it were like getting a disease or a shot (I had English last year, so now I'm immune!). The very fact that school is compulsory, he argues, undercuts the possibility that it can liberate. Instead it becomes a mechanism of enforcing conformity and dullness. "Free schools" are no answer either—they are still jails, just with fewer rules and nicer keepers.

Holt (1976/2004) stresses that freely chosen interactions must be reciprocal and depend on students' initiative rather than structural incentives of school. I try to create enactments to match. If it is spring, maybe we go on a picnic or otherwise meet in some inviting indoor space that is open to others, too. Students may bring musical instruments, food, games. Then interesting outsiders show up—such as local "Unschoolers," parents and their children who practice what Holt preaches (not homeschoolers either, by the way, who often just reproduce school at home). They are simply present, joining in whatever may happen, if students want to talk or do something else together (Williams, 2017). I pointedly just hang out and talk, too. Certain opportunities are here; will they discover them? What will they make of them?

Some students think this is just an occasion to take it easy and relax. And of course, to be consistent, relaxing into the scene is certainly one possible response. Others keep wondering whether "something is going to happen." They wait. More forward students may interview a homeschooler or a parent—making something of the opportunity before them. Meanwhile other things may be going on, only visible through Holt's glasses. In the last picnic, my students realized only after the fact that one of the teenage homeschoolers had taken the opportunity to check them out, big time: to try to figure out college, to which otherwise she hadn't had a lot of exposure. They were mostly waiting for something to happen, but *she* took a striking initiative. What might this say about her (un)schooling versus theirs? And about what this enactment was intended to offer?

Another day a worksheet may ask students to name two or three things they would really love to learn and/or places they would like to go, or the like. What is your dream? What do you really want to do in your life? The worksheet then asks them to research a rough plan, along with a light budget, for learning/doing this on their own—outside of school (Wimsatt, 1998)—and to find at least two specific contacts that can help them put their plan into effect right now. Detail the information, I say. Write down the phone numbers. Bookmark websites.

At the end, they try to give me their worksheets, like good students turning in their work. No thank you, I reply—I don't need them, but you do. Another shocking moment. You might (or might not) have treated this as an academic exercise, I say, but what you actually did was draw a roadmap for your own liberation. You could go off right now and make those calls. So why don't you do it? Really, why not? Answer that question and at least you have come to grips with Holt (Box 8.5).

BOX 8.5
No Show!?

If the course's offering of enactments start entirely dominated by the professor (e.g., in the lecture), then the logical polar opposite must be . . . what? For the final Holt (1976/2004) enactment, and usually the last for this class, I simply don't show up.

I hide out, in fact. Sometimes I am not even on campus. Students can't just come to my office and ask what is happening. It makes a scary and fascinating moment for everyone (me too) and worth every bit of "lost" class time, once they realize that I am actually nowhere to be found *on purpose.* Oh my God. What are they to do?

What *do* they do, we ask in the most astonished of debriefs—and why? They could have class by themselves, of course, and there usually is plenty to do. Still, clearly Holt would consider this just a form of inertia. What else is possible? Some students just leave—after debating how long they need to wait before hightailing it. (Most universities even have rules about this—and what are the presuppositions of *that*, my friends? This too is typically an impassioned theme in debrief.) My favorites are students who take the occasion to get completely out of school: going off and flying a kite or jamming or cooking a surprise feast for their lovers. Still, these change nothing fundamental. Real liberation, many argue in debrief, takes more than students occasionally getting more space within school. Such as . . . what?

Parting Shots

This is only a sampling of the pedagogical scenarios I have staged over the years. Still, by now I am sure that you can see why I hold that a Philosophy of Pedagogy course is not only teachable but also *superlatively* teachable as an Impresario with a Scenario. The very theme of the course allows me to stage a wide variety of scenarios, wholesale and unreservedly, because here it is essential to make the staging visible, and the more highlighted and even exaggerated, the better. I stage each pedagogy transparently, then, even flamboyantly, and unpredictably—just for starters, the fact that every single day is different, usually dramatically different, is profoundly intriguing and appealing all by itself—so as to celebrate the occasion to recognize and articulate each pedagogy's underlying assumptions, as well as to criticize them, by themselves and by way of contrast to others that the course also enacts.

Sometimes students are surprised to hear, at the start of the course, that there even *are* 20 or 25 distinct pedagogies. Actually, of course, there are a great many more. Why they (or we) don't know this already is a good question. Then, as the course enacts some of those pedagogies, it may take a few iterations to get the point: to recognize that the staging is posing them as *questions*. Even so, the too-familiar, too-literal, too-close view never quite entirely goes away. It is not easy to unlearn the old habit of just accepting whatever comes along pedagogically, especially when it is almost always the same old thing over and over again. In this class, a new kind of awareness generally does dawn for the students, and that is the most vital point.

The course brings the theme home from the opposite direction as well. The final project for each student is to design their own school or other educational alternative, starting with their philosophies and ending with a physical and pedagogical realization that can be presented to the class as a whole. On occasion, we have also redesigned a classroom on our own campus—again looking at even the physical layout and furnishings of a classroom as an embodied philosophy of education.

Again, that this is actually a *question* is a key recognition. To recognize that every pedagogy is a philosophy in action, I argue, is to recognize, inescapably and vividly, that pedagogies—like classrooms and every other practice and institution in school and indeed beyond—are open-ended, unfinished, continuously being remade, and hugely varied in the contemporary world and even in our own institution. Often, also, those pedagogies bring forth the kinds of personalities and pedagogical habits that they begin by positing (Bottenberg, 2015). They can be a kind of self-fulfilling prophecy—which is a recognition that actually widens the range of real possibilities (Weston, 1996a). What students are like, or become, under one kind of pedagogy is not necessarily what they become under others. Thus the real range of alternatives is far broader than we usually think, and beyond them in turn there may be far better alternatives yet awaiting our imagination and our courage. The one scenario that rules them all is, finally, a scenario of *freedom*.

9

UNDER THE OPEN SKIES

The fundamental scenario of my environmental courses is *rejoining the world*. Cast this way, the theme may sound intellectual, but it must be realized in a much more personal and sensory way. To truly know that the world is vastly bigger than we are, we must *feel* it as such, and not just passingly either. To truly know that we nonetheless have a home in the world, we must at least catch a glimpse, beyond the usual ignorance and stereotype and fear, of what it would be like to feel at home in it. This realization is both unsettling and deeply reassuring and grounding, and I believe it is one of the most profound and powerful offerings I can make to students. Best of all, I can only make it by rejoining the world—with them—myself.

We try in small ways close to home. When my Environmental Ethics and Environmental Visions classes move to the campus garden or university farm, at least for that time we manifestly enter the larger living world, which is after all our theme. Special dispensation to snack on the tomatoes or beans drives it home—we eat right from the land.

A fair number of my students have never actually camped out, and many more may have camped out only as a social experience. So we camp out together too, when we can, and also try for good stretches of solitude. Yet another enactment in my Philosophy of Education class may be an evening and a night alone in the woods (I and others there, but at a distance, for reassurance), cellphones and laptops back at school, sometimes with special attention to what other beings or Earth elements manifest themselves in the spaces thereby opened up (Foster, 1989). Here we *live* the deepest meaning of environmental studies: that the world *is* vastly larger than the thoroughly

Portions of this chapter also appear in my essay "Moments of Grace," in Steven Cahn, Alexandra Bradner, and Andrew Mills, (Editors), *Philosophers in the Classroom: Essays on Teaching* (Hackett, 2018).

anthropocentric and anthropocentrized cocoon in which we spend most of our time—and likely vastly more fabulous as well (Weston, 1994, 1996b, 2003).

For most of us, though, it may take much longer to feel the beginnings of a real shift in perception—to awaken into the larger world, to the winds and weather and the great rhythm of light and dark, to the creatures and the powers of place. For original peoples, of course, it took a lifetime—or rather, it just was life. Where enough of original culture remains to offer even a glimpse of the world in that key, there is still no other way that they can imagine wanting to live. Native peoples around the world still seek the constant company and presence of the other-than-human, on all scales. To them, the whole world is alive, and each place, as the magician–philosopher David Abram puts it (1996), has its own more-than-human state of mind. *More* than human: that is, it exceeds the human in multitudinous directions, yet we are part of it too.

Into the Bush

In 2004, Patsy Hallen, Australian teacher–activist–writer–dreamer, invited me to co-teach her Radical Eco-Philosophy course out of Perth's Murdoch University, which she organizes around 2 long backpack trips into the out-back. Thus in my 50th year I found myself quite literally all the way around the world from my Carolina home, traipsing overland with adult students, master's-level mostly, in their 20s and 30s, from all over the world—through the red desert and along the shores of the tumultuous Southern Ocean, sleeping for weeks under the shimmering unfamiliar stars, and later car-camping with my family up and down the west coast and among the great monadnocks of the Red Centre and in the rainforests of the Northern Territory.

Something is going on out there. This group of co-adventurers felt it especially strongly at the awakening of the Earth at dawn in the bush. The fast-shifting clouds, the countless purposeful insects, the lilting birds, the last full exhale of the soils' pores before the coming heat of the day, the quizzical but poised rocks—there is something immense and powerful in that land, seemingly just out of reach, even a hint of numinous more-than-human fellow-travelers.

Australian Aboriginal peoples speak evocatively of Dreamtimes. With permission, we followed some of their tracks through the land, winding our way between billabongs and tingle trees, meeting for talk or sometimes more or less silent wonder under the wide-open skies, joined by sea eagles or kangaroos on occasion. Our nights were filigreed by vivid and unprecedented dreams, our days sustained both the ongoing multiple human dialogues that wove through our walkabouts and constant time "alone"—meaning not with other humans but tuned to the countless other beings and presences in a desert landscape that at first seemed featureless and barren.

We are *never* "alone," Aboriginal people say. The whole world is alive, as an entirety and in all its parts (Wren, Jackson, Morris, Geddes, Tlen, & Kassi, 1996). From this perspective the question of ethics seems far too limited, almost arid—only a formal articulation of something far deeper: a felt sense of belonging (Leopold, 1949).

To the Center of Things

Co-adventuring like this out on the edge of hyperanthropocentrized modernity (Weston, 1991b) is to come to the very *center* of the world if one looks at things from a larger-than-human perspective. Thus a 2006 and 2007 summer class out of Royal Roads University in Victoria, British Columbia, part of a master's-level curriculum in environmental education and communication overseen by Professor Rick Kool, took Rick and me and 20 students, mostly Canadian environmental organizers or teachers themselves, up Vancouver Island to Tofino in vans. From there we climbed aboard a small boat that services mostly logging operations up that roadless, precipitous, primeval coast and its islands to drop us at a site called Cougar Annie's Garden—once the homestead of a legendary though problematic local figure (that's "Annie"), now being restored as a residential study facility on temperate rainforests as well as a historical site, part of Hesquiaht First Nation traditional land.

There we lived for a week in small cabins up the mountainsides, no electricity, no contact with the outside world, just the forest and the bay, grizzlies foraging by day and the dance of the nebulae at night. We took turns doing meals and between sessions hiked for miles along logging roads and Hesquiaht trails, as well as the cedar plank-ways and occasional shrines or other structures being built onsite as a labor of love by the current owner and main resident, winding between 800-year-old trees and, incongruously, hothouse-type flowers from bulbs that the eponymous Annie used to grow for sale.

Hobbitty little outhouses invited us to help fertilize semi-wild gardens below, down the steep mountain slopes while we gazed through ornately crafted windows dozens of miles across the bay. We swam in a small and spectacularly frigid lake behind the site with the mysterious Whale Rock in the middle—in native lore, a site of great power—that showed itself, with exquisite delicacy, to only a few of us, just as the ancient stories, credited by none of us at first, told us it would. Again we were living and learning—no real distinction—in the midst of a vastly larger world: this time the whole numinous Pacific Northwest surround, the fjords and tumbling waters of the west coast of Vancouver Island, at the edge of a familiar world but at the very center of another. It was not "remote" at all—quite the contrary. The grand scenario was immersion, a continuously unfolding encounter, in an uncompromisingly larger-than-human frame.

Classes and small study groups met constantly on the decks, in a small half-open chapel near the lake, or in the gardens. Students worked on a sign-posting project for one of Rick's classes (how do you present such a site—diplomatically, informatively, provocatively, honestly?). For mine, the theme was storied modes of inhabitation or co-presence, as I called them—one mode of "environmental communication," surely, or what my late friend and wilderness companion Jim Cheney (1989) called "ethics as bioregional narrative" (p. 117). Out loud as well as outside, we read the works of the Haida Gwaii storyteller Skaay (John Sky) of the Qquuna Qiighawaay, a long Sapsucker narrative in particular (Skaay, 2002), while savoring the voice of the land itself under its own open sky and surging waters, the mewling and drumming sapsuckers themselves right around us.

I invited the students to take the next step too. One of the main projects for my class that week was for each participant to find (or be found *by*) what I called a *Storied Token* of the place: some natural being or object or specific process, emblematic of the place, around which both their own human and the place's more-than-human stories might crystallize. Of course, the Token had to show itself in the first place. Tokens and their stories may come to each of you in specific ways, I said: Your first task is chiefly to be open to them. This is environmental communication as well, but in a far more ancient and mysterious mode than we have learned to expect.

Students responded with immense heartfulness and variety. Days were spent preparing, feeling their ways back into the natural world, attending to the solicitations, as Abram puts it, of specific more-than-human Others right around us. We finally spoke of them together on our last long late-summer afternoon before heading back to "civilization." Some Tokens were small pieces of wood, invoking the tree elders, scraps maybe from the boardwalks whose rough waviness brought out a certain quirky and fleeting magic in the place at the same time, counterpoint to the gravity and immensity of the trees. One Lebanese woman linked the massive ancient cedars of this faraway temperate rainforest to the legendary cedars of her homeland—now reduced by millennia of depredations to a few small plots, slowly regenerating in the hearts of the people as well as tenaciously on the eroded hillsides.

Another participant brought us a set of nested crab shells and spoke of molting—shell-shifting—as lifestory, both literally and as metaphor. When she finished, her friends in the class, knowing her own lifestory, spontaneously stood up and honored her as doing the same thing. She's beaming and sobbing at the same time. Another brought a mini-version of the Whale Rock. She had not seen it in the lake herself, she tells us, but in the very midst of her irritation—it was going to hide from all the women, *really?*—she decided that the rock was actually manifesting itself to her in another way, as something she could carry with her and warm with her own body's warmth.

I brought my own Storied Token, a little totem that came to me on a previous kayak trip in this region: an oyster shell that welded itself to a small rock, the ensemble, held at the right angle, irresistibly bringing to mind the wing of the Winged Victory, the famed although still mysterious Samothracian (fragment of a) monument now in the Louvre. A winged rock, then, quite literally. It flew home with me from my previous trip and flew back for this one. More allegorically, it is a symbol, to me, of how the whole spirit of the place, literally the fusion of life and rock, itself can take flight in our own imaginations and, yes, our environmental communications. Ancient stories tell us that rocks are alive—they just move at a different tempo, but they do indeed move: all over the surface (by water, by ice, by us) and by plate (think tectonics), up and down, into crust and mantle; and even through space. This one . . . flies.

Affinity Beings

As an exercise in many of my classes—in fact, whenever I can find a way to include it—I ask my students to consider the animals, places, or forces of nature with which they identify and whose power or presence they feel they may share in some way. Many name specific animals: they become Cat or Dog, Dragonfly, Elephant, Stingray, Deer. A runner may be Cheetah. Some pick favorite places, places that speak to them, like Beach, or specific beaches. Some are Waves, there is the occasional Sycamore or Oak, sometimes Wind or Rain or Lightning or Sun. One African American student at heavily White Elon declared herself Chameleon. A partly Native American student was Buffalo. In his dreams he becomes a buffalo, runs with his fellows, and can ask them to take him other places or into other identities in turn. And unlike most students, he did not choose this affinity being: It was given from birth, his clan animal.

Actually, I say, no one should think that they are doing all the choosing. As with the Storied Tokens, there is a more of a dance here. It is at least as true that other beings/powers choose *you*. Are there animals, I ask, that regularly come to you, in dreams or awake? Perhaps you have even had specific encounters, numinous or electrifying, that stay with you (Weston, 2014).

Of course it is possible to pick an affinity being in a superficial way. Nonetheless, there turns out to be a kind of magic in opening this door even a crack. I have found repeatedly that the beings with whom my students embrace affinities show up in unprecedented numbers and in striking ways—across our paths, on the Internet, in our dreams. I had not seen rabbits for years on campus until one of my first-years declared herself Rabbit one spring. Within days we were stumbling over them. Another in the same class was Shark, partly on account of a face-to-face diving encounter. Long after the class was over I was still sending him links to shark films that would not stop turning up on my electronic mailing lists. Yet another was Dragonfly, and what followed was the summer of, of course, dragonflies.

Of course it may be said that dragonflies and rabbits and wind and all the rest are always around anyway, and we just notice them more when we or someone else identifies (with) them. It is true: They are always there. But why is this itself not the magic? Maybe the greater task is to learn receptivity and welcome to more beings more of the time. It is also arguable that this kind of welcome may in turn have consequences in the world. Why wouldn't creatures and other spirits be more apt to come to those who long and look for them? Part of the lesson is that others beyond the human can be at least as unpredictable, surprising, provocative, and enigmatic as we ourselves. To expect otherwise is another way of missing the point (Mathews, 2005).

Usually my classes invoke our other-than-human affinities outside, around a fire if possible—fire being a presence too, of course. The results may be uncanny. After a Fire Circle for our co-taught Philosophy of Education class—for the ritual invocation of other-than-human identity is "education," too—my colleague Frances Bottenberg wrote a striking note:

> I actually had an eerie sense that [students'] faces and postures took on something of their animal (or plant or elemental) alter-egos when they began to speak about their connections to their totems . . . . Bear had a growl in his voice I hadn't noticed before . . . . Cat seemed calmly twitchy like cats are, ready to spring or lounge at the drop of a hat . . . . The way Otter moved her hands as she talked reminded me of the way otters play with objects in the water, turning them over and over . . . . Cloud was always glancing up, maybe taking all this lightly, as if from above . . . . Shark's teeth glinted, especially when she said she "always follows the blood"! Oh, and of course there was kindly but stern Owl, so owl-awkward trying to read his poem with one eye, and then the other . . . . I could list more (F. Bottenberg, personal communication, 2013).

One first-year class met for our council at dusk around an off-campus fire pit. Storms were predicted—a major front was coming through—and the evening skies were gray, but we gathered outside anyway, stoked up the fire, and began to speak. Each participant offered gifts as well as warnings to the others. Turtle offered his patience, deliberateness, precisely the ability to go slow. Moose, his gangliness—elegance, to a Moose. Shark, the reminder that the world's most self-congratulatory animal (guess who) needs to seriously temper his arrogance in the waters. Sun offered eternal light.

Between the circle speakers, the crickets and the frogs spoke up. We gave them their turns too, waiting until they paused for Owl (that was me, in my owl-head costume and academic gown—my personal affinity being is Daddy Longlegs, but philosophy's disciplinary totem is the owl) to sound the drum for the next student speaker.

We made it all the way around. At the end, Owl made a toast to the class. It was our final meeting, and the last class of the year for most of the students, the very end of their first year of college. I offered them best wishes for the summer. As I raised my paper cup at the end, just after my last word, came the first peal of Thunder. A startling grace note, perfectly timed. A Thunderous Amen.

The students drank their sparkling cider. Now it really was time to say goodbye. Shedding owl head, I invited them to fill their cups in their imagination with whatever they wanted to leave behind from this first year of college, as well as whatever part of their affinity being they now wanted to give back to the world—and then to throw their "full cups" into the fire. In they went—cautiously, angrily, reluctantly, each student in his or her own way.

The flames leapt up one last time. But by now the lightning was close and leaping, too. The winds were lifting (there is no other word for it), and we could hear the rain not so far off. Rushed embraces. Have a great summer. Then they sprinted across the woods for their cars—or jumped or galloped or crawled or flew, only half returned to human. In the next flash of lightning I had the distinct apparition of an animal stampede. Thunder followed on top of it. Then, within half a minute, it was pouring, the start of a solid day of desperately needed hard rain.

Lakota philosopher Vine Deloria (2002) writes about how Europeans consistently misunderstand Native people's rain dances as means of manipulating or producing rain. Observers turned cynical when they realized that the shamans only began rain dances when it appears that rain was in the offing anyway. But of course, replies Deloria. The function of the rain dance is not to produce rain but, as he puts it, to "participate in the emerging event" (p. 50). Wedding dances don't produce weddings, do they? That is why you only dance when the rain is practically upon you. So this, so to say, was our Thunder dance—our participation in a remarkably thunderous emerging event.

The Heron

Sometimes the Environmental Visions course meets at the Lodge, a nearby former church camp with a lake, a few shelters, a building with a fireplace for when it is too cold to meet outside, and large grassy areas where we can sit in the sun on blankets in a circle. Most of all it offers relative quiet, the chance to be outside without distraction, with alert senses for once, in good company with the always-active winds, the turkey vultures wafting about and checking us out along with the occasional hawk and chittery kingfisher, much sun and the falling leaves, and, at the start of one especially memorable fall term, lots of rain and thunderstorms as a succession of hurricanes brushed by. We spent most of our first few weeks meeting in the shelters.

That fall we declared our affinities around a smoky bonfire on a cool afternoon. Windy, too, with low clouds scudding by. Smoke blew everywhere, and there was a lot of it, so we all went to our next classes smelling like we'd been camping all week. That year it turned out I had Rain, Dolphin, Jaguar (a Mexican woman with Huichol roots, whose distant shamanic ancestors might well have been jaguars too), Salmon, Bear, and many others.

We also had Great Blue Heron. As it happened, we had seen a Great Blue at the lake below the Lodge, once, early in the term. But the heron had never been back, although one end of the lake seems like fine heron feeding-ground. Still, the heron's appearance that day was part of the reason D chose it for her affinity being, I think. The other part was some kind of quiet grace, a body that could be ungainly but in fact had an unmatched elegance; and a quickness too. Long periods of utter stillness punctuated by the lighting strike of the beak. Imagine the inner life.

Then came the day that D, who was also Great Blue Heron, was to present her term project on animal–animal, cross-species communication. We'd spoken often of human–animal communication, but she wanted to go several steps further, to look at a bigger picture. Usually she'd been very quiet and did not say much, although she was a perceptive and animated person when she got going. Now she had just begun to speak, maybe half a sentence, already with that same animation and self-possession. Everyone sat up a bit straighter and smiled.

D was sitting with her back to the lake. But now just as quickly our eyes were drawn up and behind her. Suddenly a shadow was floating by to her right and then spiraling down toward the water. Today of all days, this exact moment of all moments, Great Blue came back.

She floated down to the brilliantly sunlit end of the lake, in full view, the deeper part where feeding is (I'd think) not so good, and landed in the most graceful way right in the brightest sun. There she stood for a minute, looking us over and showing herself just enough, and then just as elegantly took back off, skimmed the water down to the other end of the lake, landed and proceeded to hunt up the stream and out of sight.

We were stunned into silence. No missing the magic here. I seriously wanted to end class right there, despite just having begun. What could you do after that? It was D's day, though, and she had a lot to say. So after a time we collected ourselves and began to speak again, haltingly and unwillingly, for in a certain way everything had already been said. We came back to that Visit in every reflection on the class for the rest of the term. No one who experienced that moment could have any doubts that animals "communicate," indeed in a far deeper way than any one of us, even D herself, had yet named or even imagined. Great Blue's Return was something primal, a brief upwelling of a communicative flow far more powerful than language itself, something for which our only available word may once again be "magic" but that hints at far deeper receptivities and harmonies possible in the larger world.

Like the Daddy Longlegs that keep turning up in my tents and on my shoulders, Herons actually keep coming to my classes—always, strikingly, in the mode of punctuation or emphasis, opening or closing some process, though never again as such epiphanies as on D's day. Of course, as Deloria (2002) says, you have to be open to them in that way. And for starters, obviously, you have to be outside. Again, again, again: The natural world is not some kind of stage scenery or piece of clockwork—not if we "participate in the process." Here there can be immense gifts out of pure generosity, hints of pervasive unseen flows, a deeply felt sense that the whole world really *is* alive.

I am thrilled for my students when such moments come. And for myself. In the end, every teacherly self-consciousness gives way before awe.

REFERENCES

Abrahamson, S. (1997). Good planning is not enough. In D. Boud & G. Feletti (Eds.), *The challenge of problem-based learning* (2nd ed., pp. 53–57). London, UK: Kogan Page.

Abram, D. (1996). *The spell of the sensuous: Language and perception in a more than human world.* New York, NY: Pantheon.

Ainger, M. (2002). *Gilbert and Sullivan: A dual biography.* Oxford, UK: Oxford University Press.

Amundsen, C., Saroyan, A., & Frankman, M. (1996). Changing methods and metaphors: A case study of growth in university teaching. *Journal on Excellence in College Teaching, 7*(3), 3–42.

Andersen, E., & Schiano, B. (2014). *Teaching with cases: A practical guide.* Cambridge, MA: Harvard Business Review Press.

Anderson, D., Mcguire, F., & Cory, L. (2011). The first day: It only happens once. *Teaching in Higher Education, 16*(3), 292–303.

Annerino, J. (1999). *Apache: Sacred path to womanhood.* New York, NY: Marlowe & Company.

Appleman, P. (2001). *Darwin* (3rd ed.). New York, NY: Norton Critical Edition.

Armstrong, E. (1997). A hybrid model of problem-based learning. In D. Boud & G. Feletti (Eds.), *The challenge of problem-based learning* (2nd ed., pp. 137–150). London, UK: Kogan Page.

Artaud, A. (1988). For the theater and its double. In S. Sontag (Ed.), *Antonin Artaud: Selected writings* (pp. 242–251). Berkeley, CA: University of California Press.

Asal, V. (2005). Playing games with international relations. *International Studies Perspectives, 6,* 359–373.

Asal, V., & Blake, E. (2006). Creating simulations for political science education. *Journal of Political Science Education, 2,* 1–18.

Auman, C. (2011). Using simulation games to increase student and instructor engagement. *College Teaching, 59*(4), 154–161.

Bain, H., & Hershey, J. (1971). Geology on the moon. *Engineering and Science 35.* Retrieved from http://calteches.library.caltech.edu/301/1/moon.pdf

Bajak, A. (2014). *Lectures aren't just boring, they're ineffective, too, study finds.* Retrieved from http://www.sciencemag.org/news/2014/05/lectures-arent-just-boring-theyre-ineffective-too-study-finds

Barbour, C., & Barbour, N. H. (1997). *Families, schools, and communities.* Englewood Cliffs, NJ: Merrill/Prentice-Hall.

Barkley, E. (2010). *Student engagement techniques: A handbook for college faculty.* San Francisco, CA: Jossey-Bass.

Barnes, L., Christensen, R., & Hansen, A. (1994). *Teaching and the case method.* Cambridge, MA: Harvard Business School Press.

Barr, R., & Tagg, J. (1995). From teaching to learning: A new paradigm for undergraduate education. *Change, 27,* 6.

Barrows, H. (1996). Problem-based learning in medicine and beyond: A brief overview. *New Directions for Teaching and Learning, 68,* 3–12.

Belenky, M. F., Clinchy, B. M., Goldberger, N. R., & Tarule, J. M. (1986). *Women's ways of knowing.* New York, NY: Basic Books.

Bell, I. (1999). *This book is not required.* Newbury Park, CA: Pine Forge Press.

Bent, H. (1970). Why lecture? *Pure and Applied Chemistry, 22,* 23–28.

Bergmann, F. (1981). *On being free.* Notre Dame, IN: Notre Dame University Press.

Bergmann, J., & Sams, A. (2012). *Flip your classroom.* Washington DC: International Society for Technology in Education.

Berk, R. A., & Trieber, R. H. (2009). Whose classroom is it anyway? Improvisation as a teaching tool. *Journal on Excellence in College Teaching, 20*(3), 29–60.

Bernstein, J., & Meizlish, D. (2003). Becoming Congress: A longitudinal study of the civic engagement implications of a classroom simulation. *Simulation and Gaming, 34*(2), 198–219.

Big List of Reacting Games. (2017). Retrieved from https://docs.google.com/spreadsheets/d/1GkDM2eHFRl5zv0NA7tz6HZKRsKum603sl8k343MFXsc/pub?output=html

Birch, T. (1993). Moral considerability and universal consideration. *Environmental Ethics, 15*(4), 313–332.

Black, H. (1983). *Scotland Yard photo crimes from the files of Inspector Black.* New York, NY: Simon and Schuster.

Blackburn, R. T., Pellino, G. R., Boberg, A., & O'Connell, C. (1980). Are instructional improvement programs off target? *Current Issues in Higher Education, 2*(1), 32–48.

Blecha, B., & Haynes, B. (2017). *Teaching with simulations.* Science Education Resource Center (SERC) portal. Retrieved from http://serc.carleton.edu/sp/library/simulations/examples.html

Bligh, D. (2000). *What's the use of lectures?* San Francisco, CA: Jossey-Bass.

Boal, A. (2000). *Theater of the oppressed: New edition.* London, UK: Pluto Press.

Bonwell, C. C., & Eison, J. A. (1991). *Active learning: Creating excitement in the classroom* (ASHE–ERIC Higher Education Rep. No. 1). Washington DC: The George Washington University School of Education and Human Development.

Bottenberg, F. (2015). Power-sharing in the philosophy classroom. *American Association of Philosophy Teachers Studies in Pedagogy.* Retrieved from https://www.pdcnet.org/pdc/bvdb.nsf/purchase?openform&fp=aaptstudies&id=aaptstudies_2015_0001_0033_0046

Boud, D., & Feletti, G. (Eds.). (1997). *The challenge of problem-based learning* (2nd ed.). London, UK: Kogan Page.

Bragg, E., & Rosenhek, R. (1998). *The Council of All Beings workshop manual: A step by step guide.* Retrieved from http://www.rainforestinfo.org.au/deep-eco/cabcont.htm

Bransford, J., Brown, A., & Cocking, R. (Eds.). (2000). *How people learn: Brain, mind, experience, and school.* Washington, DC: National Academy Press.

Burgan, M. (2006). In defense of lecturing. *Change, 38(6)*, 30–34.

Burgess, H., & Taylor, I. (2000). From university teacher to learning coordinator: Faculty roles in problem-based learning. *Journal in Excellence in College Teaching, 11(2&3)*, 83–96.

Burke, B. A. (1995). Writing in beginning chemistry courses: Personalizing the Periodic Table with student creativity. *Journal of College Science Teaching, 24(5)*, 341–345.

Burke, L. A., & Ray, R (2008). Re-setting the concentration levels of students in higher education: An exploratory study. *Teaching in Higher Education, 12(1)*, 119–133.

Burns, A. C., & Gentry, J. W. (1998). Motivating students to engage in experiential learning: A tension-to-learn theory. *Simulation and Gaming, 29(2)*, 133–151.

Burns, R. A. (1985, May). *Information impact and factors affecting recall.* Paper presented at the annual national conference on Teaching Excellence and Conference of Administrators, Austin, TX. (ERIC Document Reproduction Service No. ED 258 639).

Buskist, W., Cush, D., & DeGrandpre, R. J. (1991). The life and times of PSI. *Journal of Behavioral Education, 1(2)*, 215–234.

Cahill, A., & Bloch-Schulman, S. (2012). Argumentation step-by-step: Learning critical thinking through deliberate practice. *Teaching Philosophy 35(1)*, 41–62.

Carlson, S. (2005). The net generation goes to college. *Chronicle of Higher Education, 52(7)*, A34.

Carnes, M. (2014). *Minds on fire.* Cambridge, MA: Harvard University Press.

Caspary, W. (1991). Ethical deliberation as dramatic rehearsal: John Dewey's theory. *Educational Theory, 47*, 2.

Cheney, J. (1989). Postmodern environmental ethics: Ethics as bioregional narrative. *Environmental Ethics, 11*, 117–134.

Cheney, J., & Weston, A. (1999). Environmental ethics as environmental etiquette: Toward an ethics-based epistemology in environmental philosophy. *Environmental Ethics, 21*, 115–134.

Cherif, A. A., Adams, G. E., & Cannon, C. E. (1997). Nonconventional methods in teaching matter, atoms, molecules & the Periodic Table for nonmajor students. *The American Biology Teacher, 59(7)*, 428–438.

Christenson, S., Reschly, A., & Wylie, C. (Eds.). (2012). *Handbook of research on student engagement.* New York, NY: Springer.

Clark, C. (2001). Lost in the melee. In P. Schwartz, S. Mennin, & G. Webb (Eds.), *Problem-based learning: Case studies, experience, and practice* (pp. 34–39). Sterling, VA: Stylus.

Clark, R. (2013). *Scenario-based e-learning: Evidence-based guidelines for online workforce learning.* San Francisco, CA: Pfeiffer.

Cocconi, G., & Morrison, P. (1959). Searching for interstellar communications. *Nature, 184(4690)*, 844–846.

Corcoran, T., & Allen, B. (1994). Mastering the elements. *The Science Teacher*, *61*(9), 44–47.

Costello, M. L., & Brunner, P. W. (2008). Helping students adapt to an empowered classroom. *Journal on Excellence in College Teaching*, *19*(1), 63–79.

Cowan, J. (1998). *On becoming an innovative teacher*. Buckingham, UK: Open University Press.

Cranton, P. (1998). *No one way: Teaching and learning in higher education*. Toronto, Canada: Wall & Emerson.

Crawford, C., Gordon, S., Nicholas, J., & Prosser, M. (1998). Qualitatively different experiences of learning mathematics at university. *Learning and Instruction*, *8*(5), 455–468.

Crider, A. (2015). Final exams or epic finales? *Chronicle of Higher Education* online. Retrieved from https://www.chronicle.com/article/Final-Exams-or-Epic-Finales/231871

Crider, A., & Weston, A. (2012). Experiential education on the edge: SETI activities for the college classroom. *Astronomy Education Review* 11. Retrieved from http://aer.aas.org/resource/1/aerscz/v11/i1/p010202_s1

Crossley-Frolick, K. A. (2010). Beyond Model UN: Simulating multi-level, multi-author diplomacy using the Millennium Goals. *International Studies Perspectives*, *11*, 184–201.

Csikszentmihalyi, M. (1996). *Creativity: Flow and the psychology of discovery and innovation*. New York, NY: Harper.

Dahlgren, M. A., Fenwick, T., & Hopwood, N. (2016). Theorising simulation in higher education: Difficulty for learners as an emergent phenomenon. *Teaching in Higher Education*, *21*(6), 613–627.

Darwin, C. (1845/2001). The Galapagos archipelago, from *The voyage of the Beagle*. In P. Appleman (Ed.), *Darwin* (3rd ed., pp. 67–91). New York, NY: Norton Critical Edition.

Darwin, C. (1859/2001). Recapitulation and conclusion, from On *the origin of species*. In P. Appleman (Ed.), *Darwin* (3rd ed., pp. 158–174). New York, NY: Norton Critical Edition.

Davis, R. H., & Alexander, L. T. (1977). *The lecture method: Guides for the improvement of instruction in higher education* (No. 5). Lansing, MI: Michigan State University Press.

De Graaf, E. D. U., & Miersen, D. S. (2005). The dance of educational innovation. *Teaching in Higher Education*, *10*(1), 117–121.

Deignan, T. (2009). Enquiry-based learning: Perspectives on practice. *Teaching in Higher Education*, *14*(1), 13–28.

Deloria, V. (2002). *Evolution, creation, and other modern myths*. Golden, CO: Fulcrum Publishing.

Dewey, J. (1897/1959). My pedagogic creed. In M. Dworkin (Ed.), *Dewey on education* (pp. 19–32). New York, NY: Teachers College Press.

Dewey, J. (1899/1959). The school and society. In M. Dworkin (Ed.), *Dewey on education* (pp. 33–90). New York, NY: Teachers College Press.

Dewey, J. (1902/1991). *The child and the curriculum*. Chicago, IL: University of Chicago Press.

Dewey, J. (1916). *Democracy and education*. New York, NY: Free Press.

Dewey, J. (1938). *Experience and education*. New York, NY: Macmillan.

Diamond, M. R., & Christensen, M. H. (2005). Bravo! Do acting games promote learning in the college classroom? *Journal on Excellence in College Teaching, 16*(2), 55–67.

DiCicco, J. (2014). National Security Council: Simulating decision-making dilemmas in real time. *International Studies Perspectives, 15*, 438–458.

Diener, L., & Moore, J. W. (2011). It's elemental! Using the Periodic Table Live! to teach students about the elements. *Science Teacher, 78*(5), 40–43.

Digeorgio Lutz, J. A. (2010). Becoming global citizens without leaving home. *Teaching in Higher Education, 15*(6), 715–720.

Dittmer, J. (2013). Humour at the Model United Nations: The role of laughter in constituting geopolitical assemblages. *Geopolitics, 18*, 493–513.

Dittmer, J. (2015). Playing geopolitics: Utopian simulations and subversions of international relations. *GeoJournal, 80*, 909–923.

Donham, R., Schmieg, F., & Allen, D. (2001). The large and the small of it. In B. J. Duch, S. E. Groh, & D. E. Allen (Eds.), *The power of problem-based learning* (pp. 179–193). Sterling, VA: Stylus.

Duch, B. (2001). Models for problem-based learning in undergraduate courses. In B. J. Duch, S. E. Groh, & D. E. Allen (Eds.), *The power of problem-based learning* (pp. 39–46). Sterling, VA: Stylus.

Duch, B., & Groh, S. (2001). Assessment strategies in a problem-based learning course. In B. J. Duch, S. E. Groh, & D. E. Allen (Eds.), *The power of problem-based learning* (pp. 95–108). Sterling, VA: Stylus.

Eagen, K. (2002). *Getting it wrong from the beginning*. New Haven, CT: Yale University Press.

Engel, S., Pallas, J., & Lambert, S. (2017). Model United Nations and deep learning: Theoretical and professional learning. *Journal of Political Science Education, 13*, 171–184.

Evans, R. C., & Boy, N. H. O. (1996). Abandoning the lecture in biology. *Journal on Excellence in College Teaching, 7*(3), 93–110.

Fancy, A. (1999). This hour has too many minutes (an interrupted lecture): The case for edu-prop drama. *Journal on Excellence in College Teaching, 10*(2), 95–123.

Felder, R. M., & Brent, R. (2009). Active learning: an introduction. Retrieved from https://www.researchgate.net/publication/242102584

Felman, J. L. (2001). *Never a dull moment: Teaching and the art of performance*. New York, NY: Routledge.

Fink, L. D. (2003). *Creating significant learning experiences*. San Francisco, CA: Jossey-Bass.

Finkel, D. (2000). *Teaching with your mouth shut*. Portsmouth, NH: Heinemann.

Foer, J. S. (2010). *Eating animals*. New York, NY: Back Bay.

Foster, S. (1989). *The book of the vision quest*. New York, NY: Touchstone.

Fox, R., & Ronkowski, S. (1997). Learning styles of political science students. *PS: Political Science and Politics, 30*, 732–736.

Frank, K. (2008). Problem-based learning in the literature classroom: Empowering students through literal and metaphorical collaboration. *Journal on Excellence in College Teaching, 19*(1), 5–36.

Freeman, S., Eddy, S., McDonough, M., Smith, M., Okoroafor, N., Jordt, H., & Wenderoth, M. (2014). Active learning increases student performance in science, engineering, and mathematics. *Proceedings of the National Academy of the Sciences, 111*(23), 8410–8415.

Freire, P. (1970). *Pedagogy of the oppressed.* New York, NY: Continuum.

Funaro, J. (1994). The evolution of COTI. *CONTACT: Cultures of the Imagination.* Retrieved from http://www.contact-conference.com/c02.html

Gagnon, G., Jr. (2001). *Designing for learning: Six elements in constructivist classrooms.* Thousand Oaks, CA: Corwin Press.

Gardiner, L. (2000). Why we must change: The research evidence. *Thought and Action: The NEA Higher Education Journal, 2*, 121–138.

Garrett, E. (1998). *The Socratic method.* Retrieved from https://www.law.uchicago.edu/socrates/soc_article.html

Gatto, J. T. (2002). *Dumbing us down.* Gabriola Island, British Columbia, Canada: New Society Publishers.

Gatto, J. T. (2009). *Weapons of mass instruction.* Gabriola Island, British Columbia, Canada: New Society Publishers.

Gettinger, M., & Walter, M. (2012). Classroom strategies to enhance academic engaged time. In S. Christenson, A. Reschly, & C. Wylie (Eds.), *Handbook of research on student engagement* (653–674). New York, NY: Springer.

Giroux, H., & Penna, A. (1983). Social education in the classroom: The dynamics of the hidden curriculum. In H. Giroux & D. Purpel (Eds.), *The hidden curriculum and moral education* (pp. 100–121). Berkeley, CA: McCutchan.

Goldsmith, J. (2009). Pacing and time allocation at the micro- and meso-level within the class hour: Why pacing is important, how to study it, and what it implies for individual lesson planning. *Bellaterra: Journal of Teaching & Learning Language & Literature, 1*(1), 30–48.

Goodman, P. (1962). *Utopian essays and practical proposals.* New York, NY: Vintage.

Goodnough, K. (2006). Enhancing pedagogical content knowledge through self-study: An exploration of problem-based learning. *Teaching in Higher Education, 11*(3), 301–318.

Grant, T. (2004). *Playing politics.* New York, NY: Norton.

Greenblatt, C. S. (1981). Seeing forests and trees: Gaming-simulation and contemporary problems of learning and communication. In C. S. Greenblatt & R. D. Duke (Eds.), *Principles and practices of gaming-simulation* (139–153). Beverly Hills, CA: Sage.

Gross Davis, B. (1993). *Tools for teaching.* San Francisco, CA: Jossey-Bass.

Gustav, A. (1969). Retention of course material after varying intervals of time. *Psychological Reports, 25*, 727–730.

Harland, T. (2002). Zoology students' experiences of collaborative learning in problem-based learning. *Teaching in Higher Education, 7*(1), 3–15.

Harrington, C., & Zakrajsek, T. (2017). *Dynamic lecturing: Research-based strategies to enhance lecture effectiveness.* Sterling, VA: Stylus.

Harvard Business School. (2015). *The case method in practice.* Retrieved from http://www.hbs.edu/teaching/case-method-in-practice/resources/

Heiland, D. (2011). Approaching the ineffable: Flow, sublimity, and student learning. In D. Heiland & L. Rosenthal (Eds.), *Literary study, measurement, and the sublime: Disciplinary assessment* (pp. 115–131). New York, NY: Teagle Foundation.

Hegel, G. W. F. (1977). *Phenomenology of spirit.* Oxford, UK: Oxford University Press.

Hertel, J. P., & Millis, B. (2002). *Using simulations to promote learning in higher education.* Sterling, VA: Stylus.

Hess, F. (1999). *Bringing the social sciences alive.* Boston, MA: Allyn and Bacon.

Higgins, P. (2001). Excitement on the first day? *College Teaching, 49,* 2.

Hmelo-Silver, C. E. (2000). Knowledge recycling: Crisscrossing the landscape of educational psychology in a problem-based learning course for preservice teachers. *Journal on Excellence in College Teaching, 11*(2&3), 41–56.

Hockings, C. (2005). Removing the barriers? A study of the conditions affecting teaching innovation. *Teaching in Higher Education, 10*(3), 313–336.

Hohti, R. (2016). Now—and now—and now: Time, space, and the material entanglements of the classroom. *Children and Society, 30,* 180–191.

Holt, J. (1976/2004). *Instead of education.* Boulder, CO: Sentient Publications.

hooks, b. (1994). *Teaching to transgress.* New York, NY: Routledge.

Huizinga, J. (1950). *Homo ludens: A study of the play element in culture.* Boston, MA: Beacon Press.

Hume, D. (1779/1983). *Dialogues concerning natural religion.* Indianapolis, IN: Hackett Publishing Company.

Johnson, D. W., Johnson, R. T., & Holubec, E. (2008). *Cooperation in the classroom* (8th ed.). Edina, MN: Interaction Book Company.

Jones, L. (2007). *The student-centered classroom.* Cambridge, UK: Cambridge University Press.

Junco, R., & Mastrodicasa, J. (2007). *Connecting to the net generation: What higher education professionals need to know about today's students.* Washington DC: Student Affairs Administrators in Higher Education.

Kagan, S. (1992). *Cooperative learning.* San Juan Capistrano, CA: Resources for Teachers.

Kaunert, C. (2009). The European Union simulation: From problem-based learning (PBL) to student interest. *European Political Science, 2,* 254–265.

King, A. (1993). From sage on the stage to guide on the side. *College Teaching, 41,* 30–35.

Kitcher, P. (2006). *Living with Darwin.* Oxford, UK: Oxford University Press.

Krain, M., & Lantis, J. S. (2006). Building knowledge? Evaluating the effectiveness of the Global Problems Summit simulation. *International Studies Perspectives, 7,* 395–407.

Krain, M., & Shadle, C. (2006). Starving for knowledge: An active learning approach to teaching about world hunger. *International Studies Perspectives, 7*, 51–66.

Kreber, C. (2001). Learning experientially through case studies? A conceptual analysis. *Teaching in Higher Education, 6*(2), 217–228.

Kubrick, S. (Director). (1968). *2001, a space odyssey* [Motion picture]. United States: Metro-Goldwyn-Mayer.

Kumrai, R. R., Chauhan, V., & Hoy, J. (2011). Boundary crossings: Using participatory theatre as a site for deepening learning. *Teaching in Higher Education, 16*(5), 517–528.

Lammers, W., & Murphy, J. J. (2002). A profile of teaching techniques used in the university classroom. *Active Learning in Higher Education, 3*(1), 54–67.

Lang, J. M. (2015). Small changes in teaching: The minutes before class. *The Chronicle of Higher Education.* Retrieved from http://www.chronicle.com/article/Small-Changes-in-Teaching-The/234178

Langer, E. J. (1997). *The power of mindful learning.* Cambridge, MA: Da Capo.

Lean, J., Moizer, J., Towler, M., & Abbey, C. (2006). Simulations and games: Uses and barriers in higher education. *Active Learning in Higher Education, 7*(3), 227–242.

Leopold, A. (1949). *A Sand County almanac.* Oxford, UK: Oxford University Press.

Levin, B. (1995). Using the case method in teacher education: The role of discussion and experience in teachers' thinking about cases. *Teaching and Teacher Education, 11*(1), 63–79.

Loui, M. (2009). What can students learn in an extended role-play simulation on technology and society? *Bulletin of Science, Technology, and Society, 29*(1), 37–47.

Lovie-Kitchen, J. (2001). Reflecting on assessment. In P. Schwartz, S. Mennin, & G. Webb (Eds.), *Problem-based learning: Case studies, experience, and practice* (pp. 149–155). Sterling, VA: Stylus.

MacFall, J. (2012). Long-term impact of service-learning in environmental studies. *Journal of College Science Teaching, 41*(3), 26–31.

Maitland, B. (1997). Problem-based learning for architecture and construction management. In D. Boud & G. Feletti (Eds.), *The challenge of problem-based learning* (2nd ed., pp. 211–217). London, UK: Kogan Page.

Margetson, D. (1997). Why is problem-based learning a challenge? In D. Boud & G. Feletti (Eds.), *The challenge of problem-based learning* (2nd ed., pp. 36–44). London, UK: Kogan Page.

Mathews, F. (2005). *Reinhabiting reality: Toward a recovery of culture.* Albany, NY: SUNY Press.

Mazur, E. (1997). *Peer instruction: A user's manual series in educational innovation.* Upper Saddle River, NJ: Prentice Hall.

McDaniel, K. (2000). Four elements of successful historical role-playing in the classroom. *The History Teacher, 33*(3), 357–362.

McGinn, C. (1993). *Moral literacy.* Indianapolis, IN: Hackett Publishing Company.

McIntosh, D. (2001). The uses and limits of the Model United Nations in an international relations classroom. *International Studies Perspectives, 2*, 269–280.

McLeish, J. (1968). *The lecture method.* Cambridge, UK: Cambridge Institute of Education.

Merseth, K. (1996). Cases and case methods in teacher education. In J. Sikula (Ed.), *Handbook of research on teacher education* (pp. 722–744). New York, NY: Macmillan.

Middendorf, J., & Kalish, A. (1996). The "change-up" in lectures. *TRC newsletter.* Retrieved from http://www.iub.edu/~tchsotl/part3/Middendorf%20&%20Kalish.pdf

Miflin, B., & Price, D. (2001). Why does the department have professors if they don't teach? In P. Schwartz, S. Mennin, & G. Webb (Eds.), *Problem-based learning: Case studies, experience, and practice* (pp. 98–103). Sterling, VA: Stylus.

Millis, B. J. (2014). Using cooperative structures to promote deep learning. *Journal on Excellence in College Teaching, 25*(3&4), 139–148.

Millis, B. J., & Cottell, P. G., Jr. (1998). *Cooperative learning for higher education faculty.* Phoenix, AZ: American Council on Education/Oryx Press.

Milton, O., Pollio, H. R., & Eison, J. A. (1986). *Making sense of college grades.* San Francisco, CA: Jossey-Bass.

Mintz, A. (2009). From grade school to law school: Socrates' legacy in education. In S. Ahbel-Rappe & R. Kamtekar (Eds.), *A companion to Socrates.* Hoboken, NJ: Blackwell.

Mlodinow, L. (2015). *The upright thinkers.* New York, NY: Vintage.

Mould, D. (2003). Lessons from two service-learning projects: How teamwork, technology, and problem-based learning techniques can make a difference in communities. *Perspectives in Higher Education Reform, 12,* 129–141.

NASA. (n.d.). *Mars Pathfinder egg drop challenge.* Retrieved from http://www.nasa.gov/pdf/544868main_E3_MarsPathfinderEggDrop_C5.pdf

Newbury, P. (2013). You don't have to wait for the clock to strike to start teaching. Retrieved from http://www.peternewbury.org/2013/08/you-dont-have-to-wait-for-the-clock-to-strike-to-start-teaching/

Newton, B. (1998). *Improvisation: Use what you know—make up what you don't! Improvisation activities for the classroom.* Scottsdale, AZ: Gifted Psychology Press.

Obendorf, S., & Randerson, C. (2013). Evaluating the Model United Nations: Diplomatic simulation as assessed undergraduate coursework. *European Political Science, 12,* 350–364.

O'Connor, K. (2004). *Dialectic.* The Chicago School of Media Theory, Keywords Glossary. Retrieved from http://csmt.uchicago.edu/glossary2004/dialectic.htm

Olivares, C., Merino, C., & Quiroz, W. (2013). Fostering competencies in chemistry by redesigning the periodic table. *Procedia–Social and Behavioral Sciences, 116,* 1955–1957.

O'Neill, G., & Hung, W. (2010). Seeing the landscape and the forest floor: Changes made to improve the connectivity of concepts in a hybrid problem-based learning curriculum. *Teaching in Higher Education, 15*(1), 15–27.

Paley, W. (1802/2001). *Natural theology* (selections). In P. Appleman (Ed.), *Darwin* (3rd ed., pp. 41–44). New York, NY: Norton Critical Edition.

Palleschi, M. (2005). The commedia dell'arte: Its origins, development & influence on the ballet. Retrieved from http://auguste.vestris.free.fr/Essays/Commedia.html

Paul, R., & Thompson, R. C. (Producers) & Bridges, J. (Director). (1973). The paper chase [Motion picture]. United States: 20th Century Fox.

Pellegrino, A., Lee, C. D., & D'Erizans, A. (2012). Historical thinking through classroom simulation: 1919 Paris Peace Conference. *The Clearing House, 85*, 146–152.

Pettenger, M., West, D., & Young, N. (2014). Assessing the impact of role play simulations on learning in Canada and US classrooms. *International Studies Perspectives, 15*, 491–508.

Postman, N., & Weingartner, C. (1971/2009). *Teaching as a subversive activity.* New York: Random House.

Quinn, D. (1992). *Ishmael.* New York: Bantam/Turner Books.

Raghallaigh, M. N., & Cunniffe, R. (2013). Creating a safe climate for active learning and student engagement: An example from an introductory social work module. *Teaching in Higher Education, 18*(1), 93–105.

Rawls, J. (1970). *A theory of justice.* Cambridge, MA: Harvard University Press.

Reacting to the Past (2013). Retrieved from http://reacting.barnard.edu/

Regan, T. (1983). *The case for animal rights.* Oakland, CA: University of California Press.

Reid, E. S. (2004). Uncoverage in composition pedagogy. *Composition Studies, 32*(1), 15–34.

Rolston, H. (1999). Ethics on the home planet. In A. Weston (Ed.), *An invitation to environmental philosophy* (pp. 107–140). Oxford, UK: Oxford University Press.

Ross, J., & Smythe, E. (1995). Differentiating cooperative learning to meet the needs of gifted learners: A case for transformational leadership. *Journal for the Education of the Gifted, 19*, 63–82.

Rosselli, J. (1984). *The opera industry in Italy from Cimarosa to Verdi: The role of the impresario.* Cambridge, UK: Cambridge University Press.

Rousseau, J.-J. (1762/1979). *Emile, or on education* (A. Bloom, Trans.). New York, NY: Basic Books.

Saarinen, E., & Slotte, S. (2006). *Philosophical lecturing as a philosophical practice.* Retrieved from http://www.society-for-philosophy-in-practice.org/journal/pdf/6-2%20007%20Saarinen%20-%20Lecturing.pdf

Sandy, L. R. (1998). The permeable classroom. *Journal on Excellence in College Teaching, 9*(3), 47–63.

Sasley, B. E. (2010). Teaching students how to fail: Simulations as tools of explanation. *International Studies Perspectives, 11*, 61–74.

Savery, J. R. (2006). Overview of problem-based learning: Definitions and distinctions. *The Interdisciplinary Journal of Problem-Based Learning, 1*(1), 9–20. Retrieved from https://pdfs.semanticscholar.org/549c/9ea78fe19aa609a66e84ea0b2ecda5e731bf.pdf?_ga=2.19238781.436034065.1534096240-1707771849.1534096240

Savery J. R., & Duffy, T. M. (2001). *Problem based learning: An instructional model and its constructivist framework* (Technical Report #16-01). Bloomington, IN: Center for Research on Learning and Technology, Indiana University.

Savin-Baden, M. (2014). Using problem-based learning: New constellations for the 21st century. *Journal on Excellence in College Teaching, 25*(3&4), 197–219.

Scerri, E. R. (2006). *The periodic table: Its story and its significance.* Oxford, UK: Oxford University Press.

Schick, T., & Vaughn, L. (2014). *How to think about weird things* (7th ed.). New York, NY: McGraw-Hill.

Schwartz, P. (1997). Persevering with problem-based learning. In D. Boud & G. Feletti (Eds.), *The challenge of problem-based learning* (2nd ed., pp. 58–63). London, UK: Kogan Page.

Schwartz, P., Mennin, S., & Webb, G. (2001). *Problem-based learning: Case studies, experience, and practice.* Sterling, VA: Stylus.

Sedaris, D. (1997). *Naked.* New York, NY: Little, Brown, and Company.

Senge, P. (1992). *The fifth discipline: The art and practice of the learning organization.* New York, NY: Doubleday.

Shipman, H., & Duch, B. (2001). Problem-based learning in large and very large classes. In B. J. Duch, S. E. Groh, & D. E. Allen (Eds.), *The power of problem-based learning* (pp. 149–164) Sterling, VA: Stylus.

Singer, P. (2011). *The expanding circle.* Princeton, NJ: Princeton University Press.

Skaay of the Qquuna Qiighawaay. (2002). *Being in being: The collected works of a Master Haida Mythteller* (R. Bringhurst, Trans.). Lincoln, NE: University of Nebraska Press.

Sorin, R., Errington, E., Ireland, L., Nickson, A., & Caltabiano, M. (2012). Embedding graduate attributes through scenario-based learning. *Journal of the NUS Teaching Academy, 2*, 192–205.

Spolin, V. (1986). *Theater games for the classroom: A teacher's handbook.* Evanston, IL: Northwestern University Press.

Stevens, R. (2015). Role-play and student engagement: Reflections from the classroom. *Teaching in Higher Education, 20*(5), 481–492.

Takahashi, S., & Saito, E. (2011). Changing pedagogical styles: A case study of the trading game in a Japanese university. *Teaching in Higher Education, 16*(4), 401–412.

Thaler, R. H., & Sunstein, C. R. (2008). *Nudge: Improving decisions about health, wealth, and happiness.* New York, NY: Penguin.

Thomas, W. (2004). *What are old people for?* St. Louis, MO: Vander Wyk & Burnham.

Tormey, R., & Henchy, D. (2008). Reimagining the traditional lecture: An action research approach to teaching student teachers to "do" philosophy. *Teaching in Higher Education, 13*(3), 303–314.

Trigwell, K., Prosser, M., & Taylor, P. (1999). Relations between teachers' approaches to teaching and students' approaches to learning. *Higher Education, 37*, 57–76.

Viachopoulos, D., & Makri, A. (2017). The effect of games and simulations on higher education. *International Journal of Educational Technology in Higher Education, 14*, 22.

Vocabulary.com. (2015). Retrieved from http://www.vocabulary.com/dictionary/scenario

Wardrip-Fruin, N., & Montfort, N. (2003). From theatre of the oppressed. In N. Montfort & N. Wardrip-Fruin (Eds.), *The new media reader* (pp. 339–352). Cambridge, MA: MIT Press.

Watson, J. (2012). Time to retire the phrase "guide on the side". *KP Blog*. Retrieved from http://www.kpk12.com/blog/2014/05/time-to-retire-the-phrase-%E2%80%9Cguide-on-the-side%E2%80%9D/

Weir, K., & Barankowski, M. (2008). Simulating history to understand international politics. *Simulation and Gaming, 42*(4), 441–461.

Weston, A. (1991a). Uncovering the hidden curriculum: A laboratory course in philosophy of education. *APA Newsletter on Teaching Philosophy, 90*(2), 36–40.

Weston, A. (1991b). Non-anthropocentrism in a thoroughly anthropocentrized world. *The Trumpeter, 8*(3), 108–112.

Weston, A. (1994). *Back to Earth: Tomorrow's environmentalism*. Philadelphia, PA: Temple University Press.

Weston, A. (1996a). Self-validating reduction: A theory of environmental devaluation. *Environmental Ethics, 18*, 115–132.

Weston, A. (1996b). Instead of environmental education. In B. Jickling (Ed.), *Proceedings of the Yukon College symposium on ethics, environment, and education* (pp. 148–157). Whitehorse, Yukon Territory: Yukon College.

Weston, A. (1998). Risking philosophy of education. *Metaphilosophy 29*, 145–158.

Weston, A. (2003). What if teaching went wild? In S. Fletcher (Ed.), *Philosophy of education 2002* (pp. 40–52). Urbana, IL: Philosophy of Education Society.

Weston, A. (2004). Multicentrism: A manifesto. *Environmental Ethics, 26*(1), 25–40.

Weston, A. (2013). *A 21st century ethical toolbox* (3rd ed.). New York, NY: Oxford University Press.

Weston, A. (2014). Working the dark edges. *Canadian Journal of Environmental Education, 19*, 70–79.

Weston, A. (2015). From guide on the side to impresario with a scenario. *College Teaching, 63*, 3.

Weston, A., & Sibelman, B. (2012). *Graxes rock*. Epic poem alien-world visualization for Cultures of the Imagination (COTI) conference. Retrieved from http://wiki.solseed.org/Graxes_Rock

Weston, A. (2018). Moments of grace. In S. Cahn, A. Bradner, & A. Mills (Eds.), *Philosophers in the classroom: Essays on teaching*. Indianapolis, IN: Hackett Publishing Company.

Whitehead, A. N. (1967). *The aims of education*. New York, NY: Free Press.

Williams, K. (2017). Unschooling in class: College students gain first-hand insight into the intrigue of unschooling. *Tipping Points*. Alliance for Self-Directed Education. Retrieved from https://www.self-directed.org/tp/unschooling-in-class/

Wimsatt, W. (1998). How I got my DIY degree from the planet Earth. *Utne Reader*, (May–June), 50–51.

Wismath, S., Orr, D., & MacKay, B. (2015). Threshold concepts in the development of problem-solving skills. *Teaching and Learning Inquiry*, *3*(1), 63–73.

Woods, D. (1997). Some difficulties in implementation in an otherwise conventional programme. In D. Boud & G. Feletti (Eds.), *The challenge of problem-based learning* (2nd ed., pp. 173–180). London, UK: Kogan Page.

Wren, L., Jackson, M., Morris, H., Geddes, C., Tlen, D., & Kassi, N. (1996). What is a good way to teach children and young adults to respect the land? Panel discussion of Yukon Territory First Nations elders. In B. Jickling (Ed.), *Proceedings of the Yukon College symposium on ethics, environment, and education*. Whitehorse, Yukon Territory: Yukon College.

Wright, D., & Mitchell, S. (n.d.). *Mendeleev periodic table simulator* [game]. Burlington, NC: Carolina Biological Supply.

Wyman, R. (2008). *The Stanislavsky system of acting: Legacy and influence in modern performance*. Cambridge, UK: Cambridge University Press.

Yong, E. (2014). Zombie roaches and other parasite tales. TED talk. Retrieved from http://www.ted.com/talks/ed_yong_suicidal_wasps_zombie_roaches_and_other_tales_of_parasites?utm_source=newsletter_weekly_2014-03-29&utm_campaign=newsletter_weekly&utm_medium=email&utm_content=top_right_image#t-758996

Zaitsev, A. (2002). Design and implementation of the 1st theremin concert for aliens. Retrieved from http://www.cplire.ru/html/ra&sr/irm/Theremin-concert.html

Zeeman, E., & Lotriet, M. (2013). Beyond the expected: An enriched learning experience through learner engagement and participation. *Teaching in Higher Education*, *18*(2), 179–191.

Aboriginal peoples, of Australia, 198–99
aboriginal species, of Galapagos Islands, 53–54, 61–62
Abram, David, 198, 200
activation
    of dialectic, 77–78, 93, 98, 125
    of student energy, 34, 36, 41–43, 72–74, 97, 171
active learning
    advantages of, 6, 27–28, 33
    enjoyment of, 10–11
    environment for, 40, 42
    for ethics, 172–75
    games for, 15–16
    passive learning versus, 6, 15–17, 27–28, 37
    periodic tables and, 31–32
    as student-centered, 34
    of students, 5–6, 10–11, 37, 165–66, 170–71
    teachers and, 36–37, 38
activity, physical, for retention rate, 27
advantages
    of active learning, 6, 27–28, 33
    of staging, 19–20
affinity beings activity
    rejoining the world scenarios and, 201–03
    ritual for, 202–03
aim. See goals
alien encounter role-play, 146–47, 150–56, 157–60, 161–64, 165–66
All Mother! (COTI #3), 161–64
alternatives
    to lecture model, 32–33
    to traditional pedagogy, 2, 5, 26, 31–32, 41, 56, 178–79, 192
Anderson, D., Teaching in Higher Education by, 99–100
Arab League simulation, 107–08
arguments, in "the expanding circle" scenario, 145–46
Asal, V., 14, 73–74, 86, 109, 110–11
assessments. See testing
assumptions about education, 15, 179, 181
Auman, C., 11, 19
Australia, Aboriginal peoples of, 198–99

Barnard College, 111–13
Belenky, M.F., Women's Ways of Knowing by, 189
Bell, Inge, 190, 191
Berk, R.A., 13
Bernstein, J., 19, 109
Blake, E., 14, 73–74, 86, 109, 110–11
Blecha, B., 51
Boal, Augusto, Theater of the Oppressed by, 90–91, 183
The Book of the Vision Quest (Foster), 192
Bottenberg, Frances, 182, 202
Boud, D., 102
Brunner, P.W., 11
Burgan, Mary, on lecture model, 29–32, 183
Burns, A.C., 86

Cahill, Ann, 79
California Institute of Technology, 39

Teaching the Whole Student

Engaged Learning With Heart, Mind, and Spirit

Edited by David Schoem, Christine Modey, and Edward P. St. John

Foreword by Beverly Daniel Tatum

"For nearly a decade, higher education has been abuzz with the educational power of 'high-impact practices'—a family of interactive, hands-on pedagogies through which students and faculty work together on complex, important questions. *Teaching the Whole Student* reaches through the hype to explore—in rich, evidence-supported detail—how these engaged pedagogies kindle students' own sense of purpose and build commitment to help create a more just, inclusive, and sustainable future."
—*Carol Geary Schneider*, *Fellow, Lumina Foundation: and President Emerita, Association of American Colleges & Universities*

This book offers models for instructors who care deeply about their students, respect and recognize students' social identities and lived experiences, and are interested in creating community and environments of openness and trust to foster deep-learning, academic success, and meaning-making.

22883 Quicksilver Drive
Sterling, VA 20166-2019

Subscribe to our e-mail alerts: www.Styluspub.com

Creating Wicked Students

Designing Courses for a Complex World

Paul Hanstedt

There's a lot of talk in education these days about "wicked problems"—problems that defy traditional expectations or knowledge, problems that evolve over time: Zika, ISIS, political discourse in the era of social media. To prepare students for such wicked problems, they need to have wicked competencies, the ability to respond easily and on the fly to complex challenges. Unfortunately, a traditional education that focuses on content and skills often fails to achieve this sense of wickedness. Students memorize for the test, prepare for the paper, practice the various algorithms over and over again—but when the parameters or dynamics of the test or the paper or the equation change, students are often at a loss for how to adjust.

This is a course design book centered on the idea that the goal in the college classroom—in all classrooms, all the time—is to develop students who are not only loaded with content but also capable of using that content in thoughtful, deliberate ways to make the world a better place. Achieving this goal requires a top-to-bottom reconsideration of courses, including student learning goals, text selection and course structure, day-to-day pedagogies, and assignment and project design. *Creating Wicked Students* takes readers through each step of the process, providing multiple examples at each stage, while always encouraging instructors to consider concepts and exercises in light of their own courses and students.

(Continues on preceding page)